'The world is a book and those who ⟨ *page'*

St Augustine

Tales from the Hamlet

Memories of Italy

Cassandra Campbell-Kemp

Notices

For Ugo

Thank you my friend

'Women, like princes, find few real friends.'

Contents

Prologue
'Please allow me to introduce myself...' 1

Chapter 1
'Every cloud has a silver lining'... 13

Chapter 2
Love at first sight... 33

Chapter 3
Of food - and vertiginous roads 45

Chapter 4
An unexpected offer... 59

Chapter 5
Bad news, better news and wonderful news 71

Chapter 6
Bureaucracy, xenophobia and a wonderful Christmas 89

Chapter 7
Leaving Verona... 113

Chapter 8
Playing House.. 127

Chapter 9
The country life 141

Chapter 10
History, a castle and a proposal.. 153

Chapter 11

'Be fearless in the pursuit of what sets your soul on fire...' 169

Chapter 12

'All great discoveries are made by those whose feelings run ahead of their thinkings' 189

Chapter 13

Thelma and Louise...! 203

Chapter 14

'Bikers Welcome' 215

Chapter 15

'Our friends are lenses through which we read our own minds' .. 229

Chapter 16

"Ben tornata a casa! Welcome home!" 243

Chapter 17

'Getting to know you, getting to know all about you...' 253

Chapter 18

Meeting Pink Floyd and Steve McQueen 265

Chapter 19

'an Englishman's house is his castle...' 279

Chapter 20

'Degustibook' Luisa's ladies 293

Chapter 21

'The Woman who changed the course of history' 303

Chapter 22

Of house hunting and shiny things... 315

Chapter 23

Magic is afoot.. 327

Chapter 24

Chocolate, trout and goosebumps 339

Chapter 25

Priests, Partisans and Oratories 353

Chapter 26

Lunch, laughter and an unexpected gift.. 365

Chapter 27

Castles, choirs and supper.. 377

Chapter 28

Florence, Cantuccini, Vin Santo and a sobering meeting 391

Chapter 29

'All things must pass' 401

Chapter 30

The eleventh hour of the eleventh day of the eleventh month........ 413

Postscript 427

Acknowledgements... 430

Prologue

'Please allow me to introduce myself…' The Rolling Stones,
Sympathy for the Devil

All my life I've been a 'square peg in a round hole', 'in the world but not of the world' and all the other cliches of those destined to walk a different path.

Different from what or whom? From the norm. From the many millions of people who choose to live safe, careful and convenient lives; who conform to the norms of society and who rarely venture outside their comfort zones.

I realised I was different when, at the age of 10, I found myself disconsolately wandering around the garden at home, in floods of tears and literally begging Aslan (the Lion from the Lion, the Witch and the Wardrobe) to come and take me to Narnia. An odd thing to request and an even odder thing to hope for, nay expect, a response.

What was it about Narnia that so attracted me? How come I'd felt the lure, an almost desperate desire to live in another land - and why?

I had an immensely privileged childhood yet felt emotionally and mentally apart from my family.

My father, a massively charismatic and hugely intelligent man was flawed (and occasionally floored) by his alcoholism. My mother, an elegant yet emotionally remote woman didn't like me and always assumed that I was lying to her. Which I usually wasn't!

She would stonewall me when I tried to engage with her and although it took me a few years, I had worked it out by the time I was ten, she was afraid of me. Frightened of my "difference" of my "wildness" and the fact that I seemed to march to a different tune.

I recall hearing her tell Daddy one night, when, as was their usual practise, they came to check on the children before going to bed themselves. Standing beside my bed she turned to him and said, quite clearly, "I don't know where she's from, but she's definitely not ours". I lay still, eyes tightly shut, running through a gamut of emotions for, despite the hurt and the palpable rejection, I felt she was right. Perhaps that's why I'd called Aslan to come and spirit me away to a place where I knew I WOULD be accepted. Years later I still wonder what made her say that for I have pictures of us shortly after she gave birth to me, so I know I wasn't a foundling! It was an odd thing for her to have said.

Then there were The Twins. A brother and sister, three years younger, who used to gang up on me, with that peculiar closeness of twins and alienate me from their games, refuse to allow me to join them in their makeshift chocolate-stuffed camps made from chairs and blankets and, worst of all, they'd sequestered Cartwright our beloved black Labrador who'd love anyone who gave him biscuits!

Yet, despite feeling isolated and different from my family, I wasn't unhappy. I enjoyed my solitude and my own company. I did my own stuff in my own way and, apart from the Aslan episode, felt pretty content. Though Mummy's pronouncement had left me somewhat baffled.

Boarding school was much the same. People put up with me because I was funny and bright and I soon discovered that by making people laugh, I could survive without too much unpleasantness.

I had an enquiring mind, a lively intelligence and a thirst for knowledge. I was fascinated by geography and, it appeared, was good at languages. I also had, to my mind, the immensely useful faculty of seeing things in a different way to how others saw them. An early manifestation of 'thinking outside the box' I guess.

Yet my distinctiveness earned me the epithet 'mad'. Which hurt. It seems that I was too young to be labelled 'eccentric' - a soubriquet, to my mind, usually reserved for fabulously flamboyant and wonderfully interesting people who express and celebrate their 'otherness' and individuality by living in a vibrantly colourful fashion - usually accompanied by some wildly glamorous vice like chain-smoking Black Russian cigarettes or imbibing Absinthe from an oddly-shaped glass pipe or passing away their days having extraordinary insights gleaned through a haze of opium or hashish.

Yes, I was a precocious child and such characters absolutely fascinated me. They seemed to have harnessed their peccadilloes into a way of living that enabled them to indulge their oddities without actually alienating their peers. After all the British adore a bona fide eccentric.

My own eccentricities didn't yet extend to Absinthe or Hashish, they were more confined to painting my bedroom dark purple (so very Biba!) with Schiaparelli pink woodwork, or smuggling Gordons Gin into school, cunningly hidden inside a Baby Lotion bottle (it tasted

3

disgusting). My admirers would send me packets of Embassy cigarettes (alas not Black Russians or Sobranie Cocktails) cunningly disguised as boxes of soap which would appeal to Maiden Aunts and which escaped Matron's beady eye. I'd sit in one of the Temples in the school grounds (there were several, dedicated to various Greek gods) smoking happily and wondering how little revision I could get away with before sitting my 'O' levels.

Education was, to me, all about furnishing me with the right tools for broadening my horizons and not taking boring and, to my mind, unnecessary exams.

My arrogance was my undoing, I achieved an all-time low of getting just 3 'O' levels in a school lauded for its high pass rates. But these 'O' levels were in English, French and Russian and they were all 'A' grades. Actually I got double A's in French and Russian!

Despite this, my parents were horrified, having spent enormous sums of money on a superb private education. But what I lacked academically, I'd made up for personally by learning so much about how to integrate as an outsider, how to talk to other nationalities (we had many foreign pupils from all sorts of amazing and exotic places), how to negotiate my way out of trouble with either the

teachers or fellow students and how to survive many long hours on my own with just my thoughts for company. Oh, and how to avoid getting caught smoking!

Despite my interest in distant lands and the temples to the Greek gods, I'd been arrogant enough to refuse to study either Latin or Greek and had ensured that my father had written to the Headmistress accordingly. This however proved to be a distinct lack of foresight as, two decades later, I'd been sent to live and work in both Italy and Greece. My personal jury is still out as to whether studying the ancient languages would have facilitated the learning of the modern ones. Somehow I doubt it. Did I really need to know all the five declensions of 'table' in Latin, its six tenses or its conjugations? Or what the ablative was? Would my life be any the poorer for not knowing this? Probably not.

So it was that I left school with very little in terms of actual qualifications and an enduring memory of Matron chasing me around the car park demanding that I change out of my sheepskin coat and velvet trousers into my school uniform which I told her I'd burnt! Not only did I have the very latest in 1970's cool fashion but I also had a healthy enquiring mind, a lively intelligence and the exciting prospect of a 6th form college in which to retake some 'O' levels, study for some 'A' levels and meet BOYS!

The boys bit was fun - the education bit was not - more of the same, but I managed to get offered an interview at Cambridge University on the strength of my 'S' level English paper. I'd written at length about Ancient Civilisations and how and why they'd failed; concluding my piece by wondering how long it would be before our own civilisation failed and what and when would be our apogee?

To my father's horror, despite being quite proud of myself for having even been offered the interview, I refused point blank to attend it, explaining in my teenage disdain that I'd 'had enough' of education and that I needed to explore Europe.

5

Family holidays in Italy and pre-partitioned Cyprus had led to a lasting interest in culture and Mediterranean men. I'd spent many happy hours avoiding the family on our various trips, discovering my burgeoning and sometimes quite worrying sexuality while using the excuse to visit an historical site to indulge my passion for ruins and canoodling! Not necessarily in that order.

I was attracted to men much older than myself, not callow spotty youths and actually spent many happy hours having interesting conversations with them while being plied with Bacardi and Coke! I was aware of the law regarding sex with underage girls so was extremely careful not to compromise them in any way. Interestingly while obviously lusting after my youthful and somewhat abundant ripeness, they too enjoyed intelligent discussion and I actually learnt a lot from them about their history and cultures. They were rightly proud of their heritage and were most generous in sharing their knowledge with me.

I realised that, from a psychological viewpoint, I liked men much more than I liked women. Men seemed to take the bull by the horns and actually do things whereas women seemed, to me, to be too risk-averse, too timid and therefore missing out on so much. Of course I generalise, but that is my right!

I also realised that perhaps Mummy was right - maybe I WAS from somewhere else. This way of thinking definitely did not constitute "normal".

Accordingly most of my friends in my late teens were male, I only really had two female friends - both from my Boarding School and one, who has known me since we were ten, is still my best friend. She, like me, has a keen intellect and though her group of friends is more evenly balanced between the sexes, she relates to men in a way that they find interesting and are comfortable with. I still have several male friends that I met in the early 70's and though we are getting older and creakier by the day, we still retain that love of conversation, discussion and dissemination.

There are of course, exceptions to the rule and we have all met men who seemed to feel threatened by intelligent and self-aware women. And we have also met women who feel the same. Their loss.

My parents, despairing that, due to my woeful academic record, I would turn out to be unemployable had decided to enrol me in the Harrods Management Training programme, closely followed by enrolment on a course for a Diploma in Interior Design after I'd been 'let go' by Harrods as a result of, to my mind, showing a little too much initiative!

Both were useful - I learnt a lot about management techniques from the former and how to produce a workable electrical wiring diagram from the latter.

However my parents were keen to leave me to my own devices as they had decided to move to a beautiful 200 year old house in a village on the outskirts of Palma de Mallorca. Visiting them as often as I could, while trying to hold down a seemingly-endless series of boring secretarial jobs, I found that I managed to pick up Spanish quickly so added that to my French and Russian.

I really enjoyed trying to communicate with other cultures and simply couldn't understand how the British could be so rude as not to attempt to learn the language - even just the basics of 'please' and 'thank you', 'hello' and 'goodbye' - of the country in which they found themselves. They missed out on so much by not trying to integrate with the local people and their culture.

Even my parents attempted to learn Spanish and Daddy would sit at his desk laboriously poring through endless grammar books and dictionaries. The resulting phrases would be oddly stilted though comprehensible. My mother on the other hand was totally fearless and managed to bring an entire shop to its knees by walking in and asking for "four blue velvet testicles"... the words for cushion and testicle being worryingly similar!

Several years of pretty unexciting jobs culminated in the most spectacular piece of luck - or was it Fate? I'd been working in the commercial property sector for several years - on the marketing side and, to my delight and the astonishment of my colleagues, I was head-hunted by an international multiplex cinema operator who wanted someone who 'spoke languages' to open up Europe for them. They wanted to start with Italy, a country I'd come to know pretty well through my then partner having a number of Italian friends; thus we'd spent as much of our holidays as possible in that beautiful country. I'd added rudimentary Italian to my lexicon of languages - mostly because the wonderful old housekeeper of the house we stayed in spoke not a word of English and she was so interesting (and cooked such delicious meals!) that I'd wanted to get to know her better!

So I sallied forth into Europe - ultimately spending almost 30 years living and working in Spain, Greece and Italy for some pretty high-powered employers and, unknown to me, creating a sort of mythos around myself in the process!

Physically I am large, unfit and with a lot of very curly hair. Basically a big buxom lady with a naughty grin and who couldn't and wouldn't wear business suits! Mentally I was sharp, with an enquiring mind and an uncanny ability to see potential pitfalls - and potential solutions. Emotionally I was afraid of very little and I welcomed the opportunity to explore new countries and cultures, learning their regional differences and to combine my expertise in my profession with an innate understanding - almost a sixth sense - of their ways of living and doing business.

I also travelled to many other countries, including those behind the former Iron Curtain. I did business with and made friends in all of them, Poland, Romania, Albania, Czech and Slovak republics, I'd visited Hungary and Austria, I knew Spain, Portugal, Italy and Greece like the back of my hand (seemingly better than most of the citizens due to the fact that I'd had to travel extensively in each country) and I'd even managed to endear myself to the notoriously diffident French - apart from one very bad-tempered Mayor of a small town near Toulouse. In Poland my Russian had come in useful - surfacing after a lapse of 20 years or so to rescue me when I'd been stopped for speeding. Thinking that I was KGB, the policeman had hurriedly let me go!

Visiting all these countries also meant that during the annual European conferences and industry functions which I was required to attend, I'd become pretty well-known and, I'm told, well liked and well respected; with, thankfully, a reputation for being completely honest.

I was always greeted with affection and, as far as I knew, my somewhat unorthodox way of doing business (I had no time for stilted conversation!) had offended no-one. In fact my independent thinking had earned me many friends and gratifyingly few foes.

I loved working abroad, I was totally comfortable and liked nothing better than to go exploring - so much so that rather than fly home, I'd stay on at weekends to discover more about the country in which I found myself, my former partner having vanished into the ether several years earlier.

To my lasting astonishment, and also that of my mother, I'd managed to become Senior Management in not one, but two, major international companies and all without any formal qualifications. What is more I'd never attended an interview - having always been head-hunted. My USP was my languages, my address book and my ability to communicate and connect with people; of thinking outside the box, of understanding my markets and how to integrate my employers' product into them. Also by being respectful of authority, systems and management practices but also feeling able to express my opinion as and when required - whether solicited or not!

When I landed my first six-figure salary my mother told me that she was incredibly proud of me and promptly invited me to a celebratory lunch. She said that although Daddy had done well in business, he had done it with help, whereas I had done it on my own and without the benefit of qualifications or degrees. That meant more to me than anything and I still think that my being 'different' had contributed to my success.

Chapter 1

'Every cloud has a silver lining'...

For the first part of the Noughties I'd been working in Greece, returning in 2005 to work in London as my mother's health was failing and she needed me home. Daddy had, 20 years earlier, finally succumbed to his alcoholism, dying uncomfortably and hugely regretful of his folly.

Starting my rehabilitation into UK life I'd taken a job with an international firm of Property Consultants and while I had thoroughly enjoyed the work my own health had started to give me cause for concern. So it was that when my mother passed away in 2010 I had moved to a 17th century cottage in a charming edge of Cotswolds town in the South-West of England, not far from Bath and within easy reach of London if necessary.

Wanting to do something different and more sustainable, I'd started, with a wonderfully fun, knowledgeable and impressive woman, a Sustainability consultancy. We had no real qualifications for working in this emerging sector but none of it was rocket science and our first client had been one of the City of London's most iconic buildings. We'd managed to save them seven figures by adopting sustainable operating and management practices and though the business was doing well the toll on my health caused ever-increasing problems, leaving me no option but to retire and leave the running of the company in the capable hands of my friend and business partner.

It took me five years to recover my health and my equilibrium and I was now ready to return to work, to find something that challenged me intellectually while paying me a decent salary, yet without too much flying - for that is what had caused the initial health problems and I didn't want to jeopardise my newly-found wellbeing. I'd also adopted a rescue cat, a beautiful and hugely intelligent Siamese and I simply couldn't abandon her to resume my globe-trotting.

Actually I'd had a gastric bypass - losing over half my body weight in just over 18 months - and I was looking good, feeling good and hoping that someone, somewhere would like to invite me back into the corporate fold. But on my terms. Not least because carrying my previous weight had ruined my knees and I found walking difficult and painful. But that didn't mean that my brain didn't work.

I was down to my last pennies and after meeting with several London-based headhunters I was told that, despite speaking several languages, being well regarded in the industry, having an encyclopaedic knowledge of the Southern European commercial property market and an address book to die for, I was now too old for consideration for employment by a British company. "That's illegal" I muttered, horrified that there was, seemingly no-one who wanted to employ me. They were looking for energetic and dynamic 45 year olds who could end up on the Board, I was nearly 60, not awfully mobile and probably way too outspoken for consideration as a Board member!

A timely phone call from a former colleague who, as the CEO of a very forward-thinking property company in northern Italy, had decided he needed me to put together a new property fund by finding properties on or off market for purchase, telling me "You are the ONLY person I know that can do this job, so I need you and I need you here as fast as you can get here."

The job offer had come literally out of the blue and at the most propitious time as I was beginning to despair of ever finding any work, other than on the checkout of the local supermarket.

And so it was that I found myself at an age when others were taking early retirement and drawing lump sums from impressive pension pots, heading across Europe once again to start a new role and with an elderly Siamese cat in tow.

Announcing my departure on Facebook I'd received many responses from my FB friends, ranging from "you're mad", through "how brave you are" to "you're so inspirational" and finally from those who knew me best, metaphorical rolled eyes and "what is she up to now?". It had taken me two months to pack up the house, do the necessary paperwork, find lodgings in Verona and apply for the Italian *Codice Fiscale* (fiscal code number - without which you literally do not exist). My best friend had agreed to drive over with us and 'ride shotgun' as Geisha and I headed off to a new life in Italy. Full of excitement and plans.

The dream had not lasted long. How wrong I had been to assume that I could just slot into Italian corporate life. The job had turned out to be more difficult and problematic than any of us had foreseen so, 15 months after having turned my back on 'Merrie Englande', I was to be made redundant leaving me with not enough money to return home and, without any prospects; adrift in a city I loved but which would not have any employment opportunities for a foreign female of my age and abilities.

Yet the Gods move in mysterious ways, for, when I had worked in Milan twenty five years earlier, I had made a good friend. A charming, cultured educated and wickedly funny gay Italian man, Ugo, with whom I'd immediately clicked. He'd looked after me, taught me how to survive life in that fast-paced Italian city, helped me negotiate the mire of bureaucracy, found me somewhere to stay and thus as a lone British female adrift in one of the most ruthlessly commercial cities in the world, I had survived.

Now, 25 years later, and both of us older and greyer, we had reestablished contact. In my new role, I'd been able to offer him consultancy work enabling us to pick up where we had left off and settling back into our familiar, amusing and mutually affectionate friendship. We'd meet for long lunches after having suffered through interminable meetings with impossibly intransigent people who still did business the 'old-fashioned' way. Full of formalities and business etiquette. Yet we enjoyed it and, even better, got to travel a lot together - especially in the south and in Sicily (which I'd adored).

What I hadn't enjoyed - and what had made me feel old and inadequate - was that after about nine months my employers had asked me to take on a slightly different role - one for which I simply didn't have the necessary skill set. Uncharacteristically I kept my mouth shut about my misgivings and tried my hardest. Which wasn't good enough. I wasn't used to feeling inadequate and out of my depth, my stress levels soared and I became unhappy and withdrawn.

After 15 months of getting nowhere with the projects we'd endeavoured to set up with such hopes and enthusiasm, Ugo wasn't surprised when I'd rung him and told him that I was about to be made redundant. He'd been hearing rumours and also knew that my immediate boss had left suddenly. So he'd seen the proverbial writing on the wall and knew it was just a matter of time before I was to be set adrift. He also expressed doubt that I would get much of a payoff.

I however was naively hopeful that I could get something reasonable - more of a gilded life vest than a golden parachute, but something nevertheless.

Out of curiosity I'd consulted an employment lawyer and was told, more or less unequivocally, that if I was wrongfully dismissed, she could get me the equivalent of two years' salary (a not inconsiderable amount) but that due to the slowness of the Italian legal system, I might have to wait several years before it came to court.

Although, in my changed role, I'd not performed according to their expectations, what I was now required to do had not been written into my offer letter nor my contract. The owners hadn't even raised their concerns with me, nor had they asked me to meet them to discuss the matter, instead they had simply told the CEO to get rid of me.

Thankfully as a foreign female, my age and my 75% Italian civil invalidity (the arthritic knees and a perilously bad back) worked in my favour, thus I was somewhat protected.

There was however an added complication. The CEO, (another former colleague and old friend) had originally stuck his neck out by hiring me and my inadequacies were now reflecting badly on him. I'd never taken advantage of our friendship during business hours, but we were close and I felt that he was as uncomfortable as I with the situation. His COO was even less comfortable and was almost in tears, saying that it was regrettable because on the one hand I had done most of my job brilliantly! The part for which I thought I'd been hired!

I was scared, feeling very vulnerable, very alone and I knew that I simply had to leave with a reasonable payoff.

In a state of nervous apprehension and armed with my disability certificate I arrived in the CEO's elegant office at 8.00 sharp on the Monday morning. He was embarrassed, as was I, but I was determined to protect myself, so as he started to officially give me verbal notice I (somewhat rudely!) interrupted him and with a smile. I told him that since we had known each other for twenty five years surely the whole experience would be much less unpleasant if we approached it as friends and not the CEO and his soon-to-be superfluous employee. He agreed, seemingly relieved, and we sat down at his desk to work out how to resolve the situation. I told him what I needed financially, having worked out what I could live on for the next few months.

He gulped when I mentioned the figure. "I can't give you that. Italian employment law does not provide for redundancy payments, other than the mandatory TFR which is a small percentage of your salary based on the length of service. And you've been here for just fifteen months." I pointed out that I had moved at his behest but at my own expense to Italy - a not inconsiderable investment - and that being of a certain age and with the disability, any Court would, in all likelihood, take a dim view of my being treated in this way by my soon-to-be former employers. There was nothing in writing from them to the effect that they were dissatisfied with my work and I'd not actually done anything wrong!

He looked at the paltry figure written on the piece of paper I handed him and said he'd see what he could do. I told him that I knew he was a gentleman and that I trusted him to do the right thing. I'm pretty sure he was recalling the instance of role reversal many years earlier, when due to circumstances outside his control, he'd found himself in an extremely delicate and potentially damaging situation with my then employers. I had interceded on his behalf and he had been able to extricate himself with his reputation and the working relationship intact. Our friendship had always been based on honesty and mutual respect, for which, in the present uncomfortable circumstances, I was thankful. I left with my fingers crossed and my faith in his equanimity intact.

Two hours later he phoned me. It was all settled, the owners had agreed to my terms and I was instructed to go into the office the following day to sign various (and undoubtedly incomprehensible) bits of paper to formally terminate my employment. In the meantime I was to work with the COO to agree the text of my redundancy notice. That was a huge boon and I was grateful for the opportunity to do so. We worked on the document together, elegantly wording it so that any potential future employer would not view me as completely useless! I was grateful for and touched by his kindness and his regret at my leaving. The document had to be publicly stamped in some State office or another and I had to go with the company lawyer to sign it in front of witnesses. It basically said that we'd agreed Terms and that once having signed it, I would have no comeback against the company.

I agreed, met the charming lawyer at the appointed place and time, appeared suitably solemn in front of the official, signed on the dotted line and was told that I could now claim unemployment benefit if I chose to, given my disability. While my condition had prevented me from walking far, standing for too long or doing anything overtly energetic, I'd been living with it for so long that I'd got used to it and had just tailored my life accordingly. It had never occurred to me to claim benefits.

I walked out free, with enough money to tide me over for a few months if I was careful and immediately dialled Ugo. "Darling" he purred down the phone "you must come for the weekend to my home in the mountains…" this invitation rescued me from my fear and despair and I accepted with pleasure - first making sure that Geisha could stay with her 'second Mamma' Cheila, my wonderful Brazilian cleaning lady, who had fallen in love with Geisha as soon as she'd seen her - and vice versa!

Ugo and I agreed to meet, the following Friday, at one of the exits on the A22 motorway from Verona to Modena - it intersects the main Milan-Rome A1 not far from where he lived. Thus it had become one of the main meeting places on our travels, there being an incredibly good restaurant close by. Ugo had offered to buy me a celebratory/commiserating lunch there before we headed to the railway station in convoy to pick up his partner who was coming down from Milan for the weekend. I accepted with pleasure, just sad that we couldn't avail ourselves of too much of their excellent wine list as the *Polizia Stradale* had an office by the '*Casello*' - toll booth - and Italy was starting to crack down on not only drink-driving but speeding too.

La Barchetta is not easy to find, so I sat and waited for Ugo in the car park by the *Casello*. It was mid September but still uncomfortably hot in the *Padana* - the great plain of the Po river in north central Italy. Not only was it hot but stiflingly humid and permanently infested with voracious mosquitoes - which adore my sweet English blood! The longer I sat in the car, the greater my respect for the doughty inhabitants living as they do in a sort of insect-infested minestrone!

Ugo is a rare Italian - in many ways. He not only speaks excellent English which is unusual for older Italians, but he also really understands the Anglo Saxon mentality and mannerisms - including

being punctual! I knew he would, as always, be on time! This does not make him any less Italian but it does add a certain cachet when introducing him to British or North American colleagues or clients. They immediately feel comfortable with him and he is as honest as the day is long which is always reassuring, given that most foreigners are, rightly or wrongly, very concerned about the Mafia. He is also completely transparent in his approach to people and if he thinks you're wrong or ill-advised he will tell you - in an utterly charming and respectful way.

The road - well more of a lane really - to the restaurant ran along a route constructed on high dykes with mosquito riddled boggy ditches suppurating several metres below. I wondered how many people drove over the edge after dark, having imbibed too much of the excellent wines and grappas on offer in the restaurant! The lane wound around the incongruously placed massive concrete pillars of the recently-constructed *Alta Velocità* railway and as we circumnavigated them the restaurant came into view. Cars were parked along the ditches for several hundred metres and I wondered how we were going to find somewhere that didn't necessitate an uncomfortably long stroll in the hot and humid 'mosquito minestrone'. We were lucky - there were two spaces right in front of the main entrance, so we parked and went into the blessedly cool and inviting interior.

As we waited to be greeted and seated, I looked at Ugo. Properly looked at him, for though I had known him for years, I'd got into the bad habit of looking but not seeing. Of medium height and medium build, he looked toned and tanned. I knew he, like most Italians, spent as much time as he could in the summer sun, skin changing colour from the creamy beige of winter to the deep dark bronze of the beach. Italians are never as white or pasty as us northern foreigners, particularly the almost marble white of the Brits - which is probably why we are known as '*Mozzarelle*', the mozzarellas of the skin pigmentation world! Soon, with overexposure to the fierce Italian sun, we become '*Aragoste*', lobsters!

His hair was short, mid brown and well cut, his salt and pepper beard was magnificent, somewhat reminiscent of Tsar Nicholas II or his cousin King George V of England, it was well shaped and well maintained. Completely at odds with the wild Rasputin look he'd favoured some years earlier when we'd met in Florence. He saw me appraising him and grinned, his berry-dark eyes gleaming with suppressed amusement.

"Darling, what are you doing? You are making me uncomfortable".

"Don't be paranoid, I'm just thinking how well and fit you look".

"Yoga and Pilates my dear" he said looking pointedly at me and somewhat askance at my bountiful *embonpoint*!

My Italian friends simply cannot understand why I'm pretty unconcerned about my appearance. I'd found the national obsession with the art of looking good, quite difficult to comprehend and I remember incredulous stares from women in the supermarket when I wandered in with almost no makeup and in comfy clothes, for they were immaculately turned out, even in casual wear and always perfectly coiffured and made up. Yet I am, by all accounts, an attractive woman, though my bounty is not to everyone's taste! I scrub up well when required but have been known to go all day with a blob of mascara on my nose, because when passing one I simply never look in a mirror. Total anathema to the stylish Italians!

I made a moue at him and thankfully was rescued from a lecture on my lack of interest in exercise by the arrival of the waitress, who showed us to our table, my favourite, the one in the corner. Ugo grimaced and reaching up removed the cashmere jumper which had been casually yet elegantly slung across his shoulders and put it on. Whereas I was hot in linen!

In high summer the tables are outside, but as soon as September starts, irrespective of the weather, they are moved back inside - for which I was thankful. Bringing us a glass of cool Prosecco to sip while we studied the huge and inviting menu, the pretty and friendly waitress, one of the owner's daughters, took us through the daily Specials. The food is the absolute best of the local traditions, all home-cooked by the Matriarch and her team in the enormous steamy kitchen behind the Reception desk. For being situated in the lower Padana, the artisan production of sublime pasta, charcuterie and cheeses is what the area is rightly famed for.

The Italians tend to eat enormous lunches comprising an *Antipasto* or Starter, a *Primo Piatto* (pasta or risotto), a *Secondo Piatto* (meat or fish), *Contorni* (vegetables and potatoes) *Insalate* (salads) and *Dolci* (desserts). All washed down with copious quantities of delicious and usually-local interesting wines and followed by coffee and a digestif. Baskets of freshly made bread and carafes of water come as standard accompaniments to the meal.

I cannot begin to describe the myriad mouthwatering options open to us and endeavouring to do so would not do them justice. Suffice to say that the food from the Modena, Reggio Emilia and Parma areas as well as Bologna half an hour further south, is probably the absolute pinnacle of Italian cooking. It is no coincidence that Fico World Eataly, the food-centric Theme Park in Bologna, the 'capital of Italian gastronomy' is just down the road. Featuring eateries, pop-up stores, demonstrations and hands-on exhibits from field to fork it pays homage to long-standing regional traditions and is an extraordinary place to visit. In an area of incredible cuisine, *La Barchetta* was no exception.

The wine list - for an oenophile like me - was heavenly with wines from small local producers using mostly native grape varieties. Each area has a different wine and artisan wine production has become big business in Italy over the past few years. *Vinitaly* in Verona every spring is the largest wine exhibition in the world promoting Italian and other nationalities' wines of all types, including organic and biodynamic, to tens of thousands of visitors from over 145 countries. *La Barchetta's* owner, obviously an aficionado, went out of his way to suggest various wines to accompany our choices. He even, most intelligently, offered them by the glass. No doubt ever-conscious of the sadly - and worryingly - vigilant *Polizia Stradale* 500 metres away!

Since we didn't need to meet Ugo's partner until the late afternoon we were able to eat at a leisurely pace and lingered, long after the other clientele, had gone back to their offices or continued on their journeys up and down Italy's concrete arteries, with coffee and gentle conversation.

Ugo asked me what I was going to do, now that I was unemployed. "Are you going to go home?"

"No. I can't afford it, my house is let and I'd have nowhere to stay. Anyway I like living here and I think I might be able to get some consultancy work from a couple of people I met recently." I knew that Ugo himself had had a hard time being a consultant and wondered if my 'foreignness' might be a disadvantage or an advantage. I'd recently met some lovely business people - four brothers - and been well-received by them, they had been most appreciative of my skills and know-how and I'd hoped that they would see fit to retain me to assist them to deliver a particularly exciting project we'd been working on. I knew that my former employers had no interest in continuing with it as it had been very much 'my' project and I had the blessing of the CEO to try and agree terms with the brothers. I could even get Ugo involved if they were interested in our joint approach.

We chatted about this and a couple of other possibilities and then I asked him about his house in the mountains. "Wait and see" was all he said! I was intrigued.

Soon it was time to leave, we were meeting Sandro at the *Mediopadana* station just outside Reggio Nell Emilia. Situated on the relatively new high-speed railway line between Milan and Rome the *Frecce* (the Italian equivalents of the French TGV trains) made the long trip in just over 3 hours in sublime comfort and on time.

The station was famed for its cutting edge architecture and I recall the first time I had seen it on my return to Italy the previous year. Designed by the hugely talented Spanish Architect/Engineer, Santiago Calatrava, the pure white building is in the form of a long undulating wave of astonishing beauty in its fluid and simple perfection. It is breathtaking, but as it is situated right alongside the main Milan-Rome motorway, I'm surprised it hasn't caused multiple pile ups as drivers slow down to contemplate its majestically organic form and, though gorgeous, I'll bet it's a bugger to clean!

Resembling a fan or a series of rippling waves it rises out of the flat featureless landscape like some sort of dream. Getting to it however is more like a nightmare! Situated seemingly in the middle of nowhere there is not a designated main road leading to it, rather one has to go up to the next motorway exit, execute a series of perplexing and badly signposted manoeuvres around several roundabouts and under several impressive bridges (also designed by Calatrava) before getting onto a small road leading to what appears to be a gigantic car park with the station rising above it. Close up however, the building was oddly depressing; it was dirty, it looked badly maintained and the gorgeous glass panels between the ripples of the 'fan' were fly-blown and in need of a good clean. The facilities seemed inadequate (although the lavatories were spotlessly clean) and the car park simply wasn't big enough with cars parked everywhere in true Italian fashion! We parked where we could, just as the *Freccia Rossa* (Red Arrow) from Milan pulled silently - and punctually - into the station above us.

Sandro appeared a minute later, gliding down the escalator looking cool in a dark blue polo shirt and stonewashed jeans, his dark hair curling around the nape of his neck and his dark, almost black eyes, hidden behind impenetrable Ray Bans. He and Ugo made a handsome couple and I had visions of them working out side by side in the *Palestra* in order to maintain their form and looks. Having hugged him hello, we climbed into our respective cars and I followed Ugo back around the confusing roundabouts to the motorway, heading towards Modena Nord, our turn off for the distant mountains - only just visible through the soupy heat haze.

Coming off the motorway we drove fast down a very bumpy dual carriageway liberally peppered with speed cameras towards the hills, passing through Sassuolo, the centre of the Italian ceramic industry. Like the outskirts of all industrial towns there seemed to be little of beauty or interest to see and everything seemed to be covered with a fine layer of white dust. It was a depressing place but my heart lifted as we headed out of the area onto a country road, signposted towards the *Passo Delle Radici* the mountain pass that divides this part of the province of Emilia Romagna from Tuscany. In medieval times it was all Tuscany - but that is another story for later on! The landscape changed from dusty industrial to one of undulating fecundity for it is in the hills of this area that the land is given over exclusively to the production of the world-famous *Parmigiano Reggiano* - Parmesan cheese. Pastures for grazing, fields for growing animal foodstuffs, huge *stalle* (cowsheds), vast milk co-operatives together with artisan cheesemakers and organic butchers lined the side of the road, all interspersed by old - some ancient - clay quarries. The extremely complex geology of the area (dating from the Pleistocene and Pliocene eras) means that the clay of this section of the Apennine mountains is perfect for the production of tiles of all types. Thus for many many years - centuries in fact - Sassuolo has been a major centre for that industry.

Another benefit of the geology is that this part of the Appenines, whilst prone to earthquakes like all of Italy, is actually situated on clay so that the land wobbles rather than cracks during the majority of local seismic activity. Unlike the beautiful medieval towns in Umbria and

Eastern Tuscany, buildings tend not to collapse but to rupture. The town of Norcia, not far from Perugia in Umbria, was devastated by two earthquakes in quick succession in August 2016 with a heartbreaking loss of life and the ruin of many beautiful and historic buildings. Of course there have been earthquakes in the area of the Emilian Appenines and many landslides but, apparently, nothing truly apocalyptic for many hundreds of years.

I knew none of this as we drove along the course of the river Secchia, still heading due west towards the enticingly-named Passo delle Radici. I looked around me with interest as we passed several small but prosperous-looking towns. This area of Italy is one of the richest, being the centre of not only food production, Parma ham (*Prosciutto*) from Parma, Parmesan from the area around Reggio Emilia, Balsamic Vinegar from Modena but also the home and production centres of the world-famous Ferraris and De Tomaso cars from Maranello and Modena with Maserati and Ducati based in Bologna forty minutes away.

As the main road leads to the mountain passes and then down into the coastal stretch of Northern Tuscany life here is quiet and contemplative with the accent on living and playing well - away from the freneticism of the cities. The people, mountain people, still speak the local dialect, their accent is thick and lyrical like Cornish in England and they are naturally suspicious of 'incomers'. There are ski resorts, Winter Olympic gold medallists grew up in these mountains, there is trekking, hiking, cycling (both on and off-road), there is climbing, rafting and, with some of the clearest skies in Europe, stargazing. The area is a UNESCO biosphere and the air is fresh, clean and the scenery pastoral and spectacularly beautiful - dominated (on a clear day) by the mountains of *Cimone* and *Cusna* overlooking the ancient passes into Tuscany and the evocatively-named area known as *Lunigiana*, named for the ancient Goddess *Luni*.

Dragged from my reverie, I noticed that Ugo was turning right. Up a steep hill. Changing down through the gears to keep the revs up, I followed him, amazed at the way the road climbed so steeply winding sinuously and strenuously through beech woods to emerge onto a verdant plateau with spectacular 360∘ views. Small stone farmhouses and some bigger, more modern houses stood dotted about. Up on a hill I glimpsed the remains of what looked like a medieval stone tower. Everything looked prosperous and inviting. I turned off the a/c and opened my window breathing in cool and sweet air. It must have been eight degrees cooler up here. In the distance the mountains rose majestically into a cerulean blue and cloudless sky. After approximately ten minutes of ever steeper gradients, Ugo indicated right again, slowed down and drove through the gap between two low stone barns into a gravelled yard, round a large and handsome stone house and a couple of pretty crumbling barns into a courtyard where he parked. I followed him. My jaw hit the floor for we had parked in a gravelled forecourt in front of the most beautiful, majestic yet serene manor house, bathed in late afternoon sunshine, its ancient stones gently aglow and the weathered wooden shutters of its four storeys giving away no clues as to what lay within. It was enormous.

To our left was a huge barn, the upper part open to the elements via patterned air bricks, '*gelosie*' in Italian, in the style of the traditional *Fienile* (hay barns) of rural Italy and covered with swathes of already autumnal-coloured creeper. An arched portico at ground level gave tantalising glimpses of huge and obviously ancient wooden chests, a variety of garden furniture and many massive terracotta pots filled with fragrant plants. Further buildings, some restored, some barely standing, surrounded a central courtyard area, set off by a magnificent stone archway which had seemingly once been the main entrance to the manor which still sat portentously amongst its vassal buildings.

I climbed out of the car as if in a dream and wandered over to Ugo who was grinning at me with undisguised glee as he saw my astonishment. "Welcome darling. Welcome to my house".

I stood speechless, gazing at the faded beauty, the slumbering magnificence of this perfect place, a medieval *Borgo*. A hamlet with, at its heart, the *Casa Signorile*, the Manor House, surrounded by its attendant structures. I fell instantly and irrevocably in love.

Chapter 2

Love at first sight…

"Your house? How come...?" I asked, still drinking in the awe-inspiring splendour of the sun-washed stones radiating warmth in the September evening.

"My sister, Luisa, is married to Alberto, the son of the owner, Signor S. It was his family that built it in the 17th century". Ugo explained as we started unpacking the cars. Hearing a crunch on the gravel behind us he turned with a big smile as a serenely beautiful Arab woman, head tightly swathed in the traditional Hijab and wearing a very untraditional and gloriously colourful outfit that looked like velour lounging pyjamas, appeared from the smaller house behind us.

"*Buon giorno*" she said, coming towards us with a shy smile. A small thin girl with mischievous brown eyes peered around her to see who the newcomer was. Ugo introduced us.

"Cass this is Farah our housekeeper and this is her daughter Ayesha".

"*Buon giorno, sono* Cassandra" I shook at Farah's hand and grinned at Ayesha while introducing myself in Italian and explaining that I was English. Both looked amazed that I was not Italian and Ugo went on to tell them that he and I were old friends and had known each other for many years.

Sandro joined us, crouching down to say Ciao to Ayesha who was visibly torn between shyness and huge curiosity at the sight of a foreigner. He told her that now she'd started school she should practice her English with me. She giggled and said, haltingly, in English, "Hello". We all laughed delightedly.

Gathering up our bags and, with the help of Farah and Ayesha, we trudged towards the great front door, our feet crunching on the gravel. As we neared the door, the bush to my left rustled and out shot two tabby cats racing across the forecourt to the safety of the nearby portico where they sat and watched us curiously.

Less excitable and lying insouciantly on a huge bench which had obviously been hewn from a massive tree truck, was another tabby who stood up, purring, as Ayesha bent to stroke her.

"This is Mimi the house cat. The others are farm cats," explained Ugo as he opened the door and deposited the bags he was carrying onto an antique wooden settle opposite the door. Beckoning me in, he opened the door to his right and we entered a dark and slightly smoky room, absolutely stuffed with furniture.

Four windows on two sides were set into massively thick walls about a metre thick but little light penetrated the room and what light there was, wavered as the leaves danced on the trees outside and fluttered in the breeze. Ugo reached for the light switch and turned on the light. I was enchanted to see that the switch and wiring were also ancient and that the switch was not pressed but actually turned. A Bakelite knob in the switch housing being the only way of turning it on.

To the left of the door a huge walk in fireplace took up most of the wall with the soot-blackened bricks proclaiming centuries of use. A fire was already laid, a variety of fireplace tools and an extraordinarily colourful pair of bellows at the ready for poking and encouraging the fire, while above, suspended from a wicked-looking long hook hung a cast iron cauldron. A comfy and obviously much-loved armchair stood beside the fire behind which was a door leading into what looked like a kitchen, judging by the tantalising glimpses of copper utensils hanging from an ancient wooden wall rack.

The floor was covered in the traditional *cotto* baked brick tiles, their deep oxblood red colour burnished by centuries of polishing.

To the right of the kitchen door was another long wooden settle, possibly the twin of the one in the hallway, comfortably upholstered with a green woollen bench cushion which Mimi was now enthusiastically kneading with her claws. A series of charming antique Botanical prints hung in matching frames along the wall and at the far end stood another comfy armchair wedged in between the settle and the window.

Between the two windows on the end wall stood a massive full height dark oak dresser, its glazed upper doors displaying an interesting array of half empty bottles, each containing varying amounts of coloured liqueurs. Massive, carved and heavy-looking drawers opened above a big cupboard and the top was covered with an array of cruet and glassware. All old and all beautiful.

Another armchair anchored the third corner beside which was another enormous piece of furniture. This time it was a sideboard, as ornate and intricate as its companion piece. It was also crammed with stuff including an old-fashioned corded telephone and a somehow out of context medium-sized flat screen TV. The final armchair rested beside it.

In the middle of the room was a huge old wooden table, easily seating 10 and surrounded by wooden chairs with woven rush seats, some covered with seat pads. A great terracotta dish stood in the middle.

Despite the portentous furniture there actually seemed a lot of space and the room was comfy and welcoming and smelt of beeswax and woodsmoke and floor polish. The energy of the room felt redolent of good living, good food and good company. I longed to sit quietly in the big chair by the fireside and just 'be'.

Fortuitously my wish was almost immediately granted for Ugo suggested that I sat down while he, Sandro and Farah finished emptying the car and put everything away. I started to protest, then realised that I'd only get in the way, so demurred and sank gratefully into the welcoming embrace of the chair. Almost immediately Sandro appeared from the kitchen bearing a glass of dark red, almost purple, wine and gave it to me. Putting it carefully down on the brick hearth beside my chair I thanked him, leaned back and sighed deeply. A sigh of pure pleasure and of release. This place was already working some magic on me for I felt more relaxed and happier than I had for a very long time.

Mimi, recognising the sound of a fellow sybarite, jumped up onto my knee, briefly kneaded it with razor-sharp claws, circled once and lay down purring like a diesel engine and drooling with pleasure as I caressed her pretty head. I loved her for that simple act of welcome and acceptance - even more so when Ugo appeared carrying bags of delicious goodies, saw her in situ and remarked that this was unheard of as Mimi only loved Signor S...!

Gratified I sipped my wine appreciatively listening to Ugo and Sandro chatting companionably as they stowed the provisions. Not for the first time was I glad that my Italian was fluent and I smiled as I heard Ugo affectionately chiding Sandro for putting the wrong cheese in the wrong container! Mimi, upon smelling food, shot off my lap looking for titbits and leaving me to savour my wine.

"This Lambrusco is great." I said, grateful that I had a pretty good grounding in the better-known Italian wines. Usually I found its sparkling pinkness too sweet and sickly for my taste, But this was dark and full-bodied, robust and uncompromising with a hint of fizz and, seemingly, contained a high level of alcohol!

Lambrusco is, according to Wikipedia, 'both a grape and a wine from the Province of Emilia–Romagna with four distinct zones around the central provinces of Modena, Parma, Reggio Emilia and Modena.' The wine has a long history with archaeological evidence indicating that the Etruscans and the Romans after them cultivated the vine. Apparently it yielded vast amounts each harvest with one harvest "enough to fill 300 amphora"!

I'd remembered drinking it in London in the 1970's when it was cheap and plentiful and really not liking it. But this was from the manor house's own vines and was bottled in the *cantina* (just off the kitchen) by Alberto every autumn and it was delicious.

Ugo smiled, appreciating the fact that I knew what I was drinking - and really enjoying it. It was relaxing me perhaps a little too quickly, so I put the glass carefully on the top of the wooden mantel above the fireplace and wandered through to the kitchen to see if I could help.

The room was long and narrow with a stone sink under the window at one end and an intriguing dark door between two ancient built-in cupboards at the other. Along one wall was a massive marble worktop into which was set a large gas hob with electric oven beneath. On the wall above and running the entire length of the room was an incredible array of saucepans, pots, lids and cooking utensils all hanging, somewhat incongruously on IKEA kitchen hooks from massive wood and iron battens.

On the opposite side of the room was another great wooden chest, like the one I'd seen in the portico. I later found out that these chests were used not only for storing linens, but, historically, bread and dry goods as they were difficult for rodents to get into. Above this were full length wooden shelves groaning under the weight of an array of terracotta cooking vessels, copper pots, sieves, Bain Maries, copper jelly moulds and great bunches of dried herbs. The only hint of the twenty first century, apart from the hob and oven were a dishwasher and a microwave perched jauntily atop the large fridge/freezer in the corner.

The floor was also of dark red *cotto* upon which sat Mimi's food and water bowls.

Kitchens in Italy are for cooking in. Italians tend to eat in the main room which serves as both dining room and living room. Comfy seating takes second place to the great table at which centuries of delicious family meals will have been eaten, lives discussed and wine drunk. There was no seat in the kitchen so I perched on the great chest while Sandro and Ugo busied themselves with preparing supper.

Once again I offered to help. Once again I was refused: "You are our guest" was the response. Italians are incredibly hospitable people and I loved watching the boys evidently enjoying putting together a meal. Wanting a glass of water I headed for the sink where I'd seen a glass on the old wooden draining board and turning on the tap I wondered briefly, like some concerned tourist, whether the water was drinkable. I should have known better. In these rural areas the water comes from wells, not the mains and, of course, it was delicious, cold and sweet. As I filled my glass I looked out of the window onto a small herb garden. It may have been small in size but it was literally crammed with bushes and plants of every conceivable type of herb. Birds and insects buzzed their way around it, the only sound other than the murmuring of Ugo and Sandro as they shared the tasks.

Reaching a point where there seemed to be a little time before the next task was due, Ugo asked me if I'd like a look around. "Absolutely" I responded, and indicating the intriguing door between the cupboards he ushered me into total Stygian gloom.

I could see nothing in the all-encompassing blackness. Turning yet another light switch, he waited for a second while the low energy bulb glimmered into life, bathing everything in a warm glow.

As my eyes became accustomed to the dim light I saw another long room lined with yet more huge wooden chests upon which stood piles of crockery, urns and dishes, while an adjacent table groaned under the weight of glassware, bottles, carafes, flagons, goblets and jars. It was as if the hundreds of years of continuous occupation by one family were represented in their houseware lying casually about, completely undisturbed, apart from a regular dusting. For everything was spotless. No dust, no cobwebs, no dirt.

Along the right hand wall were a series of enormous oak barrels, like the ones into which Bilbo Baggins put Thorin Oakenshield and the Dwarves when they escaped from the Wood Elves in the Hobbit! In front of these was piled all the paraphernalia of viticulture. Vast Demijons of thick glass sitting in straw baskets, huge funnels for decanting wine and row upon row of empty wine bottles on the shelves of the wall opposite.

Between the shelves was another opening into a smaller room. A fully-stocked wine cellar. Additional full height shelves and several tables supported bottles of various types of spirits (I was delighted and amused to see not one, but two bottles of my favourite single malt Whisky) as well as many bottles of Champagne, Prosecco, Spumante and Franciacorta the great Italian sparkling wines together with intriguing-looking bottles of liqueurs - some darkly inviting, some worryingly colourful!

In the room opposite, placed impressively on a large oak table, stood a Berkel Volano, the Ferrari of meat slicers, its bright red powder-coated metal contrasting sharply with the gleaming silver of the ferocious-looking circular blade, all accompanied by a beguiling array of knobs and handles. Alongside the table stood a chest freezer, another fridge/freezer and an entire larder of bottled and pickled goodies in glass Kilner jars of varying sizes.

The whole house, or the bit that I'd seen so far, was designed around the vitally important activity of living well. What Signor S' ancestors must make of tiny kitchen areas in modern city centre flats is worth consideration! For living well is good for the soul and the Italian diet is known to be one of the best in the world. Though how copious quantities of pasta, meat, cheese and oil can be good for one is difficult to imagine. I think it's all about moderation. Less being more.

Returning to the main room we quickly laid the table and sat down. I tested all the rickety-looking wooden chairs before selecting the most robust; I had no intention of ending up on the perfectly polished *cotto* floor!

Meanwhile Sandro had decided that it was cold, around 20 degrees, so he'd lit the fire. I laughed delightedly, for 800 metres down on the plain it was probably 28-30 degrees while up here we were lighting a fire - in the second week in September! Yet it was decidedly chilly and I welcomed the warmth. My Anglo Saxon blood was obviously acclimatising to living in Italy. 20 degrees in the UK is considered warm! As the flames licked the wood, I'm told a mixture of birch, beech, chestnut, oak and hornbeam, I reflected upon my physiological changes and went to fetch a shawl.

The table laid, we discovered a gastronomic crisis - there was no bread and it was too late to go to the village and get some. Luckily Farah was able to give us some of hers otherwise it would have turned into a catastrophe! Italians eat huge quantities of bread with their meals but unadorned by butter or oil. The breads are all of artisan production and the local bread, "normal" bread was not unlike a Sourdough and vital for mopping up delicious sauces or just nibbling between courses.

The meal was deceptively simple - yet it was a feast - for everything was fresh, nothing was precooked or packaged. Before meeting me Ugo had been shopping, sensibly putting his purchases into a cool box in the boot of his car. The prosciutto had been sliced in front of his eyes earlier in the day, as had the salami with fennel seeds. The tortellini in *brodo* - tiny packets of meat-filled pasta cooked in an aromatic broth - had been handmade by the lady in the shop and the broth came from the Hamlet's freezer, being constituted from the rendering of chicken bones, bouquet garni, onions and herbs, all from within the fridge and larder of the house.

The *Barzigole*, flattened pieces of meat sliced from the belly of a sheep had been bought at the organic butcher on the main road and were cooked to perfection in a very hot dry frying pan with a pinch of rock salt, ground pepper and fresh rosemary from the herb garden to season it. Even the salad was a simple mix of local lambs lettuce, radicchio and butterhead lettuce. Cold pressed extra virgin olive oil from up the road and balsamic vinegar completed the repast.

Everything was washed down with copious amounts of the Hamlet's Lambrusco and a jug of ice cold tap water.

Conversation flowed, lights flickered, the fire hissed and crackled and Mimi prowled round the table like a mini tiger on the lookout for stray pieces of prosciutto and *Barzigole*.

After the meal, in companionable silence, we sipped Luisa's *Nocino*, a bitter liqueur made from the Hamlet's walnuts. The silence was that of good friends who do not feel the need to speak, each gazing reflectively into the glowing fire. But no one had warned me that the Nocino was lethal and I was suddenly overtaken by a wave of tiredness. Musing upon this I realised that this was the first time I'd actually been able to properly relax in a long long while.

Ugo, noticing my sudden exhaustion suggested he and I take my stuff upstairs to my room, make the bed and ensure that the room wasn't too cold for me.

So off we went through the hall, to another twisty light switch and a stone staircase, worn in the middle of each step by centuries of the comings and goings of the house's many inhabitants. I was too tired to do much more than briefly notice prints, maps and paintings on the walls as we climbed the stairs to the first floor. A great chestnut door opened into a lovely inviting room with its own en-suite bathroom. Like the rest of the house the furniture was large and of dark wood, but it was not at all oppressive. The bed was massive and covered with what I call a 'Princess and the Pea' mattress. The old fairy tale by Hans Christian Andersen recounted a Princess so sensitive that she could feel a pea under a mattress if it wasn't thick enough. Well she'd not have felt a golf ball under this one, so deep was it!

Together we quickly made the bed, Ugo showed me where the light switch was for the bathroom, delved into a big cupboard and produced a cozy-looking huge woollen blanket "in case you get cold with just the duvet", hugged me goodnight and headed out of the door, pausing just long enough to tell me that I might get a visit from one of the resident ghosts.

I was so tired I didn't care about ghosts. Anyway in a place like this they were bound to be friendly, after all they were Signor S' family, so mentally saying hello and goodnight to them, I cleaned my teeth and climbed into bed, having opened the window slightly so that I could hear the owls hooting in the trees. Thus I descended into the arms of Morpheus.

Chapter 3

Of food - and vertiginous roads

The next morning, breakfasting on warm, newly-baked Arab bread thoughtfully provided by Farah with little glass bowls of homemade fruit compotes from the recesses of one of the mysterious cupboards, we discussed our plans for the day. I thoughtfully sipped my large cup of black coffee, ignoring the horrified glances of the boys as I'd added a lot of hot water to an espresso while they downed theirs scaldingly hot and, to my mind, very over-sugared from tiny cups. " Darling how can you drink that stuff? It's disgusting. You don't even take sugar?"

"Come on Ugo, you know I love espresso but I need a long coffee in the mornings and I really don't like cappuccinos". They laughed as I grimaced at the thought of the hot milky frothy coffee that the Italians had in the mornings - usually with some sort of '*brioche*' the word for a sweet pastry or croissant. Many years ago when I'd arrived in Italy for the first time, Ugo had taught me that cappuccinos were only drunk until 11.00 am and that you could always tell a foreigner as no self-respecting Italian would be seen dead drinking one after that hour. Cafe owners, waiters and bar staff all over Italy still snigger when unsuspecting tourists order a cappuccino after their lunch - or worse, their dinner!

We were all keen to go out and get some provisions, especially the local and, apparently, rightly famous bread, the Pane di Valestra made by the local bakers in the village so we agreed to eschew the tour of the house and grounds until later on.

45

Piling into Ugo's sensible and very comfortable Fiat Panda, I noticed with amusement that, as we'd approached the parked cars, small scampering felines disappeared under mine and that the bonnet was already coved in dusty paw marks - a sign that my car met with the approval of the farm cats!

We turned right out of the driveway and I drank in the landscape, opening the window to sniff the air. We were set in the midst of rolling pastures, dotted here and there with clumps of deciduous trees and further up the hillside woodlands stretched away as far as the eye could see. The road meandered around a series of curves climbing gently towards the landmark that was Monte Valestra. At this altitude it was not much more than a hill, but from the plains below it could be seen for many kilometres. The fields undulated gently near the road, becoming much steeper in places and I wondered idly about ploughing them, for some of the escarpments were vertiginous. All were lushly carpeted in bright green - despite the torrid summer - for it seems that up here rain was fairly regular (and fortuitously mostly nocturnal) which explained the fertility of the fields. In the distance a couple of lakes glinted in the sunlight and Ugo explained that Signor S had created them and stocked them with fish then leased them to two local fishing clubs.

As we drove towards the village I spied a couple of houses perched high on the crest, facing north east. Neither were of the same antiquity as the Manor House and the Hamlet, but one looked a couple of hundred years old, radiating a sort of fading gentility as it sat solidly among steeply plunging gardens, mostly filled with some fruit trees and shrubs dotted randomly about the lawn. The state of pride in its upkeep was evident in the meticulously mown grass, which must have been a feat in itself!

The second house was a modern chalet-style house. Obviously built to accommodate two families, for it had two distinct main entrances, one on each storey. It was terraced and balconied, both of which boasted a pretty display of lush plants and small trees in terracotta pots. The house looked prosperous and welcoming and as we drove by, an elderly lady sitting taking the sun on the upper terrace waved at us in response to Ugo's friendly toot toot of the horn. It's just as well he'd done that, for lurching massively towards us, round a tight bend was an enormous red tractor, closely followed by an equally large blue one. All three vehicles simultaneously stood on their brakes and we carefully manoeuvred our way past each other, much to the interest of the old lady.

We rounded another bend and I gasped in amazement for, laid out before me was an astonishing view. Far below us, to my right, stretched kilometre upon kilometre of the *Padana*, the fertile plain of the Po valley. A brown smudge in the shimmering heat haze clearly indicated the route of the A1, the Autostrada del Sole, Italy's great arterial motorway from Milan, to Bologna, Florence, Rome and Naples. It is the oldest European highway and the most important in Italy. At 759.6 kilometres (472 miles) it was constructed in 1964 and runs through 6 Provinces and I knew it like the back of my hand, having spent an enormous part of my working life rushing up and down it, from one appointment to another. Yet I'd never looked up, to see the hills over which we were now driving and it gave me an odd feeling to know that they had always been here, quietly overlooking the frenetic activity below, both areas coexisting side by side yet, somehow disconnected by a spatial or temporal shift. Up here, 700m above sea level, it was, literally a different world, with different rhythms, priorities and ways of being.

The brown smudge which ran along the line of the motorway for as far as the eye could see was sad testament to the pollution of the plains and the communities therein. Up here the air was sweet and everything seemed to sparkle in the autumn sunshine.

On the outskirts of the village we pulled off the road and parked in front of a long low white building. A sign pronounced it to be the *Latteria Sociale* di San Pietro, the local cheese factory. I was informed by the boys that this was the International award-winning dairy producing the world famous unpasteurised and lactose-free Parmesan cheese to which the Region gives its name - which is not to be confused with the lesser-quality *Grana Padana* from the plains.

A small glass door in the corner opened into the shop, the remainder of the vast place being given over to production. Inside was a large chiller cabinet literally crammed with various types of Parmesan - ranging from the sweetest, aged 12 months (which is the minimum seasoning duration) to the more mature and robust 30 months version with the 20 month variety in between. There were great slabs pre-packed in vacuum packs, whole round cheeses with the San Pietro logo stamped on the curved sides and buckets of fresh ricotta, a whey cheese produced from the leftovers of the Parmesan production. There were also half kilo pats of butter ready-wrapped in waxed paper and all stamped with the seal of the dairy.

In a corner stood a small table and display cabinet loaded with cheese-related paraphernalia such as Parmesan knives, cheeseboards with magnetised knife holders, wooden troughs for displaying the cheese, wines, local jams (eaten with the cheese) and huge golf umbrellas, together with chefs aprons all proudly bearing the logo and a copy of the gold medallion awarded for the world's best unpasteurised cheese.

I'd never seen a Parmesan knife before and on close examination realised how sensible they were. This cheese was nothing like the small cardboard barrels of grated cheese that resembled dust, or the liberal sprinkling of dryish powder that we get on our pasta in Italian restaurants outside Italy (along with ground black pepper from the phallic oversized pepper mills that waiters worldwide love brandishing with a knowing leer!). This Parmesan was solid, a robust cheese full of flavour and to enjoy it properly it needs to be cut into chunks or shards to nibble on. Hence the knife with its drop or leaf-shaped blade (not unlike a Stone Age obsidian adze) and sturdy wooden handle.

I quickly stocked up on the goodies, amassing an enormous pile by the till and the friendly lady behind the counter beamed with delight as I chatted with her, exclaiming to the boys that she'd never met a *straniera* who spoke such good Italian. We discussed the various merits of the 3 versions of ageing of the cheese.

The production of *Parmigiano Reggiano* is strictly controlled to maintain quality and authenticity. The milk comes from cows who are fed hay solely from the fields we'd driven through and, at certain times of year, also graze on the rich grass. They are milked twice a day with the milk being immediately trucked to the dairy where it is poured into massive copper lined boiling vats, rennet is added and the mixture is stirred by hand by the Master Cheesemaker. No preservatives or additives are permitted in the process. Once the desired consistency is reached the cheese is then poured into moulds where the briny rind forms, it is then stamped with the Cheesemaker's mark and left to mature.

The 12 month version is used for grating or nibbled as an *aperitivo*. The 20 month is the oldest version of the cheese with over 1,000 years of history behind it and is used in daily cooking as it is the best cheese to eat for a healthy diet. The oldest, the 30 month old is reserved for 'a more refined palate" and for more refined cuisine! This Parmesan is so rightly lauded that it makes for a wonderful and gratefully received gift.

Having decided to go for the 20 month version I ordered a kilo slab but the lady wouldn't countenance giving me a pre-packed piece. Instead she selected a huge whole cheese and rolled it to her marble topped preparation area where she deftly sliced it in half using a lethal-looking cheese wire and cut, by eye, a slab which weighted almost precisely a kilo. This she placed between two sheets of monogrammed plastic wrapping and putting it into an enormous machine vacuum packed it for me. Totting up my purchases she added a tub of Ricotta to them, explaining that this was a gift for the *Signora Inglese* who was so *simpatica*!

I thanked her profusely quietly marvelling at the price, €15 for the kilo which, in any supermarket in the UK would have cost well over double that amount and the quality would not have been anything like as good!

Staggering beneath the weight of our purchases we stowed them in the boot, noting that the little space had filled up fast with eager customers, some of whom drove considerable distances to get here, such was the Latteria's fame. We pulled out of the parking area and headed into the village for our next gastronomic treat. A visit to *Il Forno*, the village bakery.

Having wrestled to get through the mandatory fly curtains we entered the shop and were warmly greeted by a smiley welcoming couple. Mauro the Baker was tall and grave-looking with a handsome face that reminded me of the Welsh actor Jonathan Pryce. Luisa, his slim beautiful wife, her wildly curly hair (a remnant from some Celtic warrior passing through centuries before?) safely tucked into her white Baker's hat, came forward to show us what they had baked today. For everything from the different types of bread and rolls, to cakes, biscuits and pies were freshly made daily in the huge bakery behind the shop, as well as the various types of pasta.

Ugo swiftly sequestered two large loaves of the *Pane di Valestra* the Bakery's speciality, telling me that they were organic. He then turned his attention to the goodies in the display cabinet.

"You must try this" he said indicating a sort of flat pie that reminded me a bit of the Greek *Spanokopita* - spinach pie. " This is *Erbazzone*, made from local herbs, greens and cheese. Luisa please tell my friend how you make it." With a lovely smile Luisa obligingly explained that it was a traditional pie from the province of Reggio Emilia and that the herbs and greens are picked locally, sautéed with onion and pancetta. Parmesan is added to enhance the flavour and then encased in a thin crust (called *pasta matta*) made from unleavened flour enriched with olive oil or lard and then baked. She cut out a sliver and offered it to me to try. It was absolutely delicious and I immediately asked for half the entire pie to share with the boys when we got home.

Meanwhile Sandro was at the other end of the shop, chatting with Mauro who was busily selecting salamis, prosciutto and mortadella for him to try. He was also mulling over the local cheeses - cow, sheep and goat and all from a 20 kilometre radius. I was told that, wherever possible, everything was '*biologico*', organic, and I went over to look at the chiller cabinet with its impressive range of organic locally-produced yoghurts that Ugo had pointed out to me. They were produced in the dairy at Bebbio where local milk was flavoured with fruits growing wild in the woods or organically cultivated by local smallholders.

I gave Ugo a €50 note saying that I wanted to contribute to the housekeeping and that while they were selecting the goodies I wanted to pop into the *Tabacchaio* opposite as I saw they had some interesting historical photographs in their window. Crossing the road I noticed a large building containing a small general store with adjacent bar. The tables outside were occupied by several old men, doing what old men seem to do best, sitting and watching the world go by. Their conversation was unintelligible to me as they were speaking in the local dialect and not in Italian. When I'd lived up in Verona I'd got used to their dialect which sounded very like Spanish, but this was completely different. There were also two petrol pumps outside the bar and the various comings and goings obviously provided the gentlemen with a constant source of amusement and interest.

The village also boasted a hairdresser, a shop selling interesting ceramics and jams (sadly shut) and two butchers, one of which was organic. There was also a Dry Cleaner and a very interesting municipal Notice Board onto which were affixed various notices advertising *Sagre* (festivals or fairs). Such was the local tradition of seasonal gastronomy that each municipality prided itself on its own particular produce. Not only was Valestra renowned for the excellence of its cheese, its bread and its meat, but also apparently its *pasta al ragù* (Pasta with meat sauce). It seemed that tonight there was to be the end of summer fair just down the road and all sorts of cool-sounding musicians and DJ's were advertised. In the middle of the mountains it seemed that the farming community knew how to party!

The houses were mostly constructed of the local stone, hewn from the mountain, evidenced by the scar in the side of Monte Valestra. A lovely warm grey stone, the same as the Manor House which set off the *castagno* chestnut wood of the beams, doors, window frames and shutters. All were roofed with the typical *cotto* roof tiles. I really liked this little village, it had a warm and welcoming atmosphere and the views were stupendous over the wide pastures up to the hills and the telecom mast incongruously perched on top. Wi-fi in the area was conspicuous by its absence so a Telecoms company, Eolo, had come up with the clever idea of providing Wi-fi via the mast - all one had to do was rent a satellite dish from them and as long as there weren't any trees in the way to impede the signal, excellent Wi-fi could be had by all. I'd seen an amusingly worded advert saying that "who said nothing ever happened in Baiso (a neighbouring town) Wi-fi is coming!". I suspected that broadband was desperately needed in these areas - not least so that the beleaguered farmers and local smallholders could fill in, online, the myriad forms constantly required by the tedious and time-consuming bureaucracy of Province, State and the EU.

I felt very at home here, it felt calm and safe and while I waited for the boys to finish their gastronomic spree I found a big wooden bench and sat quietly in the sun just drinking in the peace and the vibe.

They soon emerged from the *Forno*, arms full of interesting-looking packages and we all piled once more into the car.

"*Cara* we're going into Carpineti as there are a couple of small supermarkets where we can get some fruit and some vegetables as the mini market here is not always good quality".

We drove out of the village and I literally drank in the view. Great swathes of meadow, dotted with old barns and small clusters of houses and in the distance were the mountains with the peaks of Cusna and Cimone shimmering in the clear autumn air. No brown motorway smudge here! This was the Emilian part of the Apennines dividing this gorgeous place from the Tuscan coast to the west.

Lucca and the beaches of the Tuscan Riviera were just over two hours drive away but here, where we were, it seemed light years from those places and their teeming energy. How had this special, gentle place managed to remain relatively undiscovered for so long? I resolved to ask Ugo when we got back to the Hamlet.

The road veered off to the right and started climbing, tightly hugging the base of the mountain to one side with a sheer drop to the other. The view past the drop, despite bringing on my vertigo, was stunning, kilometres of verdant meadows, dotted here and there with small woods bedecked in their autumnal finery, all rolling in a natural wave towards the distant snow-capped peaks marking the border between Emilia Romagna and Tuscany. Drinking in the natural beauty I knew it would definitely be a panoramic demise should the unthinkable occur and the car plummet down the hillside. I wondered how people coped in heavy rain, ice or snow as the Armco barriers were few and far between, protecting only the steepest bits of the drop. To my right, the rock of the mountain was crumbling in places and great swathes of thick reinforced wire had been hammered into the rock face. Nonetheless there were still bulging bits of wire where huge boulders had tried to defy the constraints. As if Mother Nature was fretting at being so tightly corseted.

In places the road narrowed, barely allowing enough space for two cars to pass and I was glad that we were hugging the mountainside despite the falling rock hazard.

As Ugo expertly swung the car around several hairpin bends, I noticed a couple of interesting-looking brown signs. The ones that are used throughout Europe as providing information for tourists and wondered as to what they were referring. Another question to be saved up for Ugo!

The last hairpin bend ended at a T junction with what seemed to be a major local road. We turned left towards Carpineti and followed a much more level route along a valley dotted with small *Borghi*, hamlets like our own. Some had medieval towers, some were a cluster of rural buildings while several tiny chapels stood dotted around and there were yet more enticing brown signs! To our left there seemed to be a hive of logging activity with great piles of cut wood stacked up and several tractors and lorries loading up. Now that it was September, as we had ourselves discovered last night, a fire was necessary in the evenings.

We rounded another bend and, there, right in front of us, perched majestically atop a rocky crag was a castle. A proper medieval castle, complete with a great tower from which, no doubt, the land for miles around could be surveyed. "Wow" I exclaimed in English. Sandro, sitting behind me, leant forward and told me that this was Carpineti castle, the favourite residence of Matilda di Canossa, the Medieval 'Queen' of Italy, Margravine and Grand Countess of Tuscany. The castle was still partly intact, one could rent rooms in the gatehouse and apparently there was a restaurant at the bottom of the keep. The castle was open from March to September but Ugo said that this time we'd have to give it a miss as he was focused on shopping and then lunch! So we drove past the turning and into town.

Chapter 4

An unexpected offer...

Carpineti is a small market town of just over 4,000 inhabitants, about 30 kms from Reggio Emilia and on the old *"Lunigiana"* route from the plains over the mountains, to the ancient and mysterious area. Home for centuries, to the western tribes of the *Liguri* an ancient population once inhabiting the region now covering southern Lombardy, Liguria (from whom the province gets its name), Tuscany and the Emilian part of Emilia Romagna. Some say they were the descendants of the Trojans and there is a wine, produced in Liguria, from vines historically thought to have been brought from Troy.

We'd passed the turnoff to the great castle and as we entered the town I could see that the road was straddled not only by homes, somewhat Alpine in style, but many interesting-looking shops and businesses. There were several banks, several bars, a cafe and a small piazza which was used for parking and no doubt, on market day, for the weekly market. Opposite there was an even older piazza, which looked medieval, named Piazza Matilda di Canossa in which the *Municipio*, the town hall, occupied a portentous position, its balconies gay with hanging baskets and three flags - one for the State, the Italian *"tricolore"* (for which the eponymous salad was created from avocado, tomato and mozzarella!), the EU one with its gold stars on their blue background and a brightly coloured flag which was obviously that of the *Comune* - a wonderfully lyrical composition of leafy wreaths, a single Hornbeam tree surmounted by a coronet composed of castle walls complete with battlements as the merlons.

Gorgeous old houses, with either stone or stuccoed facades, surrounded the cobbled piazza on all sides, apart from a small access by the side of the Town Hall; the boys told me that, in summer, it became the venue for open-air concerts and *'spettacoli'* so perfect were the acoustics. Despite being so picturesque there were no bars or cafes in it, so we crossed the road and settled down at a welcoming-looking but much more modern bar with tables and comfy chairs outside. Ugo rushed off to the small supermarket, leaving Sandro and I to chat and, more importantly, to decide what to drink. The waitress came out to take our order, returning almost immediately with a large plate of assorted nibbles. I really like the incredibly civilised Italian habit of providing, with a drink, little *'assaggi'* tastes, of local produce such as thin slices of different salamis, pieces of various cheeses and crostini, small toasted bits of local bread spread with anything from tomato and mozzarella to local pates. All complimentary. Even the worst bars provided nibbles - a bowl of potato crisps, pretzels or peanuts to be enjoyed with the *'aperitivo'*.

We settled on the current rage in aperitifs, *Aperol Spritz*, the bright orange and somewhat sticky drink that had caught the popular imagination and was, I believe, being drunk in large quantities worldwide. Aperol is a bitter liqueur, dating from 1919, and is made mainly from rhubarb, gentian and *cinchona* (apparently a flowering plant native to the forests of the Andes in western South America), the liqueur is mixed with Prosecco and, sometimes, soda water; poured over crushed ice and garnished with a slice of orange. Whatever its provenance, it is definitely an acquired taste - but I was becoming used to it, though I drew the line at actually buying a bottle for myself!

As we waited, Sandro lounged upon a sort of day bed under a white sailcloth awning, I sat in a wicker chair next to him and looked around me. The piazza was modern, lined on three sides with shops. I spotted banks, a restaurant, a newsagent/ *tabacchaio*, a Gelateria (which also advertised Gin & Tonics!), a toy shop, a stationers and small launderette. Everything was spotlessly clean and upon hearing a ping from my phone, I saw that there was free wifi - with a very strong signal. What a pleasant place!

Ugo returned with his bag full and we ordered him a Spritz. He told me that Carpineti was a nice town with many good shops and craftspeople and that Signor S was well-known and well-respected here.

Across the road was a Police station, that of the local *Carabinieri*, the military gendarmerie of Italy which, along with the *Polizia del Stato* and the *Guardia di Finanza*, took care of the country's law enforcement. As I looked at it, a car drew up and a man in his 40's, dressed in jeans and smoking a cigarette (only permissible in the open air or a private house) got out. Stubbing out his cigarette underfoot he bent in and retrieved a dark suit carrier which he slung over his shoulder and, locking his car, he proceeded to the Station, using a key pad to enter a numeric code, thus gaining entry to what looked to be a long dark corridor.

The *Carabinieri* are the force with the really smart dark blue uniforms with a wide red stripe down the trouser leg. They drive matching dark blue cars, usually Alfa Romeos. The State Police are not so sartorially turned out, nor do they look as forbidding! I think the *Carabinieri* deliberately recruit the best-looking applicants for, a few minutes later, the door opened and out strode this absolute Adonis resplendent in his uniform. It was the same man, but his demeanour had completely changed. He stood taller, straighter and seemed a thousand times sexier as he strode purposefully towards a waiting squad car. It was astonishing to witness the swift transformation from mere mortal to godlike paramilitary officer. He looked a totally different person and while I would not have looked at him twice in his day clothes, dressed like this he was most definitely worthy of a second, if not third, glance!

Ugo saw me staring and remarked upon it. I confessed my love of men in uniform and the laughed "Darling, I was in the *Carabinieri* when I did my military service…"

Now, ok, he's gay, but like most gay men he's gorgeous so I sort of gulped at this revelation and my imagination went into feverish overtime! " You are such a fag hag" he teased, reminding me that, 25 years earlier, that had been his nickname for me.

I've always had gay men as friends. They are funny, smart, acerbic and they are not afraid of living for or in the moment. So naturally I'd wanted to spend time with him and his friends, earning myself the somewhat unflattering soubriquet, rather than try and negotiate the sometimes rocky waters of friendships with straight men - whose wives and/or girlfriends (sometimes both!) seemed unfairly suspicious of me and my motives.

I agreed that he was right and, despite the nibbles, we were starting to feel hungry - it must have been the mountain air for breakfast hadn't been so long ago. We finished our Spritzes, me marvelling at how the Bar could provide the drinks, the nibbles and make a profit, for the cost of the drinks had been half that of a similar bar in Verona.

I liked Carpineti, it had a good solid Borghese feel to it. Decent, unpretentious and hardworking people who were genuinely proud of their heritage, going about their daily lives in a place where the air was clean, the food delicious and the prices affordable. What was not to like?

We returned via the terrifying road and I, being on the side of the sheer drop, kept my eyes closed until we were once again on level ground.

Upon arriving back at The Hamlet, we found that Farah had preempted our idea of eating outside in the loggia overlooking the orchard and had thoroughly swept and cleaned the great long wooden table and put yellow and white cushions on the benches. She appeared from the house carrying a great tray laden with cutlery, crockery and glasses. The boys and I hurried into the kitchen and, opening all our packages, laid out a veritable feast of local produce. I enquired whether Farah would join us, to be told that, since she was Muslim, she wasn't able to eat prosciutto or salami as they were pork. She therefore preferred to eat with her family where, I'm told, she had made superb pizza and lamb-based couscous.

63

The orchard was abuzz with myriad insects all gorging themselves on the ripe and fallen fruit from, it seemed, every conceivable type of fruit tree. There was even a huge spreading fig tree which Farah had already raided and the fruit, dark purple, plump and perfect was piled onto a huge platter in the centre of the table.

Lunch was delicious, plates of bread, cheese and meats - and all produced within a few kilometres of where we sat. A tomato salad (home grown) was simply dressed with the greenest of extra virgin olive oil which had been decanted into a small ceramic jug from a massive dark green bottle - easily the size of a Methuselah of Champagne and a small flagon of *aceto balsamico* stood nearby.

I sat with my back to the wall of the woodshed, just drinking in the beauty of the '*orto*'. Tall clumps of grass rustled and swayed as Mimi and the farm cats stalked each other and the small unsuspecting furry creatures that nibbled greedily on the fruits of Nature's bounty. To our right was a long low building I'd not noticed before, with grilled unshuttered windows overlooking the orchard and three tiled steps leading up to a partly glazed wooded door. A somewhat saggy washing line hung from a pole by the door, the other end firmly tied to an apple tree. A small table and chairs sat by the foot of the steps.

"Who lives there?" I asked.

"No-one. It is the *tavernetta* which we sometimes use for guests when we have our parties and all the rooms in the house are full. There used to be a small hotel in the village and each New Year we would fill it with our friends. The owner was always most amused by the amount of screaming queens that descended on him! But he's closed it now so we put people up in here instead. It used to be absolutely freezing but my father built an ingenious method for heating it which I'll show you after lunch".

"Your father? Does he live here too?"

"No. But since my sister married Alberto, he comes every summer for a couple of months and to stop himself from getting bored he invents projects! All of which have been incredibly useful."

Farah appeared with coffees and Ugo popped into the house to get the key to the barn. Coffees drunk, we crossed the loggia past the massive brick barbecue with its deep charcoal pit, around the end of the building and into a long covered portico which linked the *Tavernetta* to Farah's house, providing a pleasantly cool and shaded place from which to sit and watch the various comings and goings of daily life in the *Borgo*. Several cats scampered behind us at a safe distance, for they were very wary of humans.

Ugo inserted a huge iron key into an oak door and it creakily swung open.

Gesturing for me to enter first, I could see his father's great engineering project acting as a sort of room divider between the kitchen into which we'd entered and a small sitting room. The room had windows all along one wall and a large stone and brick fireplace stood at one end. Sitting solidly in the middle of the two rooms was the ingenious construction - a huge wood burning stove built into a wall which rose almost to the ceiling. With spaces for wood storage either side of the stove it also featured a wide terracotta tiled shelf which ran the whole way round and on which, I was told, one could cook toast as it became so hot when fully fired up!

The wall itself was of pinky cream bricks and along the very top a slightly incongruous steel tube disappeared up into the ceiling. A clever system of small drawers on the short edge of the wall could be used for regulating airflow, as could the wrought iron and glass front to the woodburner. Ugo explained that when heated, it literally radiated heat into the whole house and, through a system of tubes and vents, connected via the tube, also carried heat to the bathroom and bedroom on the other side of the kitchen.

The sitting room's windows were set into deep walls and looked out over the orchard and the loggia. The kitchen door was between the hot wall, as I'd christened the room divider, and the sink which was set into a massive marble worktop. There was a microwave, a cooker and a fridge freezer along the back wall, surmounted by a fantastic antique wooden crockery and pan holder running the entire length above the cooker and fridge.

A door led to a passageway off which were the bathroom (complete with shower and wonderful art deco bathroom furniture of basin, bidet and wc) and a good-sized bedroom, outside which stood the massive fig tree, providing shade, for this room faced almost due south. On the other side of the passageway, were set, high up, an arched stable window which provided light and, lower down, a circular window upon whose outside sill was already snoozing one of the cats!

To the left of the front door was a selection of alcoves with shelf storage and, to my delight and astonishment, a brick-built small pizza oven inset into the wall.

I loved the place and turned to Ugo to tell him so, only to find him looking at me intently. "Cara why not move here from Verona? Would you like to rent it?"

I found my eyes filling with tears at the thought of living in this magical place and at the well-timed and incredible generosity of Ugo in suggesting this. I'd been worried about how I was to continue living in Verona, with no income and a high rent to pay.

"It wouldn't be expensive, around €250-€300 per month. Of course you would be responsible for your own gas, electricity and wood. You'd be completely private and self-contained and there are TV points in the *salotto* and the bedroom… Come let me show you where the gas tank is and where you could store your wood".

In a daze I followed him out into the far end of the orchard, the part closest to the fig tree where, securely gated, sat a massive gas tank, sunk into the ground and accessed by a no-nonsense cover which clipped onto the base. Returning to the *Tavernetta* Ugo explained that the empty part situated on the end closest to the road and open on one side, was currently used as Hassan's garage, but could be converted into an extra room for me if I needed the extra space. The electricity supply was separate and I was shown the '*contattore*' the meter, high up on the outside wall. It was perfect and I knew that Geisha and I would absolutely love living here.

"Well what do you think?" He asked gently, seeing the look on my face.

"Yes please" I answered quietly, my usual exuberance constrained by the enormity of the idea. But it felt so right…

A million thoughts flew through my brain, could I surrender my lease in Verona without paying a large penalty or losing the massive deposit I'd had to put up? I'd certainly save a huge amount of money by moving. I could see that all my furniture wouldn't fit in and I wasn't sure where I could store that which I didn't need. The Hamlet was so easily accessible from not only the motorway but also Bologna airport and the *Altavelocità* train stations. Well connected and only an hour and a half from Verona it was hard to believe that this place was real. I'd been quietly terrified as to how I was going to manage financially once my payoff ran out. I knew that I couldn't afford to return to the UK, not least because the house was let but also because of the prohibitive cost of moving. More importantly I still felt that I had things to do in Italy, that my ill-fated adventure had actually been some sort of grisly catalyst for bringing me to this country… and so on and so forth.

I shoved all my concerns to one side, feeling somehow that if it was meant to be, it would be and I hugged Ugo tightly, for once lost for words.

I knew instinctively that I'd needed to find a place in which to reorganise myself and to figure out what to do next, to buy myself the time necessary to take stock of my life and to decide whether I remained in Italy (I was already a Resident due to being an EU citizen), or whether Geisha and I cut our losses and went back to Blighty as I affectionately called my genetic and ancestral home. I felt that I was at some sort of crossroads in my life, but I wasn't ready to admit defeat, I wanted to stay in Italy and see if, against all odds, a partly disabled, lone foreign woman of a certain age could make it all by herself - in a country where the great bond of family counts for everything!

Returning to the house we sat and drank tea (how English!) and discussed the practicalities. We agreed that, subject to my meeting and being approved of by Signor S, I could rent the *Tavernetta*. There were some remedial and aesthetic works to be done but they wouldn't take long and I was already mentally planning where to put the furniture. I also knew that Geisha, while having been completely uncomplaining, had secretly hated Verona and her little balcony and that she would love to be here, warming her delicate old bones in the sunny orchard and hopefully making friends with Mimi.

After tea I finally got my conducted tour of the Manor House and as we walked up stone staircases and through room after room filled with antique beds, cupboards and chests I felt a great connection to it and to its ghosts whom I could feel whispering excitedly about the newcomer! I mentally thanked them for their friendly interest and asked that they intercede with Signor S, their descendant of many generations, so that he may like and approve of me.

After that things speeded up as Sandro had to catch a train back to Milan we had to rush around packing up. Bidding a fond farewell to Farah and promising that I would be back in a couple of weeks to meet

Signor S, after Ugo had made a quick call and we'd agreed upon a date, I climbed into my car. Looking back at the sun-washed stone, I found that I was humming the tune that Fraulein Maria sings in the Sound of Music, when she and Captain von Trapp declare their love for each other... "for somewhere in my youth or childhood, I must have done something good... for here I am standing here, loving you..."

I drove down the mountain in a state of incredulous euphoria, for it really felt as if my Guardian Angel had intervened and, through Ugo, had given me the chance to recuperate and recalibrate in this spellbinding place.

Chapter 5

Bad news, better news and wonderful news

So it was that I returned to Verona and spent the couple of weeks before I was due to meet Signor S trying to find some consultancy work to bring in some money. But as solo consultants the world over know, it is very difficult, if not almost impossible for those of us who have to work alone to survive financially if their clients - both existing and prospective - just do not exist in the same timeframe. I had several excellent and potentially lucrative projects which could keep me afloat financially but only if - and it was a big if - my clients kept to agreed timetables and, more importantly, to their decision to hire me - and remunerate me.

I had also made several friends; former colleagues and friends of colleagues who were wonderfully supportive. Their kindness and generosity in inviting me for meals, having coffees or aperitifs together and their efforts to suggest potential sources of work were so welcome. One, Carolina, even offered to come to the Veronese equivalent of the Department for Health and Social Security to see what I might possibly be entitled to. We went, one Monday morning and I couldn't decide whether to laugh or cry when I saw that she was as confused as I. We decided it was simply too much of an uphill struggle to get the requisite paperwork so, defeated, she generously invited me to lunch in a little nearby trattoria and we sat there drinking good local wine from Valpolicella and laughing about our woeful experience. She had suggested that I try again but the mountain of paperwork I faced, was simply too daunting and if I was indeed leaving Verona, I would only have to go through it all again once I was settled in the Hamlet. If I was settled in the Hamlet.

Another former colleague, Aurora, who still worked for the company, rang me to suggest we meet for lunch and when we did, firmly insisted that she needed me to help her improve her English conversation - for which she would pay the going rate. I told her I wasn't properly qualified to teach English as a foreign language and she snorted!

"Such nonsense. You are British, you speak English. You will be an excellent teacher."

I demurred and she would come to the flat every Tuesday evening; with Geisha looking on we would spend a couple of hours talking, reading from prepared texts or general comprehension. She already spoke some English but, like most Italians, had almost no practice and was therefore somewhat shy of making mistakes when she did use it. Her grasp of the subtleties of the mongrel language that is English was impressive and we found ourselves more often than not, comparing English with American English - which is pretty much a different language altogether. I absolutely loved teaching her and as a result of the lessons we became firm friends.

She even recommended me to her Acupuncturist, Aurelio, who offered to swap sessions so that in return for him sticking long thin needles into me, I would prepare him for his forthcoming holiday in Spain. I pointed out that both Italian and Spanish are Romance Languages, those that originate from Latin, so surely it would be easier for him to learn Spanish? But apparently not! He wanted to learn English conversation and we had some hysterical times role-playing when he told me he needed to know how to approach attractive-looking ladies in bars! Especially if they were British tourists with regional accents...

The first time I spoke to him in a regional accent and using slang, he looked completely dumbfounded. "What language is that?"

"English. From the north east of the country and I'm using slang. Not everyone speaks BBC English you know!"

A few weeks after I'd started the lessons, Laura, a girl who lived in my block and with whom I'd chatted whenever we'd passed each other by the entrance gate, stopped me one day and asked whether I would teach her. "I'm going to London for a long weekend in the spring with my boyfriend, and he doesn't speak any English. I only speak a little. Can you help me?" So I did and we had long discussions about Oyster travel cards, where to get the best Italian coffee, where to go shopping and how to navigate the Tube - the London Underground - with its myriad coloured routes and, to a foreigner, unpronounceable station names.

My little band of pupils was expanding and Aurelio even sent his brother to me. A lawyer who wanted to speak better English to his occasional international clients. That was a little more challenging as we had to speak business English and he had a mixture of clients who spoke either British or American English. Luckily I had once worked for an American company so knew the correct terminology. He was always very formal but I know he enjoyed the lessons because Aurelio rang me and told me that he'd been somewhat impressed.

On the recommendation of Laura I found a place for myself to do something fun and stimulating, it was a charity that offered free self-empowerment workshops for unemployed women and some of them looked really interesting. I needed something to do during the day as all my lessons were in the evening, so I looked it up. It was just down the road, but in true bureaucratic Italian fashion, I had to be registered as eligible before being offered a place on one of the workshops - thankfully this was accomplished by filling in several mind-numbing forms, with which Aurora helped and giving them my *Codice Fiscale* with a copy of my Dismissal letter.

I was accepted on the first course, something to do with 'how to find and use our strengths and weaknesses to good effect' and on the appointed day I arrived early, found a parking spot close by and not knowing quite what to expect, rang the buzzer by the firmly closed gates. Having signed in, I was pointed towards the meeting room where five other women of all shapes and sizes who appeared to know each other, simultaneously stopped talking and looked at me enquiringly - not for the first time I felt very conspicuous and foreign. But they were friendly and welcoming and by the time Marco, the workshop facilitator arrived, we were all laughing and chatting.

The day was great fun and focused a lot on the psychology of the Greek Goddess archetypes, which was something I knew quite a lot about. By the end of the day I had two more 'pupils' a mother and daughter who were heading to Scotland for their summer holidays and who spoke not a word of English. I'd also made friends with Marco who was astonished that I knew so much about the Greek deities and on discovering that I'd worked in Greece asked if we could meet for a coffee sometime. He and his wife were, in his words, Polytheists, those who worship many gods and since this was something really unusual in a staunchly Roman Catholic country and intrigued me, of course I said yes!

Thus I managed to keep my financial head above water for a few months and had also made some more friends. I was sad in a reflective sort of way that, if Signor S liked me, I might soon be leaving to live in the Hamlet for these people were open and generous and frankly amazed that I had come to Verona alone with Geisha to start a new life without husband or family. "You are so brave, crazy but brave!"

Despite my little group of pupils, I still hoped that I'd be able to work on the big project and every couple of weeks I'd phone the client to see whether he was in a position to press the button. But, as is the way of the world, what had seemed pressing and urgent when he had first mooted the idea of my working for him, now slipped and became less urgent and the commitment to the project became a vague promise, fading to disinterest then finally becoming impractical for him as other more pressing ideas and projects, with which I was not involved, took hold. Thus leaving me without work and with no prospect of earning anything substantial in the short term.

I didn't know whether to take it personally or whether it was yet another sign of lean economic times. Yet the client, an extremely rich man, had been wildly enthusiastic about working with me because of

75

my 'specialist knowledge and international contacts'. I'd worked closely with him and we'd put together a stunning proposal for investors - an upmarket and financially viable specialist leisure attraction which, at that time, had absolutely no competition and which would have been truly ground-breaking. I even had a potential investor who had asked for more detail on certain aspects - something which would require just 6 months work and minimal financial outlay on the part of my client. Yet when he put it to his co-Directors they decided that the project was not their core business and being more risk-averse then he, told him that I was no longer needed. 6 months of paying work vanished before my eyes. Admittedly I got an astonishingly good lunch from him as he, embarrassed, tried to explain their mindset to me. He even sent me a case of organic Prosecco as a parting gift! But that didn't help the bank balance and as overdrafts are illegal in Italy unless one has a personal relationship with the bank, the chance of obtaining a small overdraft with no potential income or collateral was zero.

At the same time, a long-standing friend and former colleague, a quintessential Englishman had expressed an interest in setting up business in Italy but realised that he needed someone who not only spoke Italian but also understood both the British and Italian mindsets and ways of doing business - which is why he'd called me. So I'd made introductions, researched his potential market and found him opportunities as well as running around on his behalf as his 'representative' for several months without financial recompense other than receiving vague promises of consultancy fees. I'd found him his lawyer, his accountant and his Managing Director for Italy but when I sent a small Invoice for the work I'd done on this behalf I was told I didn't merit the fee as I'd "done nothing".

I was speechless, hurt and angry. Thankfully he agreed to reimburse me the monies I had expended on his behalf as out-of-pocket expenses but not one cent was forthcoming for the enormous amount of time I'd spent working on his project - I even had been given business cards from his company. But he was a notoriously mean and litigious man and knew that I simply didn't have the temporal or financial wherewithal to fight for my fees.

The combination of the disappearing Italian project and the mean and mean-spirited Englishman meant that if it hadn't been for my trusty band of students I would have been up the proverbial creek without a paddle.

The only bright point on the horizon was the upcoming meeting with Signor S. I had my fingers (and toes) crossed that he'd like me and agree to rent me the *Tavernetta*. Getting away from the stress in Verona became my prime concern. I longed for the peace, quiet and beauty of the mountains. I'd been happy when I'd first arrived in Verona - a wonderful city where I'd spent many enchanted hours exploring its historic beauty but it was no place for a lone female - especially an unemployed one and the enchantment soon vanished. If it had not been for the support and friendship of Ugo and Aurora I would have been desperate.

Ugo and I had agreed that I would return to The Hamlet for Sunday lunch in early October and the morning dawned bright and clear.

Verona was chilly in the autumn sunshine and I was in a wonderful mood and full of optimism as I headed south towards Modena. I'd bought, at vast expense, a bottle of Single Malt Whisky for Signor S and had stopped at my local *pasticceria* where I had collected a pre-ordered tray of '*mignons*' little sweet delicacies such as rum babas, shortbreads and little eclairs filled with crème pattisière and other delectable naughtinesses!

In Italy, as in all civilised countries, it is customary for a guest to arrive with a small gift for the host. I'd been forewarned that Signor S was diabetic so the whisky was for him. I didn't know an Italian who didn't appreciate a good Scotch and a decent single malt would be deemed more than acceptable judging by the bottles I'd already seen in his Cantina! I also knew that the pastries would be equally well-received by Ugo, his sister and his brother-in-law.

The road was clear and as I headed towards the distant Appenines I passed motorway exits to wonderful and historic places such as *Mantova* (Mantua), *Gonzaga* and *Mirandola* - all names from literature and history - or both! Mantua was where Romeo had been banished after killing Tybalt, Juliet's hot-headed cousin in Shakespeare's eponymous play. Gonzaga was the ancient seat of the Gonzaga family, also dukes of Mantua, and Mirandola was where the astonishingly precocious Italian philosopher and polymath, Giovanni Pico della Mirandola at the age of 23 had "proposed to defend 900 theses on religion, philosophy, natural philosophy and magic against all comers".

His book on the subjects, "The Oration on the Dignity of Man" published in 1486 was dubbed the "Manifesto of the Renaissance" and is on a par with Dante's Inferno and Machiavelli's (a contemporary of Pico Della Mirandola) great treatise, The Prince.

Driving past these cities always inspired and frustrated me. The latter because it seems that I was always on the way to somewhere and simply wasn't able to stop and spend time in these extraordinary places - all of which are well off the usual tourist routes and thus all the more interesting to me!

My musings had by now led me to the junction of the A22 motorway from Verona with the A1 on which I was to spend precisely one minute as my junction, Modena Nord, was literally just a few hundred yards from the busy intersection. As this was my first trip without Ugo guiding me I was keen not to miss the exit so I slowed right down to make sure I didn't overshoot the turnoff, much to the noisy indignation of several faster drivers who hooted and gesticulated wildly at me before realising that not only was someone driving a car with the wheel on the wrong side, but that I was a lone bespectacled grey-haired female. I was sure I was accurately lip-reading their imprecations as they swerved around me at breakneck speed. I cared not a jot, for I have driven thousands and thousands of kilometres in Europe and beyond in both left and right hand drive cars without incident. But I always found the majority of Italian drivers to be ridiculously impatient. Even Ugo, Italian born and bred, is angry at such unnecessary behaviour and told me he always deliberately slows down with his foot on the brakes! Which pisses them off even more!

Turning off, onto the correct road without incident I headed towards the mountains, remembering to follow the signs for the Passo delle Radici, the 1529m high pass that separates this part of the Emilian Appenines from northern Tuscany. I followed the road for several kilometres until I recognised the "Marilyn I love you" graffiti on a wall near where I was due to turn off. Who was Marilyn? Monroe? Who loved her and why were they painting it on a wall in rural Italy, in English?!

Butterflies started in my stomach as I found the right turnoff and started climbing, swinging the car up and around the steeply carving bends, up and up through bright green fields with sheer drops on either side of the road - and a glimpse of the Secchia valley far below. I wound down the window and once again breathed in great gulps of the cool fresh air to try and calm myself down. I was so worried that Signor S might not like me or didn't feel that I would fit in with the Hamlet family, in which case I wouldn't be moving into the *Tavernetta* - and that left a future that was unthinkable...

Slowing down I drove into a small village - more of a cluster of houses really - narrowly avoiding a small dog lying insouciantly in a patch of sunlit road. It raised its head and grumpily got up to wander to the edge of the roadside which surprised me for I was more accustomed to the well-known game of canine 'chicken' where dogs lying by the side of the road would dash headlong at the car barking loudly and trying to bite the wheels, completely traumatising the poor driver. The driver would break out into a cold sweat at the prospect of informing Fido's (what is the Italian equivalent?!) devastated owner of their pet's grisly demise or whether it was the *'pazzo cane'* - the mad dog - who so happily and recklessly diced with death (and the blood pressure of the poor driver) only to pull back at the last moment.

Happily escaping unscathed I noticed that the village was called Levizzano where a small but open (on a Sunday morning!) shop was doing brisk business in freshly-baked bread which smelled delicious.

As I left the village the vista opened up and in the distance I could see Monte Valestra and with a quiver of anticipation I realised that I was only a couple of minutes from The Hamlet. A quick glance at the clock told me that I was going to be precisely on time and I wondered whether this was going to be an advantage or a disadvantage... I'd learnt the hard way, from many years of working in Southern Europe that my peculiarly Anglo-Saxon habit of being punctual was not always appreciated! Was Signor S a stickler for time-keeping or was he somewhat laid-back and unconcerned by such things? Well I'd soon find out!

Driving between the two stone gatehouses, I turned into the driveway, swung past the Tavernetta and Farah's house and pulled up next to Ugo's car in front of the Manor House, my tyres crunching on the gravel announcing my arrival.

The front door swung open and out came Ugo, arms wide open for a welcoming hug.

"Darling, welcome back". I smiled at him and asked if he would carry the tray of pastries into the house. Bearing the whisky before me as a sort of talisman I followed him into the house, blinking slightly as my eyes adjusted to the darker interior.

Three people rose to greet me.

"Cassandra, can I present Signor S?" said Ugo and I looked into the bright blue twinkling eyes of a tall, well-built and wonderfully patrician-looking older, but still very vigorous, gentleman. We greeted each courteously in formal Italian, he taking my right hand and bowing over it. Beside him stood his son, Alberto, equally tall and equally striking and his wife Luisa, Ugo's sister, an astonishingly pretty and vivacious-looking blonde also with bright blue eyes, all of whom smiled at me and moved to greet me in the traditional way of air-kissing twice, once on each side.

"*Benvenuta*" boomed Signor S, now with an unlit cheroot clamped between his teeth, welcoming me and indicating for me to sit beside him. The fire was blazing merrily and a delicious smell of woodsmoke and frying garlic permeated the room. Before I sat I proffered the whisky, noting that Ugo had had already taken the tray of naughty goodies into the kitchen.

I explained my Scottish origins and that I hoped Signor S would find my offering acceptable. It being, in my opinion, one of the best single malts - from the Isle of Skye. He nodded, pleased and Alberto leant over him explaining in a loud voice what I'd just said. My stomach lurched as I realised that perhaps my Italian wasn't good enough and that he was going to have difficulty understanding me. I need not have worried for Alberto turned to me explaining that his father was really quite deaf and that I'd have to speak loudly to him as he refused to wear his hearing aid!

I repeated what I'd said, louder this time and Signor S twinkled at me, "*Si, grazie*! Yes, thank you!"

As I took the proffered seat and sat down next to him Mimi appeared from the kitchen and winding herself sinuously around my legs happily head-butted me until I bent down to stroke her, at which point she jumped up onto my knee and purring, settled down. The look on Signor S' face was an absolute picture! He raised an eyebrow and looked at me quizzically. "It seems that my Mimi likes you" the possessive pronoun was not lost on me. "I love cats" I explained.

"*Bene*. We have many cats here…" he trailed off as Luisa came through bearing a huge bowl of pasta which she placed on the table. It had already been laid with crisp white napery and several place settings with a seemingly vast assortment of cutlery - how many courses were we going to have?!

Signor S got up and, talking me by the elbow, steered me to the seat on his right and took his place at the head of the table.

The others joined us and we chatted easily, stopping to repeat certain things slightly louder when Signor S had missed something. I was gently questioned about myself and about my life so far in Italy. Ugo had obviously filled them in on a fair amount because they knew that I'd worked in Milan in the early 90's - explaining to Signor S that this was where Ugo and I had first met.

He asked what I thought about the recent Brexit referendum and, looking him in the eye, I told him that I didn't want to answer in order not to offend him by using bad language. He roared with laughter and poured me more wine. To partly answer his query I explained that for the last 25 years I had spent a long time working in Europe and that I was sad that Brexit might put a stop to others having the same opportunities. "When it happens are you going to be able to stay here?"

"I don't know" I replied honestly. "It's all a bit vague at the moment, no-one knows whether I can or not."

"We'll have to find you an Italian husband!" He chuckled. I smiled.

"It might not have to come to that as my Grandfather was born in Ireland and because of that I'm able to apply for an Irish passport."

"*Brava!*"

The conversation - and the wine flowed - and as one delicious dish followed another I realised how at home and welcomed I felt among these kind, intelligent and amusing people. I gathered that Signor S' wife had passed away a few years earlier and that she was buried in the cemetery at Levizzano which I'd passed earlier. I also learnt that Alberto and Luisa had lived in Chicago for 5 years and that they had two children, both at University and that all of them spoke excellent English like Ugo.

I told them that I'd loved my years of living and working away from my home country and, with Brexit, I wasn't sure I wanted to return.

"And did you also learn the languages of the countries in which you worked?" Signor S asked, looking at me intently. "Of course" I answered succinctly, glad to dispel at least one perception of the English abroad!

"And do you speak them as well as you speak Italian?"

"It depends how much wine I have had" I grinned in response. He laughed loudly and at this, enquired as to why the English had a reputation for drinking too much.

"Good question. I don't really know. It might be something to do with our Viking and Saxon heritage or it might because the weather is so awful!" This led to a discussion of how European children are raised to have a little (watered) wine with their meals from a very early age - something the British don't tend to do. I deemed this to be very sensible and immensely civilised.

All too soon the meal was over and having had a (very small) Nocino Signor S said that he was retiring upstairs for his afternoon nap - his '*sonnellino*'. "I'm 82 you know" he said twinkling at me.

"Well you don't look it" I responded, meaning it. He embraced me and walked to the door where he turned and announced that I would be a welcome addition to the Hamlet family. I was absolutely ecstatic and spent the next hour or so excitedly discussing details and timescales with Luisa, Alberto and Ugo while we enthusiastically demolished the plate of pastries along with cups of much-needed coffee.

Ugo asked if before I returned to Verona I'd like to have another look at the *Tavernetta* and see what was needed. With enormous pleasure and relief I accepted and we spent a happy hour with tape measure and taking photos on my phone in order not to forget a single detail of my new home.

Mimi had joined us and spent time looking for spiders, I was relieved to see that she didn't find any! As we locked up and I prepared to say '*Arriverderci*' to everyone some of the other cats came over to see what was going on. Luisa had joined us and asked if I liked cats "I adore them" I answered showing her a photo of Geisha. "Oh how beautiful she is. Where is she? In England?"

"No she's in Verona. Will it be a problem to bring her here?"

"Absolutely not, no problem". I told her how Geisha had travelled from England with me, sat like an Imperial Being on a pile of cushions in the back of the car as we had

driven through France and Italy with my best friend and a huge pile of feline paraphernalia as well as our own luggage. She'd found the whole thing really interesting and had spent hours purring at lorry drivers who waved at her as she sat in the back window! It's a miracle we hadn't been arrested by over-vigilant policemen.

Luisa was astonished and said that she must love and trust me very much to endure such a thing "and without a cage".

"She'd have hated it in a cage" Luisa nodded and in her I sensed a like-minded cat lover and hoped I'd see her often!

She and the family all lived down in Reggio Emilia, Signor S too. He came to the Hamlet at the end of May each year and stayed until September or October depending on the weather. For while it was still stiflingly hot down on the plain it could get really cold up here in the evenings. Despite his absence he was, I gathered, still very much regarded as the Lord of the Manor and was hugely respected by all.

As the afternoon was wearing on Ugo suggested that I might like to leave soon, before it started getting dark, so that I could find my way down the mountain on roads that I had not yet become used to! I agreed, not least because I hate driving in the dark and after all the emotion - and too much wine - I was exhausted. I badly wanted to be at home with Geisha snuggled up under our cosy rug and making plans for our move.

"Darling you will soon be back here and you will make a great addition to the Hamlet family". We hugged each other happily - I still couldn't really believe that it was happening. Returning to the house to pick up my things, I swapped contact details with Alberto and Luisa and we agreed that we'd start things moving along so that I could move in as soon as possible.

Walking to the car I saw that it was already covered with dusty paw marks - it seems that even the cats were welcoming me!

As I opened the door, Farah emerged from her house with her husband, Hassan and we were introduced to each other. I liked him immediately, his open friendly face and his twinkling brown eyes reminding me of their daughter Ayesha. Ugo explained that I was going to be moving into the *Tavernetta* and with only a moment's hesitation, Farah moved towards me and gave me a shy hug. "Welcome Signora".

"Please, call me Cassandra or Cass. Let's use the informal, please call me 'Tu' not 'Lei'..." I said referring to the less formal mode of address between friends and family. Farah agreed happily

I climbed into the car having hugged Ugo goodbye and whispering "thank you" in his ear. He smiled and asked me to call when I was safely home. I agreed and putting the car in gear, executed a neat three point turn, and waving to everyone drove out of the drive past my new home, heading for Verona.

As promised, having arrived a couple of hours later and been held up in Sunday traffic at the motorway exit, I rang Ugo. He told me that I had been a great success with Signor S who was saying how charming I was - and how cultured! Finally it seemed that the expensive education had been worth it after all…

Chapter 6

Bureaucracy, xenophobia and a wonderful Christmas

Regretfully, leaving Verona was going to take longer than I'd anticipated. There were several remedial works to be done at the *Tavernetta*, more than we'd realised and since they were going to be done by Ugo, Luisa and Suleiman (another of the Hamlet caretakers and whom I'd not yet met) it all had to be fitted in around their busy lives. Additionally, winter was closing in fast and up in the Hamlet the snow could arrive at almost any time and would not be ideal conditions for refurbishment works. I also didn't fancy spending my first few months there gingerly driving along icy roads that, frankly, had scared me in the sunshine! So it was something of a relief to me that we agreed that we'd work to a timetable of 1st March as moving day.

Now that I knew there were still a few months before the move there was no point in becoming impatient, for there was nothing further I could do. So I turned my attention to sorting out my health.

The Italian health system is absolutely excellent but for those, like me, who don't completely understand its inner workings it can be confusing, frustrating and very very slow. Learning to successfully navigate the seemingly endless bureaucracy is an art and one in which I was not particularly proficient. Not least because I am dreadfully impatient.

As an employee I'd had deducted from my salary monthly INPS, social security payments, which covered health and pension requirements. Enrolment was mandatory and the contributions covered old age pensions, disability benefits and unemployment benefits. For self-employed people participation in the scheme was also compulsory and now required my registration as a '*libera professionista*' a freelancer.

What no one had told me was that I was expected to have some form of income and that, furthermore I was required to pay €250 a month into the scheme in order to receive treatment. A valid *Tessera Sanitaria,* the health insurance card, was needed in order to obtain treatment and without proof of INPS payments one didn't get the *Tessera.* Treatment was, literally, refused.

Furthermore I had got absolutely nowhere with claiming disability benefit as on further investigation it transpired that my my payout had taken me above the means test threshold.

I had been given my 75% civil disability status (as opposed to military!) due to a rare, painful and incurable medical condition called Lipo-Lymphoedema - elephantiasis as it had once been cruelly known. An abnormal build-up of fat cells in the thighs, legs and buttocks, combined with breakdown of my lymphatic system meant that I had huge painful legs which would never get any smaller. The condition required regular treatment which I wasn't getting, but to which I was entitled. I was supposed to have twice-weekly manual lymphatic drainage and an annual visit to a specialist clinic in Austria. I knew, from the clinic, that the Italian state recognised them as a bona fide treatment centre and sent patients to them. The condition also required the daily wearing of full-length medical compression stockings, which in Verona's heat, had occasionally proved to be somewhat hot and uncomfortable!

Determined not to become a serial invalid and not to become a victim of my condition I'd decided that while wearing the stockings was mandatory, there was no way I was going to wear the medical beige version! So with the help of a wonderful therapist in the UK I'd been told how to get them in funky colours. I had purple ones, pink ones, batik (tie died) ones in two colours and, having been away for over a year, I needed to replace some of the older ones. They were expensive, they'd been over £100 a pair in the UK but here in Italy they cost €800 a pair - and that was just for the horrid beige ones!

My local health service doctor, my *'medico di base'*, a fiercely intelligent though overworked man, with a head of curly greying hair, somewhat flyblown glasses and a very wry sense of humour, had been most sympathetic and had organised a seemingly never-ending series of appointments with various experts in various locales around the city, to diagnose and confirm my condition, with the goal of ultimately leading to an appointment with the Head of the relevant department in whose gift were the desperately-needed MLD sessions, the visit to the clinic and the supply of the hosiery.

It had taken me months and I'd still not had that appointment. My condition was deteriorating so I went to see him and explained my dilemma. He was appalled that, after all this time I'd still not seen the head honcho and took it upon himself, there and then, to make an appointment for me with the Director of the local public health centre. Moreover having confirmed the date and time he told me that he would telephone while I was there to ensure that I was fast-tracked. He apologised profusely for the unacceptable delay and said that all would soon be resolved.

I thanked him profusely and on the appointed day and hour I was sitting in front of the very charming Director of the centre when his phone rang. He was a tall man, immaculately groomed with greying hair, a small neatly-trimmed moustache and elegantly sartorial. He looked a bit like an erudite Professor and not the harassed boss of the Health Department.

"*Mi scusi Signora*" "Excuse me" he said turning to answer the phone. "*Pronto? Ah ciao Franco*" he said looking at me. "Yes she is here now" and I knew that it was my indefatigable *Medico di Base* who as promised had rung at the right time and from what I could hear, proceeded to berate the poor man volubly on my behalf, saying that the lack of treatment was inexcusable, that I was in constant pain and that unless I received, forthwith, the relevant appointment, I would become very unwell and require even more treatment.

The Director, to his credit, calmly confirmed to my apoplectic Doctor that this was indeed most regrettable and that he would, personally, ensure that I received an urgent appointment today - though not for FOR today he hastily added.

I was somewhat surprised at the vehemence of my Doctor and equally astonished that the Director had agreed not only to see me, but to take up my case. He was as good as his word, immediately lifted the receiver on one of the three telephones on his desk and summoned the Head of Department's assistant to come in as soon as she could.

As we waited for her to arrive we chatted amicably. He obviously knew my Doctor well because not only had he called him by name but had addressed him as '*Tu*'. He told me that I was fortunate to have such a champion fighting for me.

I readily agreed, going on to explain that, as a foreigner, I found the system immensely laudable but almost impossible to navigate. He nodded knowingly and told me that even for Italians the system was sometimes confusing and complimented me on my fortitude and knowledge of the language. There was a knock on the door and the Assistant appeared, a small dark bespectacled and harassed-looking woman bearing a massive tome apparently appertaining to various medical conditions and whether they qualified for treatment under the present system. In a matter of minutes she had confirmed that, yes, all was in order, I did qualify and after referring to her iPad she had found a mutually convenient appointment, with just a little pushing from the Director, just before lunch two days hence. This was further reinforced by a quick phone call from the Director to the Head of Department in question, explaining that I was an urgent case and apologising for railroading her!

"*Allora Signora*, everything is now organised. Please let me know how you get on".

I promised I would, thanking him once again for his understanding and assistance.

Two days later, I eagerly arrived at the centre, well in advance of my appointment and presented myself at the *Sportello*, the glass fronted cubicle and bullet-proofed reception to the inner sanctum of the relevant department. I wondered vaguely why it was bullet proofed.

Announcing my name slowly and succinctly, because it is very difficult to comprehend in Italian, I smiled at the lady behind the reinforced glass. She scowled and asked me to repeat it, letter by letter, in the Italian phonetic alphabet which, unlike the NATO one (alpha, bravo, charlie, delta etc) is place names. *"Como, Ancona, Milano, Palermo..."* it went on for a while not least because of having a double-barrelled surname! That didn't work, so we tried the first bit. Then the last bit. I also tried my first name. I even gave her my *Codice Fiscale*. Nothing. She told me, unequivocally that I was not in her system and that I therefore did not have an appointment. I told her that I most certainly did and that it had been made for me, by the Director. To my astonishment she looked unconvinced and I swear she actually snorted with disbelief!

I suggested that she call him to verify what I was saying. She said she'd do no such thing. By this point I could see why she was sitting behind bullet proof glass.

Her intransigence was breathtaking and there was literally nothing I could do about it. I was perplexed because, apart from this one woman, every single person I'd ever encountered in all the various government offices I'd been in, had been helpful, charming, friendly and in one or two instances, fun!

Just as I was about to give up in despair, Fate intervened in the marvellous apparition of the Director himself walking towards me, obviously on his way out for lunch. He saw me, smiled and came over, asking me how I was.

I explained, very loudly, so that the woman could hear us via her little microphone that I didn't appear to be in her system. He turned towards her looking exasperated. "Search again" he commanded "I made the appointment myself".

I resisted the childish urge to yell "I told you so!".

Sheepishly she acquiesced. Somewhat miraculously my name appeared so she printed off a sheet, handed it to me and indicated which door I should go through. I turned to the Director, smiled charmingly and thanked him - and her - for their help, almost skipping through the door in my euphoria, hurrying along a corridor until I found the relevant office and knocked on the door.

"*Avanti*. Come in".

The Head of Department, an elegant woman with magnificent silver hair and wearing some interesting silver jewellery, smiled at me. She told me that this was her last appointment before lunch so we would have to be quick. She examined me, asked a few succinct questions and while I was hauling my stockings back up my legs asked me how I coped with doing it on a daily basis. "With difficulty" I answered.

"*Ci credo*." I believe you. She typed something quickly into her laptop, printed off a sheet and handed it to me explaining that it was an urgent prescription (a red one) for 3 months of twice-weekly MLD therapy which was to begin immediately or at the latest within one week of today's date.

She explained that this was an unusual therapy and that I'd therefore have to go to a specialist unit in a hospital on the other side of the city. I told her I didn't have a problem with that, I was just so grateful to be finally receiving some help. "*Imagino*", I imagine, she smiled at me and gathering up her stuff we left her office together. She for her lunch and me to see if I'd got a parking ticket. (Eleven months later, after I'd been living in the Hamlet for several months I finally got an appointment which, now that I was no longer resident in Verona, I could not have. And I'd have to go through the entire process again - without my knights in armour.)

I decided that I too was hungry and so headed for the area in which I lived, San Zeno, and my favourite little trattoria beside the Romanesque Basilica of San Zeno Maggiore. Tradition has it that in its crypt, the marriage of Romeo and Juliet had taken place. Which may be true as it was outside the gates of the medieval city and therefore fitted the story.

The waitress, who knew me and asked me for help with her English when she was serving tourists, smiled and showed me to my usual table. Today I asked her to bring me a large glass of wine, almost before I'd sat down.

"What's happened?" She asked, seeing the look on my face. I was explained what has happened with the woman at the *Sportello* and that I'd been really upset by her attitude.

"She sees that you're a foreigner and thinks that you should not be entitled to free healthcare treatment".

"What?? That's insane...*pazza*". I was really shocked.

"She probably thinks you're a refugee.."

"Do I look like a refugee?" I asked

"Well you do wear long skirts and you don't look Italian!" She laughed it off but I was concerned. I've always dressed colourfully and worn long skirts. The latter to hide my legs, but I'd never been mistaken for a refugee...

Verona at that time was full of refugees, those fleeing Syria and those who were economic migrants from Africa and who'd suffered unbearable and inconceivable hardships on their journey to get to Europe. The harrowing daily pictures on the news of upturned boats with scared helpless people barely afloat in flimsy life jackets fighting for their lives, just for a chance of a better life, had really rattled me. Most people I had spoken to were concerned about their plight but found their habit of importuning people for a few Euros too much to take and told me so. But the lady in the *Sportello* seemed to be in a different league; to her, we were all foreign spongers. Who didn't deserve free medical treatment. When I eventually asked some of my Veronese friends they told me that, rightly or wrongly, there was a preconception that asylum seekers and economic migrants were taking money and resources that should have been spent on Italians. I finally understood. For I had seen something similar manifest in the Brexit referendum. I didn't like it, or accept it, but I could see where it was coming from.

Carla, the waitress went on to tell me that she was from Verona and that the Veronese were renowned for being naturally suspicious and distrustful of incomers. She told me that even Fabio, the owner of my favourite bar on the other side of the square, who came from Lecce in the south, had suffered racial abuse and he was Italian.

I needed a second glass of wine to help me digest this information. Sitting there, sipping it, I looked at the sun-washed facade of the breathtakingly beautiful Basilica with its magnificent bronze-panelled doors and remembered, with a wry smile, that San Zeno, the patron Saint of Verona, had himself been a black African! He was known as the *'Vescovo Moro'*, the 'moorish bishop', Moor being, at the time he was in Verona in the 10th century, the collective noun for persons of colour. His bones still rested in a glass walled catafalque in the Crypt, sumptuously dressed in rich clothing, little embroidered slippers on the bones of his feet. By all accounts he had been a wonderful man, pious and learned, yet blessed with a ready smile, was quick to laugh and who had a passion for fishing, for which he became the patron saint of fishermen and anglers! How sadly ironic.

Maybe it was just Verona, situated as it was at the crossroads of the north/south and east/west axes of the country. It had been the most northerly Roman outpost, founded in 89BC and its strategic importance lay in its position at the junction of the four main roads, the *Via Gallica*, the *Via Claudia Augusta*, the *Via Postumia* and the *Vicum Veronensis*. A veritable international crossroads and most importantly the last outpost before Germany and its Teutonic hordes, the *Teutones* - which might go some way towards explaining the mistrust of foreigners!

I had recently been approached by a lady I'd met in one of the women's refuge centres where I'd gone to apply for some part-time work. She had told me about a two week course for migrant women seeking work, saying that I might find it useful. It was run by the *Comune* of Verona and places were limited, but might I be interested in attending? Absolutely I'd said, recognising that I fell into the category for qualification. I was a woman, I was a migrant (and post Brexit I would become *Extra Comunitari*) and I was seeking work. So I signed up, partly out of curiosity and partly because it could, maybe, help me find work.

It proved to be one of the most sobering yet interesting courses I'd ever attended.

There were 12 of us, a group of women of all ages and all from different countries, apart from the two Tunisian sisters. I was the eldest and the youngest was 24 having just graduated with a BA in Engineering from the university of Gadi Ayyad in Marrakech. There were ladies from Russia, Morocco, Albania, Nigeria, Algeria, the Ukraine and... Great Britain. Almost without exception they spoke excellent Italian, having been in the country for several years and most were highly educated with university degrees. I, with my few O and A levels and lack of a degree, felt completely inadequate by comparison.

Yet all of them, despite their qualifications, were actually working as or being encouraged to look for work as '*Badanti*' Carers or Home Helps.

With an ageing population, Italy, like most of the rest of Europe, desperately needed female companions and carers to look after the needs of the elderly, infirm and vulnerable. And here were these women, most of whom had undergone tremendous hardship to get to Europe, who had not a hope in hell of working in their chosen profession. Instead they were being offered low-paid positions as glorified servants.

As the course progressed, horror stories emerged of unscrupulous families who had not obeyed the law and not given the women a legal contract, with fixed minimum wage, guaranteed rights and other entitlements under EU law, instead they had paid them in cash, often not paying them for months and then, for the flimsiest of reasons, letting them go - literally turning them out on the streets - more often than not without their back pay and no references.

So a lot of what we learnt focused on rights and contracts and recourse to agencies who could help them. But there was no information on other jobs, skilled jobs, for which many were qualified. It was just assumed that this was all they could do.

Not for the first time realised that, by being part of the EU and a 'first world' country I was so very very fortunate, despite my woeful lack of qualifications. I'd not even make a decent *Badante* as I couldn't cook and my health was so parlous I'd have been totally useless.

Their stories and experiences put life into a very different perspective and I knew how lucky I was. I couldn't even begin to imagine how soul-destroying and terrifying their experiences must have been. I realised with a frisson of real fear that my years of being head-hunted and of the six-figure salaries and expense accounts were well and truly over. I'd come to Italy because I'd even been told that

I was unemployable in the UK and now I realised that I was pretty much unemployable here too. If it hadn't been for Ugo, Signor S and his family offering me an affordable refuge, I'd be in very real trouble.

The course however ended on a bit of a high note for me. The Director of the local job centre, who had been to talk to us on our last day, had asked me to pop in and see her because she might have something for me. But first I'd have to fill in the standard European CV form. We'd been taken through it a couple of days earlier and my heart had sunk for it asked for details of qualifications. I had none. At least none that came with a bit of paper. 20 years in senior management and in-depth knowledge of the Southern European retail, entertainment and leisure sectors, it all seemed insubstantial. Even my ability to speak, write and read several languages without the benefit of a qualification in any of them was worthless.

Something that my father had said to me at fifteen reverberated around my head. "The trouble with you darling is that you are charming but useless..."it seems he'd been right and I'd been too busy being an arrogant little madam to take much notice.

I thanked the Director for her interest and explained that I was shortly moving away from Verona so therefore she might prefer if we didn't meet as I didn't want to waste her time. She thanked me and wished me luck, which was kind of her.

I was also quite cheered because, whilst I'd been on the course I'd received a couple of phone calls from people who were interested in exploring whether there was the possibility of working together. One was from a charming Florentine lawyer who specialised in Real

Estate. He offered me the opportunity to work with his small real estate team, saying that I would be paid on results, and that we could share expenses. I was grateful and seriously considered his offer, but Florence was three and a half hours from the Hamlet, was a notoriously expensive place in which to stay and petrol

and motorway tolls would have added to any capital outlay. So regretfully I turned him down, agreeing instead that if an opportunity arose where I was going to be living then I would happily collaborate with him and his team.

Another business acquaintance who knew of my current situation had enquired whether I was returning to the UK in which case he would have liked me to work with him on a massive project he was undertaking in the north of England. Sadly I had to refuse that too. But I was gratified that I was still considered commercially viable. At least by them!

I wasn't keen on returning to post Brexit referendum Britain. I needed to rest, take stock of my life and discover the area around the Hamlet. It was wildly self indulgent but I had been so stressed for so long, I seriously needed a break and some time to myself. I couldn't wait to get there, but first I had to get through Christmas and New Year.

I have always loved spending Christmas by myself. The thought of forced familial bonhomie was not appealing even though my sister had invited me back to the UK to spend two nights with them, it was a lot of money to expend on a quick visit at the most expensive time of year, especially as I was going to have to stay in an hotel in a nearby town. To be fair she'd offered to pay for that, as my Christmas present.

I thanked her and told her that apart not wanting to fork out for a flight and a hire car, I couldn't come as I had already bought a ticket for the Moscow State Ballet on Christmas night and that I really would prefer to stay snuggled up with Geisha eating smoked salmon, artisan wholemeal bread and drinking the remainder of my case of Prosecco from Andrea, the almost-client.

I had also been invited to a Christmas Eve, *'Vigilia di Natale'* supper with Aurora at her home and to meet her two cats, Merlino and Flora. They lived in an elegant small apartment in the most wonderful converted building which had once been the country estate of a Veronese nobleman, a few minutes outside the western suburbs of the city. Hidden away down a tree-lined avenue, the complex had been skilfully transformed into apartments and houses of various sizes, grouped around an attractive formal garden and with its own tiny chapel situated to one side. Approached through electronic gates and with parking for guests, I'd been given the various codes for the gates and the entryphone.

Aurora explained that I would have to enter the one for the gate quickly as they tended not to open if the code was not forthcoming within a limited time. Driving up, in the darkness of a winter evening, my heart sank as I realised that the key pad was of course situated to the left hand side, whereas I was in a right hand drive car so would have to get out, dash around to the key pad, enter the correct code in the gloom (it was illuminated badly by a most elegant lamp atop the ornate pillar) and dash back round the car in time to make it through the gates before they closed.

I failed at the first attempt and swearing volubly as I got out to try again, was embarrassed when I heard Aurora's voice emanating from the intercom. She'd been keeping an eye out for me and seen that I was having difficulties. So she offered to open the gate remotely once I was back in the car and ready to drive hurriedly through the gates. We agreed upon this course of action, which involved me yelling at the top of my voice through my open passenger window, telling her that I was *'pronto'*, ready. This time everything worked smoothly and I parked where she told me and loaded with bags of goodies as my contribution to supper plus Christmas presents for her and her feline family, headed through the ornate archway and up the impressive stone staircase to her first floor apartment.

As always she was elegant and her apartment reflected her taste. Not large but beautifully laid out with some lovely antique pieces, interesting paintings and a massive bookcase as well as two happy cats, who upon hearing a new voice, came and gently sniffed me to see whether I was worth their attention. It seemed I was, for Merlino spent most of the evening winding himself around my ankles, purring loudly.

As is the tradition in Italy, meat is not eaten on Christmas Eve, so we had a wonderful assortment of fish; spaghetti alle *vongole* (clams), thin slices of swordfish, salmon and tuna which had been smoked, and *baccalà* the famed salted cod, accompanied by various vegetables, breads and pickles.

Aurora then explained that shortly before midnight we were going down to the little chapel, which is private and only for the use of the residents, for a short service. I explained that I wasn't Christian, let alone Catholic and would this be a problem? Absolutely not Aurora said. Her friends and neighbours were expecting me.

The evening passed most convivially, once we had swapped and genuinely appreciated each other's presents, and the cats had enjoyed their treats from Geisha, Aurora told me a lot about her life. It had, it seemed, been hard in many ways and I respected her for all that she had gone through, while maintaining her elderly mother who insisted on still living in the home of Aurora's childhood, an hours' drive to the east, closer to the mountains. In return I told her about my solitary life and living and working alone in Southern Europe for many years. We recognised in each other like-minded spirits, both of whom had seen hard times and suffered loneliness, but who, now, fiercely guarded and cherished our independence.

Soon it was time to wrap up warmly and head down to the little chapel. It was stunning in its simplicity with beautifully frescoed walls and ceiling. The visiting Priest was setting up the Communion utensils and we chatted to him as others started coming in, blowing on their hands and stamping their feet, for with the sunset had come the freezing cold of a northern Italian winter's night. The chapel rapidly filled up and we took our seats. I'd never been to a Midnight Mass, let alone a Roman Catholic one so I was interested to see what happened. It was gentle and beautiful and serene. I recognised the words the Priest spoke, the universal story of the birth of Christ and in this place

105

I felt something stir within me. The open-hearted kindness and friendship of Aurora, the welcome of her friends and neighbours and the energy of this special place moved me and I felt tears pricking my eyelids. I stayed put as the others moved towards the altar for their Communion, which attracted some curious gazes. One kind lady asked me I wanted to partake and I whispered back that I was Protestant, not knowing whether or not this prevented me from participating in a Catholic communion. I wasn't Protestant at all, but it seemed the easiest way of explaining why I was not taking Communion, rather than having to explain that, horror of horrors I was not Baptised nor Confirmed. " Ahh. *Protestante*...?" She breathed and patting my arm sympathetically she moved up to take the wine and the wafer.

The profoundly moving yet simple ceremony came to an end and I reflected upon the fact that despite not being religious in any way, shape or form, I could still feel the special energy of this tiny sacred spot. And appreciate it.

As everyone gathered round to wish each other *Buon Natale*, Aurora introduced me to a handsome couple, telling me that the husband, Maurizio, had a notable wine cellar which he generously threw open to the residents of the Cortile every Christmas and that we were invited to walk across the courtyard to his house and sample what he had picked out for this year's delectation.

This was the icing on the proverbial cake! I adored discovering new wines and chatting to new people. My 'simple supper' with Aurora was turning into a veritable tapestry of gorgeous experiences, each different from the next.

The wine cellar was a revelation and, after probably too many glasses of different sparkling wines, I found myself chatting and laughing with two handsome and wildly intelligent men. Furthermore it appears that I knew of them in a professional capacity as they had worked on several projects with my former employers. Maurizio, putting two and two together, slapped his forehead in a true Italian 'Eureka' moment. "You're *that* foreign woman! I've heard about you!"

"Oh God!" I responded, "I hope nothing too awful...?"

"On the contrary..." he smiled at me and noticing that the excellent Prosecco in my glass seemed to rapidly disappear, topped me up. I realised that I'd probably had too much to drink and knew that I needed to go home, to Geisha, who would not be impressed by my late night antics and I started wondering how I could drive without being stopped and breathalysed, by vigilant policemen. There was also the problem of how to get out through the infernal gates again!

Aurora agreed that it was probably time for me to go and rushed off to get my bag of presents from her flat. I said my goodbyes to her lovely neighbours and was most gratified when Maurizio insisted that I come again the following Christmas!

I had had a lovely evening and, walking slowly across the courtyard, trying not to slip on the rapidly-icing marble pathway paused for a moment and looked around me. The softly lit old buildings glowed gently, giving off an air of permanence and respite from the real world, while above the sky was like black velvet and the stars like diamonds, the air clear and, after a couple of deep breaths, thankfully, sobering.

Aurora was waiting for me by the archway leading to the parking area and told me that the gates would open automatically as I approached them. We hugged and I was seized by a surge of fierce affection for this lovely woman. My first real friend.

I thanked her profusely knowing that words would not suffice, but I hoped that she knew how much I appreciated her invitation and her friendship. I drove home slowly with my heart in my mouth, on the lookout for police cars.

Geisha looked appalled as I weaved somewhat unsteadily in through the door and filling a large glass with water I headed straight for bed, where once she was sure I wasn't going to wriggle about, she joined me and I slept deeply, my head filled with images of dancing candlelight, star-filled skies and the convivial laughter of generous welcoming people.

The next morning I woke late and really looking forward to the ballet. After a very happy smoked salmon, Prosecco and Skype-filled Christmas Day I dressed myself in my finest, turning to Geisha for approval. She looked disgusted that I was once more venturing out into the cold and dark and disappeared back into her cozy bed.

So off I went, driving slowly through an unnaturally empty and very silent city, finding a convenient parking space just behind the Arena, the Roman amphitheatre that stands at the heart of Verona. It had been built in the First century AD and is still in use today, now famous for its legendary large-scale operas and concerts and still seating 15,000 people on the deeply uncomfortable ancient stone stadium seating. Cushions are, thankfully, for hire and attending a performance in this extraordinary place is a once in a lifetime experience and should definitely be on everybody's bucket list!

It was very dark and slightly spooky as I walked around the rear of the building, the cobblestoned piazza glistening frostily in the cold moonlit air. Only a few people were around and, muffled against the cold, they scurried past me no doubt on their way to great festive dinners. I walked slowly through the historic centre, savouring the moment to enjoy it without the usual throngs of people, locals and visitors. I walked slowly, pausing at Juliet's house, the *'Casa di Giulietta'* a very pretty medieval house dating from 1300 with its world-famous balcony and the bronze statue of the young Capulet girl whose right bosom has been rubbed to a shining patina by thousands of tourists' hands. For legend has it, that by rubbing this, love will be brought into your life.

The walls of the gated passageway leading to the inner courtyard were literally plastered with love notes, pleas and letters to Juliet, asking her to intercede on the writer's behalf. I'd seen the film Letters to Juliet and wondered whether the mooted tradition of each letter being answered by a committee of well-meaning romantics was true.

Turning down a side alley and being careful not to slip on the rapidly freezing cobbles, I came out into *Piazza Viviani* where the *Teatro Nuovo* stood in all its elegant classical splendour. Many people were milling around the entrance. I, not wanting to linger found someone from whom to buy a programme, presented my ticket to the young usher, easily found my seat and settled down - it had been worth paying the extra when I'd booked for I was in the tenth row of the stalls with a great view of the stage! Two women, possibly mother and daughter were already in the adjacent seats, so I smiled at them and wished them *"Buon Natale "* a Merry Christmas. They didn't respond, instead fixed me with a cold stare and then turned away from me. Surprised, but determined not to let such lack of manners deter me from having a good time, I muttered a few well chosen Anglo Saxon imprecations under my breath and settled down to enjoy my evening. The plush red and gold auditorium was packed with elegant people standing in the aisles chatting or peering at their tickets to try and find their seats. I loved people-watching and this was a real treat.

The Company, the Russian National Ballet, was performing the Nutcracker, the well-loved and traditional Christmas ballet and one that I always enjoyed watching, for its sheer spectacle. It was wonderful and I was soon transfixed by the story of Clara, the magical toymaker Herr Drosselmeyer and the life size Nutcracker doll. I particularly enjoyed the sumptuous costumes, watching the non dancers acting in character during the group scenes and, of course the exquisite dancing. Petipa's choreography and Tchaikovsky's music leading up to my personal highlight, the ballet's most famous dance, that of the Sugar Plum Fairy, which I believe is one of the most difficult and challenging roles in ballet and the pretty Russian Prima Ballerina did not disappoint, garnering noisy and enthusiastic applause from the appreciative audience. It was a happy couple of hours despite the miserable duo to my right! The performance ended to rapturous applause and the Company took many justly-deserved curtain calls. At the first opportunity, just after the last swoosh of the massive velvet curtains, I got up and hastily left, almost before the lights had come up. It had been a glorious evening but now I wanted nothing more than to get home, put on my nightdress and finish the rest of the Prosecco.

I walked back to the car through a now totally deserted Verona. It was magical having the city centre to myself, it was well below freezing and was so atmospheric that I was sure I could feel the ghosts of past residents gliding silently around me. I absolutely loved this city but I was not too enamoured with some of its populace! In just 24 hours I had seen the best and the worst of them. It was definitely time to move to the countryside and armed with that happy and exciting thought I drove back to the flat and a furry purring festive love-in with Geisha.

Chapter 7

Leaving Verona

I was going to miss Verona, despite occasionally feeling like a fish out of water, I'd been struck by the great vibe in the quarter of town I'd chosen as my home and had been made to feel very welcome by some of my neighbours and several of the tradespeople in our 'village', Not least the lovely lady in the Expert electrical store on the corner, who upon having learnt my surname was convinced that I was not only related to Martin Kemp from Spandau Ballet but also Naomi Campbell! I could not have looked less like either of them! The village of San Zeno, named for its great basilica which had been built on the site of a Roman lapidary, grew up around a series of small interlinked piazzas which, because they led nowhere, had happily retained their age-old character and appearance, juxtaposed, in the way Italians do so very well, with striking modern buildings which didn't detract from the very ancient heart of the village.

Situated on the edge of the river Adige and wedged between the old city walls where joggers jogged and dog walkers walked, it was a leisurely stroll along the river bank into the historic city centre with its hordes of tourists. The Village, as I'd mentally named it, was filled with interesting shops, bars, cafes and trattorias as well as the indigenous inhabitants whom, I'd learnt, were renowned for being somewhat eccentric! Thus I'd fitted in well and had become quite well-known myself as the *"Signora Inglese"* who drove a car with the steering wheel on the 'wrong side' and who was known to sit in bars

113

drinking exotic cocktails - all alone! Unheard of in a country where family and friends are everything. I'd even got an admirer, a widower in his 80's who, every day headed to the bar downstairs where he sat at his usual table reading the paper and watching the world go by.

He'd greeted me shyly one day asking whether I was confused by driving a car with the wheel on the right, as opposed to the left. I told him I'd being doing it for years, having lived in Greece and Spain before I'd come to Verona. He muttered *"che coraggio"* and offered me a coffee. Thus we had begun our weekly ritual of taking a coffee together and putting the world to rights.

His name was Giorgio, a courtly gentleman with a Roman nose and a mane of silver hair. He was somewhat short-sighted and would peer myopically at his newspaper where he took particular pleasure in reading the Obituaries. He'd been a clockmaker, an horologist, and had retired several years before. His wife had died about three years previously and I sensed that he was lonely. He was genuinely sorry to hear that I was going to be leaving, for a few months earlier his best bar buddy, another neighbour, a retired Professor, had left to return to the city of his birth, Ostuni, right down in Puglia, in the heel of Italy. "But I was going to invite you to my apartment to see my flowering balcony" he said when I told him of my upcoming move. I laughed delightedly and patted his hand. This he took to be the signal to cover my hand with his whilst give me a smacking wet kiss on the cheek. I was going to miss him.

While sitting and watching the village life one day, I'd remarked how San Zeno seemed to be becoming quite trendy *di moda* among young professionals. He agreed and said that it was a good thing because the house prices were going up and Niccolò the estate agent through whom I'd found the flat, has told him that The Professor had got a very good price for his.

San Zeno's trendiness might have been caused partly by the incredible monthly antiques market which was held, on the first Sunday, in the huge square in front of the Basilica. The piazza and the surrounding streets were crammed with upmarket stalls selling everything from genuine - and expensive - antique furniture, glass, china, paintings, statuary and weaponry to vintage clothing, books, objets d'art, records, rugs and everything in between. The place was always crammed and the cafes, bars and trattorias set around the huge square and the smaller ones did a brisk trade.

I loved my monthly meander through the market and, more often than not, picked up one or two interesting items. This time I wandered through it, looking for potential buyers. Whilst I loved all my possessions, the *Tavernetta* was simply not going to be big enough to house them. Ugo and Luisa had kindly offered to store my mid 17th century English walnut bureau and matching fall-front, which were the same age as the Manor House and which would love being stood on *cotto* floors. For when they had been made, they would have stood either on flagstones or wooden floorboards and I think that after a century of carpets and central heating they were in need of a break.

But they couldn't remain there permanently and, having looked similar items up on the internet I saw that, even in less than perfect condition, they were still very much sought after. I simply didn't know where I was going to be long term, but they had been my parents' respective desks and I didn't want to part with them. However I did want to know whether there might be some interest in purchasing them. For if I knew that they'd go to a good home and be loved and appreciated as much as I had loved them, then the sacrifice (and associated monetary gain to numb the pain) would be worth it. On one of my daily perambulations I'd seen, tucked away in a corner of the piazza closest to the river and opposite the wonderfully old and gloomy artisan pizzeria, an antique restorer, almost hidden away behind a high wall. It had been his beautifully burnished name plate and bell that had alerted me to his presence, for it had gleamed proudly and brassily on its background of sombre grey stone. A wooden door was slightly open and I'd cautiously peeped round it calling *"Buon giorno"*. A gruff voice answered and an old man, wearing a threadbare cashmere jumper filled with moth holes and a pair of very very faded Levis approached me, the unmistakeable smell of shellac coming off him in waves. I'd explained my mission and he'd agreed to come to the flat later that day and have a look at my furniture. Some bits had come off in the move from England, I still had them and had wondered if he might be able to restore them to their rightful place.

He'd turned up on time and his intake of breath as he'd seen the pieces and then lovingly stroked them told me all I needed to know. He peered at them, opened them, unerringly found their secret compartments and complimented me on having maintained the lustrous golden patina of the walnut. I told him I had used nothing but beeswax as had my parents before me. I thanked him, explaining that if he thought they were worth selling then I would like to talk to someone that might be interested in them. Perhaps he knew of someone? He'd suggested the trip to the market, to talk to the various stall holders dealing in antiques. But he explained that exquisite as the pieces were they were not for him. So, with his direction, I'd taken some good photos on my phone and armed with these I approached the stall holders. To cut a long story short, no one was interested. Well not at a realistic price. One, after having sucked his teeth and scratched his head said he'd only be able to offer me a few hundred Euros for both. I was outraged! The pieces I'd seen on the internet were belong sold for tens of thousands of Euros and I told him so. Speaking eloquently with his hands, he spread them wide while pouting and shrugging - basically saying "take it or leave it". I left it, knowing that I simply could not have parted with them unless the financial gain had outweighed the emotional loss!

I'd already checked my Lease on the flat and saw that I had to give 6 months' Notice and return the flat "to the condition in which it had been handed to me". Which meant, at the very least, that it had to be repainted - and it was huge. I knew my landlord, a lovely but somewhat exacting woman would accept nothing less, even though it was virtually spotless. She visited me, pointing out how sad she was to be losing me for I had been the perfect tenant. I apprised her of my parlous financial situation - without going into detail - and said that I was going to find it hard to pay for the repainting and might she consider taking the cost from the substantial Deposit that was being held - against damages and unpaid rent. She said that she would consider it, but that she would have to inspect the property, with the agent, at the appropriate time. I said of course and offered to help Niccolò with 'set dressing' when he came to photograph it prior to putting it on the market.

She thanked me and then looked pointedly at my bookshelves. "They'll have to be taken down as it's unlikely that anyone else would have so many books". I gulped. For one long wall was entirely taken up by 11 full height (with extension pieces!) Billy bookshelves from IKEA which contained my beloved library of over 800 books. What on Earth was I going to do with 11 Billy bookcases?!

Luckily Cheila, my wonderful cleaner and friend, a pocket-sized, curvaceous and vivacious Brazilian with flashing eyes and flashing jewellery, together with her partner Marcelo, a gentle and taciturn *Indio* musician from Bolivia offered to take them down and dispose of them. They had been in Italy for several years and rented a rambling yet cosy farmhouse about 40 minutes outside Verona in the midst of wine country. As well as cleaning and performing music, they imported all sorts of fantastic items from their respective countries and stored them in their huge barn, taking stalls at weekend craft fairs and markets throughout the Province, in order to supplement their incomes. I gladly offered them everything I didn't want or couldn't take and I could see that they were pleased.

We had become friends quickly and I was extremely fortunate that they had taken to me, for they looked after me as if I was some slightly dotty maiden aunt. Geisha adored them and when I had had to travel for work, they'd have her to stay with them. I'd load her into the car and together we'd head off into the countryside to spend several happy hours with them, having long lunches and putting the world to rights, before leaving Geisha to curl up onto her heated pad and blankets (they spoiled her rotten!) and heading off on my travels.

When I had returned from the Hamlet, and been approved by Signor S, I'd asked Cheila and Marcelo to join me for supper in a great local pizzeria, preceded by several Caipirinhas in Fabio's bar. Cheila knew that I'd lost my job and had offered to clean for me for nothing. I was hugely touched and we agreed that she'd come every couple of weeks but I'd pay her what I could. But now the time had come to tell them of my move. They were sad, but understanding. I told them about the *Tavernetta* and that I was going to have to store my books as there simply wasn't room for the shelves. I explained about the landlady and her requirements. Cheila made a disapproving noise and I looked at her surprised. "That one is all about money" she said.

That problem solved, I'd turned my attention to finding a company which could move what I was taking from Verona to the Hamlet, a distance of 85 miles (137 kms). I found several companies online and an Italian 'man with a van' website so put in my details and awaited the quotes. The estimates that I received were extraordinary - eye-wateringly expensive - the cheapest being several thousand Euros for a trip of only a couple of hours. What is more, the prices didn't include loading and unloading, which I was informed would require hiring a "*gru*" a crane. Additional expense.

The cost of bringing the whole lot out from England hadn't cost much more that what I was being quoted and that was over 1000 miles, a journey of two or more days. What is more it had included packing, loading then unloading and unpacking!

It seems that my move to the Hamlet was being thwarted at every turn and was going to cost me money I simply didn't have. I found myself sitting on the sofa sobbing helplessly, telling Cheila of my dilemma. Grimacing at the memory of the original move with which she and Marcelo had spent all day helping the movers, she told me she knew some Brazilians with a big truck, that she'd speak to them and get a price for me. She agreed that the quotes I'd received were outrageous. She knew that money was tight and that I was finding life very stressful. She hugged me and told me not to worry. I knew that I could leave it to her, that she'd find someone to help and would vigorously negotiate on my behalf to get me a fair deal.

True to her word she did. We arranged a date and I then started the horrendous task of repacking everything I'd brought out from England not two years earlier. If only I'd known... I knew that I needed help and simply could not cope on my own. Nor could I impose further on Cheila so I rang a friend in the UK, offered him a flight, bed, board, beer and €200 if he'd come out and help me. He jumped at the opportunity and we spent a sweaty 3 days packing up, boxing and storing the stuff in my bedroom. He was on a blow-up bed in the study and I was on the sofa bed in the sitting room with poor worried Geisha sitting looking mournfully at me. I called Cheila to check that the Brazilians were coming as arranged the next morning and she confirmed that they were.

Once again we were on the move! The morning dawned bright and cold but after having manhandled the entire contents of my home into the lift and onto the first of two big trucks, everyone was sweating. My friend and I had already loaded the car the night before and so, taking Geisha and all her travel paraphernalia with us, we headed off slowly with the Brazilians following behind and Cheila, tightly wedged in between them, calling me every 10 minutes or so in case they lost sight of me, for they had no idea where they were going. I'd told them that it was in the mountains and they'd blanched. It occurred to me that perhaps they were not used to driving big trucks up perilous mountain roads. I kept quiet, hoping that by the time we got there, the sun would have burned off any icy residue. Slowly, kilometre by kilometre we chuntered our way to the Hamlet where the wonderful Farah (who'd also been on the phone to me checking our ETA) was waiting with her husband, her brother in law, Farouk, and Suleiman.

We decided to unload everything into the huge portico so that I could slowly go through things and decide what went where. Farah had made up made the bed which had already been in situ and lit the fire and clever Luisa had made 4 complete sets of curtains, a matching bedspread, cushions a headboard plus curtains for the storage units in the kitchen. As we walked in with Geisha the enormous *stufa* was already pumping out heat. Everything looked homely and welcoming, Luisa had found some mad paintings of cockerels which now decorated one wall and Farah had even thoughtfully provided crockery, glasses and cutlery for the first day or so. She'd also produced sandwiches in homemade Arab bread for everyone and I'd provided bottles of beer for the Brazilians and cans of Coke and Fanta for those that didn't drink alcohol.

Cheila insisted on a conducted tour of the Tavernetta and went in dragging with her two massive suitcases which she stowed in the bedroom. I could see she was impressed for this was much more like the farmhouse she shared with Marcelo and she told me she much preferred it to the soulless flat in Verona, which she now told me she hadn't much liked!

Introducing her to Farah had been interesting as the latter was effectively taking over looking after me and I was delighted to see them hugging each other as they finally met. The unloading was accomplished in double quick time as the redoubtable Brazilians has apparently taken a sickie and were off work for the morning in order to do my job. I gave Cheila the cash to give to them and gave her a separate envelope for it was going to be the last time I saw her for a long time. Barely holding back the tears we bade each other goodbye, she looked at Farah and said, fiercely, "*guardala bene*" - look after her well - referring to me.

In that moment I realised how extremely fortunate I was to have met such amazing people - all 'incomers' to the country and all great of heart, generous of spirit and prepared to go beyond the bounds of friendship to help me. David, my English friend, was equally impressed by their kindness and affection.

Saying goodbye and wishing them a speedy return to Verona, I waved Cheila and her magnificent Brazilians off and the rest of us got back to work stowing my stuff. Geisha being totally unfazed by the whole thing, had cautiously inspected the *stufa* and deciding it to be acceptable had settled into her bed alongside it and was snoring away gently.

David was staying in the Manor House as Ugo had kindly offered him Luisa's room. That evening after having stowed as much of my stuff as we could, we sat at the kitchen table with a bowl of pasta each and a bottle of wine, discussing the day's events, exhausted but happy that the move had been accomplished without a hitch.

The next morning I drove him to Reggio and put him on a bus to the airport for his long trip home, thanking him profusely for I couldn't have done it without his help, friendship and companionship. It had also been great to be able to speak English with him! He'd loved Italy and it had been interesting watching him get used to Italian ways and I regretted that he'd not been able to stay longer so we could have explored my new surroundings together.

A couple of days later, late one Saturday morning, Ugo, Sandro and Luisa appeared. We'd agreed to meet for lunch at my table in the orchard and I'd piled plates high with cold meats, cheeses and bread from the little shop in Levizzano. Run by Rebecca and her brother Marco, the lovely and attractive twenty-something children of the owner, I'd been enthusiastically greeted by them, in halting English! They'd seen the right hand drive car and naturally assuming that I didn't speak Italian were charmingly introducing themselves. They breathed a huge sigh of relief when I'd replied in Italian, thanking them and presented them with my shopping list. Rebecca had started gathering up the cheeses, including the famed local parmigiano and

Marco was busy on the meat slicer offering me succulent *mortadella*, spicy local salami, raw (*crudo*) prosciutto and the cooked (*cotto*) version. I wandered around gathering up lettuce and tiny sweet vine tomatoes, and asked Rebecca where her bread came from. "The Forno in Valestra of course! Everything we sell here is local."They asked how long I was staying and when I said that I was moving here they were delighted. They told me that I was the second English person in the area at which I was horrified. "What? There are others?!"

It appeared that there was a couple "from the BBC" that had bought and renovated a house just down the road. I was told they came for the summer and occasionally for a long weekend in the spring and autumn. I was also told that they didn't speak Italian. Would I like to meet them? Curiosity vied with the desire to remain anonymous and not mingle with other Expats, so I cautiously said yes and left them my phone number, hoping they'd never ring me!

My list complete, they'd loaded the carefully wrapped packages into my bag, presented me with a bottle of Lambrusco as a welcome present and then told me they only took cash. My heart sank. "I've only got a few Euros". I'd said, thinking how stupid I'd been to automatically assume that they'd take Bancomat cards. So I'd started to unload my purchases wondering if I'd enough time to drive to Carpineti, the nearest cash point, and return to get the packages and then get home to greet Ugo, Luisa and Sandro. "Stop, stop! It is not a problem, you can pay us next week. Where are you going to be living?" I told them."Ah Signor S! A great man! His cousin Signora Anna lives just up the road here. Have you met her?"

"Not yet" I replied, marvelling at their laidback attitude and, reloading my bag, I bid them a cheery "*arriverdverci*" and climbed into the car, heading back up the steeply curved road to my new home and a sunlit lunch in the orchard.

Chapter 8

Playing House

Having unpacked most of the things that Geisha and I would need, I set about arranging for one of the two men who had moved me from England to Verona, to come out to the Hamlet, pick up my furniture, most of the books and many many boxes of stuff which he would store for me in his facility in Wiltshire until such time as I knew where my life was going. He and his associate had become firm friends with Cheila and Marcelo and when he was told that he wouldn't be seeing them as they were over a hundred miles away he was most upset but I promised that that he had new friends awaiting him in the form of Farah and Hassan and his brother Farouk.

Once the indefatigable Cheila and her Brazilians had offloaded the truck, Hassan and Farouk had set to work carefully stowing the antiques in the *loggia* of the *fienile*, safely protected from sun and rain by blankets and tarpaulins. The boxes of books were swathed in plastic sheeting to protect them from hungry rodents and inquisitive cats looking for somewhere new to snooze, whilst keeping a bleary eye out for possible adventures. Farah was amazed when she saw the furniture and remarked that it looked as old as the house itself. I told her it was. She then proceeded to berate the men for not paying sufficient attention to the furniture and personally took it upon herself to give everything a loving polish with beeswax "to protect it while it waits to go home" before tucking it all up once more in its protective cocoon.

Although Luisa had offered to let me store the better pieces in the house it would have involved carrying them up to the second and third floor attics and it just seemed too much of an effort to do it when Howard was arriving at the end of the following week.

While I had my boxes of books available I spent a day sorting through them to see what I'd like to keep, or couldn't live without for an indeterminate period of time. Sure enough I was going to need a couple of bookcases in the *Tavernetta* and I briefly regretted losing the Billys from Verona. Ugo, by now thoroughly conversant with my parlous financial state, suggested I pop down into Bologna one day to meet him as there were a couple of second hand furniture warehouses which sold all manner of things and apart from bookshelves I was going to need a sofa, the one in Verona being too big to get onto the van with all the other things so I had given it to Cheila who was delighted and I knew that she'd get a good price for it - which she richly deserved!

Luisa had already provided several magnificent pieces of furniture for the *Tavernetta* but I needed a big sofa to go along the front of the *stufa*. I jumped at the opportunity to visit the furniture emporia of Bologna!

The day before I headed down the mountain to meet Ugo, I decided to pop into Carpineti to see what I could pick up there. Stupidly I'd packed up most of my kitchen equipment and seeing that it was in a box destined for storage in the UK, I needed some basics.

Carpineti is a wonderful little town, it has everything. While the village, Valestra is great for the *Forno,* the butchers and the petrol station and with Rebecca in Levizzano which was more like a corner shop, Carpineti became my shopping destination of choice - and what a choice!

Along with the usual *Posta* and *Farmacia* all three banks had Bancomat cash points, there were many bars and cafes, the gin and tonic selling gelateria, three supermarkets of varying quality, a *tabbachaio*, stationers, flower shop, hairdressers, haberdashers and the most interesting-looking establishment selling ironmongery, agricultural accessories and household goods.

There was also, of course, the weekly market in the piazza, with stalls selling everything from live fowl, to local meats and cheeses, the gorgeously titled *fruttivendolo* (one of my favourite words meaning 'greengrocer') selling a vast range of organic and locally produced fruit and vegetables. Great shiny purple *melanzane*, incongruously shaped zucchini, onions of purple and brown, several different types of potato and glorious tomatoes of all shapes - from the tiny sweet piccolo to the huge beefsteak ones which you eat with mozzarella, huge bunches of various lettuces, bunches of carrots and of herbs, baskets full of apples, pears, oranges, mandarins, figs, nuts, seeds. Seasonal produce at its best and all looking so healthy!

The butchers van did a grisly trade in skinned rabbits, which hung forlornly from hooks their dead eyes staring at would-be customers. Slightly off-putting when you're queuing for some chicken breasts or mince for a Bolognese sauce! The delicatessen van did a roaring trade in prosciutto *crudo* and *cotto*. Massive chunks of marbled mortadella lay next to various salamis, the *Cacciatore*, the local mildly-spiced

129

pure pork *Felino* from, apparently, the neighbouring village, some with *finocchio* or *pepe* and some of the *Lardo di Colonnata* from just across the mountains in Carrara where Michelangelo selected his marble, no doubt munching on the salami which has been made there since Roman times. There were more types of sausage than could be imagined, but best of all were the trays of the dangerously high cholesterol *Ciccioli*, deep fried pork fat, which was effectively great slabs of crackling eaten cold and a favourite accompaniment to an aperitif.

The cheese van was situated slightly to one side as you could smell it from almost the other end of town! It groaned under the weight of many huge roundels of Parmigiano, about which I had already learned so much, as well as a bewildering array of locally-produced cheeses from cow, sheep and goat milk. The little trays offering *assaggi*, a taste, slivers of each to try were hugely tempting and that was before one got to the *pasticceria* van...!

Italians take their food very seriously but none more so than the various delicious, delicate and hugely fattening *pasticcerie*, pastries. Even the biscotti, biscuits, were dazzling in their abundance. Myriad shapes, sizes and flavours, some more exotic than others with unusual spices and combinations. All of them singing their siren song "a minute on the lips, a lifetime on the hips". To be fair that could be applied to almost every single one of the food vans - with the obvious exception of the *fruttivendolo*!

Navigating the packed pathway between these vans was no doubt an art. I half expected there to be a mobile defibrillator awaiting me at the end of the food section.

Equally fascinating were the customers - a glorious mix of *casalinghe*, the wives and mothers who stayed at home and whose culinary arts more than matched the greatest restaurants. They knew what they wanted and they were vociferous in their demands not just for service but also for quality. Sadly I understood little of what passed between them, their friends and neighbours and the vendors for they all spoke in dialect, which sounded to me a lot like French. I could see people looking sideways at me, I was new, I was female and I was alone and when I stopped at the cheese van the hush that descended on the people surrounding it was palpable. As I opened my mouth to speak as one they leaned forward to hear what was going to come out. In perfectly good Italian I asked for an *assaggio* of an interesting-looking semi hard cheese. There was a communal exhalation of breath as they heard the *straniera*, me, speaking Italian! I then asked the cheesemaker if he had a semi hard goats' cheese. He did and proffered another sliver. It was delicious, tangy and not too salty.

Normally the other customers would be impatiently waiting for me to make my choice so that could place their own orders, but such was the fascination of the goat cheese eating foreigner that I'd bought myself some time. Enough time to have a quick exchange of pleasantries with the *casaro*, the cheesemaker. "Signora, where are you from?" asked a pleasant-looking lady with amazingly chic glasses. "I'm English but I have just moved here" I explained. "How come you speak such good Italian?" she asked. The others nodded and I felt a small glow of pride. I briefly explained that I thought it rude not to learn the language of the country in which I was living. An answer that immediately elicited a flurry of wise head-nodding from many potential new friends and a small pat of ricotta from the *Casaro*.

The lady then asked me if I would give English lessons. I laughed delightedly but explained that I was not qualified to teach. "Just conversation... nothing too difficult..." she explained that she and a group of friends would meet every week at one of the cafes to practice their English conversation and it would be so wonderful to have a *"vera Inglese"* a real English woman join them and correct them. Of course I agreed, it would be great to meet some people and I'd be happy to help. Shyly she thanked me in charmingly accented English, which drew oohs of admiration from the onlookers, for they'd obviously never her heard speak English in public and we arranged to meet two days hence at 7pm when the cafe reopened for the evening. By this time we had become a sort of sideshow and were blocking the pathway through the market, so we hurriedly swapped phone numbers by waving our iPhones at each other (thanks to the gods of technology!) and were about to go our separate ways when I realised I didn't know her name or she, mine. "I'm Cassandra" I said which elicited a chorus of *"che bel nome"* from the onlookers. "I am Monica" she said with a smile and was almost immediately swallowed up by a crowd of by now somewhat impatient would-be English students!

I continued on through the market which had transformed into the non-food area and was beguiled by stalls selling capacious knickers as well as lacy thongs, push up bras, the latest mass market fashion and cocktail-coloured housecoats as well as camouflage gear for the hunters (something which I was going to have to get used to as it formed a huge part of the community's life), sensible knitted socks, long boots to protect against snakes, Viyella checked shirts (yes, here in Italy), hats with ear flaps and many assorted jumpers, jackets and gilets all in camouflage colours or bright red checks!

But what fascinated me most of all was the housewares stalls, selling everything from individual saucepan lids, to pots and pans, clothes pegs, washing lines, buckets, crockery, cutlery and a dizzying assortment of implements, the use for which I could not even begin to hazard a guess. But all of which were no doubt indispensable and absolutely necessary for life in a rural Italian *borgo*!

Exhausted by all the excitement I looked around for a place to get a coffee but the several bars and cafes were full to overflowing with farmers and their associates, all exchanging news and gossip and covertly watching the women as they walked by. My interaction at the cheese van had not gone unnoticed nor unremarked and as I walked by on my way back to the car, I was acknowledged with a brief nod by several of the farmers.

I'd parked the car opposite the Ironmongers, a wonderful place with household items to one side and farming and agricultural implements on the other. I wanted some mosquito mesh for the windows, a water jug and a couple of other things for the kitchen so I stood in the middle, uncertain as to where I should start. The owner, a distinguished-looking man with smiley brown eyes ventured forward.

"Can I help you Signora." I explained that I needed some mosquito mesh for a swing door and the windows. Hassan had agreed to make the orchard side of the house mosquito proof. There was old netting in the bedroom and bathroom windows which needed replacing and none at all in the kitchen or sitting room. The ironmonger, who introduced himself as Luca (something quite rare as formality is the norm when socialising with Italians to whom you have not been introduced) suggested that instead of making an additional door frame for the kitchen door I might consider one of the ready made versions and, indicating a magazine full of exciting looking household implements, proceeded to show me something which while no doubt highly effective just looked wrong and out of character with the architecture of the *Tavernetta*. I explained that my landlord would probably prefer me to have the made-to-measure option. "Where are you living?" I told him and with a huge smile he said "Ah with Stefano..." "Not exactly WITH Stefano I've rented the *Tavernetta*." "In which case you are right about the door, Stefano would appreciate your attention to detail". He headed off around to the farmers' area and popping his head around a huge shelving unit asked me if I wanted black or green netting. I'd have preferred the green as the black looked somewhat stygian but the house would have looked wrong with the green so black it was. A fortunate choice because when I got home I saw that it went perfectly with the black wrought ironwork of the window grilles.

We settled on 4 metres which I reckoned would be ample. He wrestled the roll to his measuring bench and assiduously measured out

4 metres using the brass ruler nailed to the edge of the bench. I sighed happily for this was a proper ironmongery, like the ones of my youth, with everything measured to one's specifications. We had a brief discussion about the type of frame (softwood) and therefore the nails I would need. While Luca wrapped them in paper (eliciting another happy sigh from me) I wandered over to browse the household shelves noting the shiny and expensive copper-bottomed saucepans, the deep black cast iron skillets and the amazing assortment of Tupperware containers, bowls, mats, more cutlery and crockery, glassware and even a Foppapedretti ironing trolley - the apogee of household implements and at over €300 way beyond my budget. It really was the most wonderful place and I knew I'd be an all-too frequent customer!

I paid and Luca offered to carry the netting and my bag of other goodies to the car, Exclaiming in admiration at my Audi A4. *"Bella macchina Signora!"* I thanked him and agreed that it was an excellent car but that I wasn't sure how excellent it would be in the snow and the ice of the winters. He nodded sagely and indicating the innumerable Fiat Panda 4x4s parked everywhere told me that that is what would be best. I agreed but the winter was a long way off and I didn't think I'd be doing much driving down lanes and through ancient trackways so the Audi would have to do. In any case if I needed to go back to the UK with Geisha we could do it in three days' leisurely and comfortable driving, whereas three hours in a Panda 4x4 was probably all we could comfortably survive!

I sang all the way home, taking my eyes off the vertiginous mountain road just long enough to blow metaphorical kisses at the beautiful landscape that had produced such gastronomic bounty.

The next day I set off down the mountain to meet Ugo in Bologna. It was strange driving down the mountain towards the smudgy ribbon of brown haze that I knew was the motorway. I'd really not appreciated how special and not of this world it was up at the Hamlet. I felt as if I was emerging from an enchanted dream as I waited at the T junction to join the stream of traffic heading for Sassuolo and the A1.

The 40 minute journey went quickly, good music helped and I'd found a really eccentric radio station called Birikina ("naughty"!) which was a hub for requests, and none of the endless and usually (to my mind) meaningless chat of the more mundane radio stations. What was interesting that the listeners all seemed to have grown up at the same time as me for their requests were a wonderful mixture of Italian, American and British hits from the 60's so I sang along happily as I drove almost missing the turnoff onto the Bologna ring road, the *tangenziale,* in my nostalgic reverie and having to dangerously traverse three lanes of fast-moving traffic in order to make the exit - much to the disgust of horn-tooting Italians. I was born in 1955 so was lucky enough to be just old enough to enjoy the hippy music scene emerging from cool places like Haight Ashbury and London's Carnaby Street and Abbey Road, but sadly not old enough to attend any of the legendary festivals!

It was a very chilled and laid-back me that embraced Ugo as we met outside a vast warehouse named *'Cose d'altre Case'*, 'Things from other houses'. We found a most convenient parking space by the entrance, thanks to my Blue Badge and walked into what I can only describe as an Emporium of Everything! I had grown up in London and the Furniture Cave on Chelsea's Kings Road in the 1970's had to be seen to be believed. This was every bit as good - if not better. Everywhere I looked there were chic displays of every conceivable type of decorative and utilitarian object. From amazing vintage clothing, complete with VERY non-pc fur coats, luggage, hats, pictures, mirrors, objets d'art, lighting, old electrical items, old mechanical items such as turn of the century - 20th century - typewriters (Italian and foreign), ceramics, glassware, cutlery, pots and pans and downstairs in the basement every possible type of furniture. Lots of sideboards, massive cupboards, wardrobes and chests of drawers in the dark wood beloved of the Mediterranean nations, as well as a plethora of 'shabby chic' distressed painted wooden furniture. Chairs of all eras and comfort abounded, from the stylish but deeply uncomfortable 1950's mustard or olive coloured occasional chairs to overstuffed leather or faux leather armchairs and sofas, bedroom stools, nursing chairs and wicker backed spindly-legged dining chairs.

I was enchanted, but my heart sank when I started looking for a sofa that a somewhat rounded Anglo Saxon posterior could lounge on in comfort. There seemed nothing that I actually wanted to sit on. Visually they were aesthetically pleasing, but less physically pleasing.

I pondered on this as we wandered through the jettisoned accoutrements of people's lives. Who had bought them and when? What stories these abandoned pieces could tell. Briefly I indulged in a mad idea to write short stories based upon various items, but Ugo was exhorting me to greater effort and so I followed him, my imagination fired by a Fellini-esque diorama, shot, naturally, in black and white...

However upon rounding a corner all such arty musings disappeared in a metaphorical haze of long-exhaled cigarette smoke and I literally screeched with delight. For there, sitting in lone splendour among less useful and more decorative pieces was the very item I was looking for. An IKEA L-shaped sofa which opened out into a double bed. I plopped myself down on it much to Ugo's surprise and recognising that this was a rare find, I refused to budge until he had found an assistant and we obtained the necessary ticket in order to pay for it. There was no way I was allowing anyone else to steal "my" sofa from under my nose. It even looked in pretty good shape and was upholstered in smart charcoal grey fabric. Scandinavian design at its most functional and understated.

"Are you sure you want this?" murmured Ugo in a tone of voice that basically intimated his disapproval that it was so un-chic!

"Absolutely. If I had been able to afford it I would have bought one in IKEA anyway. You can't beat them for sofas. How much is it?"

"Let's go and find out"

"You think I'm leaving this sofa?! No way. At least not until this is mine!"

He looked at me in that slightly reproachful way of his, but knowing that I was not going to be budged either literally or metaphorically. We tested the sofa bed mechanism which was in good working order and satisfied, he wandered off to find someone who could help us.

A few minutes later he returned with an efficient-looking young man clutching an invoice book, while he was carrying two old and somewhat ornate brass bedside lamps. I was informed that the price for the sofa was €150 and the lamps, if I wanted them were €30 for the pair. The shades looked in good condition as did the wiring and the switch so I said yes. We were given a ticket and told to go upstairs to pay for our items then come back and arrange collection. I hadn't thought of that. Somehow assuming that they would deliver. Apparently not. Ugo murmured something about having a friend with a van.

As we made our way upstairs we collected more tickets - two sturdy mahogany night stands and two bookcases (one a smart black and almost unused full-height Billy from IKEA!).

Ugo stood patiently in line while I wandered through the record section, the magazine section, the bric a brac section and flirted briefly with buying a Ferrari red set of kitchen scales. "NO!" Ugo hissed at me. I smiled disconcertingly at him and muttered something about the fact that I was not one of those people who insist on spending hours browsing through such emporia. I knew what I wanted and apart from a couple of side trips had stuck to my plan - and somewhat limited budget. There was a brief discussion at the till when Ugo presented his "*Tessera*" and I proffered my credit card. Shock horror an English credit card. Apparently it would completely confuse the accounting system if his membership card was associated with a foreign credit card so it was cash or nothing. Luckily I'd still got some left over from the day of the beatific Brazilians so rummaged around in my bag until I found the envelope and, miracle of miracles, found that I had just enough to pay the bill. But not to buy Ugo lunch. That would have to go on the English credit card!

We took the smaller items with us and drove round to the storage part of the business to collect the night tables which would fit in my car and arrange a pick up date for the larger ones.

"Next Tuesday darling. I will talk to Domenico about using his van"

"Ok, thank you." Once again I fervently thanked the gods that I had Ugo as a friend, for without him I would have been completely at sea.

Chapter 9

The country life

The next day I told Farah that I had the netting all ready for Hassan. She and I had got into the habit of having a chat every morning when she came in with wood for the *stufa*. While she cleared the ash from the previous day's fire and then laid the kindling and logs for the new daily fire we would talk about anything and everything. I learnt that she had been a Dentistry nurse back in Morocco and had had a notable amount of freedom, driving herself to and from work every day. Then she and Hassan had decided to move to Italy to give themselves and their children a better chance of life in Europe and she had found herself up a mountain with two small children and no way of getting around. I asked her why she didn't take the Italian driving test and she smiled ruefully, "My Italian isn't good enough". It was true, she spoke perfectly well and knew way more useful words than I (such as woodpile, drainage channel and gas tank) but her grasp of rudimentary Italian was poor. As I had learnt to my cost, bureaucratic Italian - such as for a driving test - challenged me, let alone her. The obtention of an Italian Licence meant passing a two-stage test, a theory test and a road test and while she would have no problem with the latter, the former would prove to be a formidable obstacle. I was lucky, as Britain was still (just) in the EU, I'd been able to swap my British licence for an Italian one with no problem, but her Moroccan one was another story.

She told me that Hassan was looking into buying her a little car which did not need a licence, the sort used by people with mobility problems - more than a mobility scooter and less than a car. I'd seen old men driving around the country roads in them and they looked great.

I told her this and asked her if she minded being isolated up at the Hamlet and she looked at me smiling "No, not at all, it is wonderful here, where would I go? Although it would be nice to be able to go to Baiso to see my cousins without having to wait for Hassan to be home from work". I agreed and offered to take her anytime she wanted to go. She smiled happily and promised that the next time they all came for a family lunch I would be invited, so that I could meet them.

I realised that she was pleased to have me there for company and she adored Geisha, making sure to greet her every morning. Geisha for her part, liked Farah and would purr welcomingly when she came in bearing great armfuls of logs.

As she worked on the *stufa* we discussed my getting my own log pile. As the *Tavernetta* hadn't been occupied I'd been using the communal log pile but it was a bit much to expect to be able partake of them on a daily basis. So as a full-time resident of the Hamlet it was now time for me to have my own supply of logs. Wood was plentiful and Farah told me that Signor S owned many hectares of land around the Hamlet which he rented out to the local farmers, part of their rent was paid in wood, part in wine and part in fish - for there was the massive fishing lake a few hundred metres away. A beautiful tranquil spot which I intended to explore when I'd settled in.

We chatted away, for she had little else to do as the children were at school. The yellow school bus arrived every morning at 8.00 sharp and Ayesha, bent double under a massive pink Hello Kitty rucksack, would erupt from the house, her gorgeous little face alight with excitement and her thick dark plait bouncing jauntily behind her. Little voices would call out to her from within the bus and I could see that she adored school and her friends. Mohammed her elder brother went to the 'big' school in Baiso and would leave earlier with Hassan in the car, so Farah and I were alone for the day, until everyone returned at 3.00 pm.

Once she had finished the fire, she stood up and shyly asked whether I'd like some Moroccan mint tea. Would I?! I adored mint tea as drunk all over the Arab world, so very happily accepted her invitation. "Stay there, I will go and prepare it and bring it back. It is warmer in here than my house." I was also conscious of a potential slight awkwardness, I was not family and therefore I was unsure whether my entering their house meant I had to encompass their traditions. As muslims, the family was accustomed to removing their shoes when indoors. Since I wore compression stockings having to remove them in order to be barefoot made things a bit complicated thus I had so far managed to avoid any invitations to their home. Farah always looked stunning in her hijab which she had to wear when any male other than her husband and son were present. But when it was just the two of us, or she was alone with the family she wore a headscarf, less all-encompassing than a hijab but still modestly

143

covering her hair. Her clothes were loose, long sleeved, full length and brightly coloured.

A few minutes later she returned bearing a silver tray complete with tea pot, water jug, a sugar bowl, some freshly-picked mint from the herb garden, two beautifully decorated tea glasses and a plate of delicious-looking biscuits which she told me were just out of the oven.

We sat at the table as she performed what I came to dub Moroccan tea magic. Pouring the hot water into the tea pot and over the leaves many times, the action cooled the drink but retained the flavour without steeping the mint too much. Did I take sugar? No I didn't, so she poured my drink first before adding sugar to hers.

The tea was sublime, fresh, minty and gently exotic - I absolutely loved it and nibbling on small shortcrust biscuits flavoured with lemon I reflected that the simple things in life simply couldn't be beaten.

Shyly Farah asked me if I intended to keep the house clean myself. I started chuckling and nearly choked on my biscuit, explaining that I hated cleaning and found it painful for my back and knees. She smiled sympathetically and asked would I like her to clean for me. I told her I'd be delighted and would she like to do some ironing too? We agreed on a rate and she smiled happily, her plan having come to fruition. As had mine for I realised that I was going to miss the indefatigable Cheila so I was glad to be able to help her in that way because she had been so warm and welcoming to me, I wanted to be able to give her something back - other than my company. She explained that it was her job to look after the manor house, the *casa signorile,* even when Signor S wasn't in residence. It took a lot of cleaning and there was also Mimi to look after. She was the manor house cat and when Signor S or Ugo and the family weren't staying, she had the run of the house to herself. Farah had learnt to keep all the doors to the upper floors closed as Mimi had a habit of sleeping on newly made beds and getting fur everywhere and then getting inadvertently shut in. She also seemingly spent a lot of time spraying her food around the kitchen such was her enthusiasm for her victuals! I remarked that it seemed such a pity that Mimi was alone in the house for months, though of course she had an open window through which to come and go during the day. At night she retreated to her boudoir, where Luisa had made her a wonderful cosy bedroom in the little barn by the loggia, complete with cardboard boxes, cat beds and her own feeding bowls. Thus in the depths of winter she could be safe and warm but still mistress of her domain.

Mimi also had the undivided love and attention of Ayesha who had raised her from a kitten and thus domesticated her, her having been born to one of the farm cats. She and the farm cats had an understanding. She was not one of them, she was a Signora and thus not part of their gang. Her interest in Geisha was touching and it was good to see Geisha understanding that this little tiger-striped cat was happy to have a new friend. When Geisha wasn't looking Mimi would come and wind herself around my legs purring like a diesel engine, looking for cuddles in the absence of her family.

Farah told me that she absolutely adored Signor S and that when he had tried to take her down to his house in Reggio for the winter she had been terrified of being cooped up and frenziedly raced around his flat yowling until he had called Alberto to take her back up to the Hamlet, seemingly preferring to be alone in her own domain without her adored *padrone.*

The farm cats lived in the barn and the *legnaia,* the wood store, where they had a very definite hierarchy. I asked Farah what they ate. She told me that the hamlet was mouse, rat and snake free thanks to the feline colony and that she and Hassan fed them their leftovers as well as the huge tins of dog food that Luisa brought. They were all fat, lazy and happy, so I had no concerns. Being as I was, a total softie when it comes to animal welfare and a *'gattara pazza'* crazy cat lady to boot!

Geisha of course was spoiled rotten, as befitted her Royal Siamese status she had the best of everything. Heated pads, beds in every room, special blankets, a ferociously expensive covered cat box complete with state of the art litter remover and various combs, brushes and accoutrements to help keep her looking beautiful.

Farah remarked that she wasn't like other cats. She was hugely intelligent and totally trusting of me, more like a companion than a pet. When we travelled in the car she sat on her pile of cushions or the passenger seat, looking out of the windows with great interest. She had a litter tray in the passenger footwell which she used - even when I was driving at great speed - and loved sitting in front of the air-conditioning vents with the breeze ruffling her fur. If she didn't get what she wanted, she would bat me with her paw. Thus I nicknamed her The Imperial Paw and her escapades kept my Facebook friends entertained.

Farah had looked aghast when we had first arrived from Verona with the car packed to the roof with stuff and Geisha sitting insouciantly on a suitcase surveying with interest the new surroundings and sniffing the delicious mountain air appreciatively. As soon as I'd left the main road and started the vertiginous climb up the winding road, I'd lowered the window just enough for her to be able to poke her elegant nose out and olfactorily investigate the myriad interesting smells wafting through the window. The air somehow felt green and I could see that she shared my sentiment and pleasure.

Ayesha had been enchanted by her and watched wide-eyed as I'd coaxed her down from her perch and carried her into our new home. Shyly she had asked if she could stroke her and I told her she'd have to ask Geisha! She did and Geisha allowed her to gently stroke her, even purring a bit. She instantly had two more love slaves!

We had drunk the mint tea and eaten most of the biscuits and I could see that Farah wanted to discuss something else but didn't know quite how to start so I gently coaxed it out of her.

She said that Hassan had offered me half of his garage, which was the continuation of the *Tavernetta*, to store my own wood. I was delighted because I had not wanted to spoil the aesthetics of our shared covered loggia by leaving a truck load of wood piled up by the door. Leaving it anywhere else would have resulted in trudging across the forecourt with a wheelbarrow - something with which my back would not have been able to cope. I asked for the phone number of the woodman and Farah fished a piece of paper out of her pocket. "My Husband gave it to me last night. He says you need to order 20 *quintale*" I had no idea what a *quintale* was but I knew that Hassan would know exactly how much wood I needed, so I nodded my agreement. "He also says that the *contattore* on the gas tank is in the red and you will have to order more gas if you are not going to run out. They come up from Reggio once a week so you should order it as soon as possible. The second number is theirs."

I was hugely grateful for their assistance and forward-thinking. I was still marvelling at my new surroundings, lost in the pastoral dream of my new existence. Everyday necessities, apart from mosquito netting, hadn't yet permeated my consciousness. Utilities such as gas, electricity and firewood now taken care of I asked Farah about telephone and wifi.

She looked uncertain and suggested I talk to Hassan when he came home from work as he knew the best and cheapest providers and they'd never had any problem with them. I mentioned that the mobile signal from my provider was almost non-existent up here. She showed me her phone, with a strong signal, but that it was with another provider. I would have to try and get out of my current contract (which was undoubtedly going to be an expensive and bureaucratically unedifying experience) and get a pay-as-you-go SIM with her provider.

I'd seen a satellite TV shop in Carpineti and noted that it also provided wifi. I wasn't sure of the technical aspects of whether we were set up for wifi in the hamlet but Farah said that they had wifi in their house, via a satellite dish on their roof which received a signal bounced off the distant phone mast. It meant that she could keep in touch with the family in Morocco via WhatsApp. It occurred to me then how much she must miss them - her parents and her sisters - with whom she was in daily contact, and marvelled at the technology that allowed us, halfway up a mountain in the middle of nowhere, to remain in touch with our family and friends.

Though I quite liked the thought that I could be unreachable for the days when I just wanted to sit and think! The luxury of being removed from the fast pace of life in the 21st century was hugely appealing. Already the magic of the place was altering me. I was sure that my blood pressure had dropped significantly in the short time that I'd been here.

We walked out into the morning sunshine together as I stood in the forecourt to get a good signal and dialled the woodman, the 'boscaiolo'.

"Tell them you live with Signor S" she advised "they all respect him and you will get a fair price".

Thanking her I waited for the phone to be answered. A gruff male voice grunted "Si" I explained who I was, where I lived and what I needed. He told me the price, €150 - which I thought really reasonable for a season's worth of wood - told me I could pay cash and that it would be delivered the next day. We agreed a time and I told Farah.

"I will help you move the wood when it's unloaded."

"What do you mean, move the wood? Surely they will stack it?"

She laughed, a great big happy laugh. "No, they unload it onto the ground and we have to stack it."

Not for the first time was I glad to have her there. As well as being beautiful and gentle and kind, she was fun. Her sparking eyes and deep chuckle enhancing her beauty. She was very engaging with an enquiring mind and she and I were going to get on like a house on fire.

The next day, right on time, the truck arrived and unceremoniously dumped several *"quintali"* of seasoned wood on the forecourt. The *Boscaiolo* explained that he had given me a mixture of woods as they all had different burning times and densities. I was intrigued and Farah gave me an impromptu lesson as we started laboriously stacking the logs. Some were slow-burning overnight big lumps which she put in a series of large baskets by my door. Most were medium density chestnut, hornbeam and birch, the larger pieces being oak. It took us a good couple of hours to select and stack the wood so that it didn't fall down in Hassan's garage. I felt like a ligneous version of a dry stone waller. An historic and attractive method of rural wall-building without mortar, it is an art and I felt that my woodpile was also worthy of being called art. Farah and I had been ruthless in our selection and placement of the logs so that not only was the pile sturdy and safe but also aesthetically pleasing - just like a dry stone wall.

All I had to do now was to learn how to build and maintain a fire! Farah was an expert and me an impatient novice!

Tired from all the lifting and stacking we returned to our respective domains, she to start baking the bread for the family supper and me to collapse in a dusty heap on the sofa which a couple of weeks earlier Ugo and Domenico had brought up the mountain ensuring that it was still in good working order and placed where I wanted it. Right in front of the *stufa*.

My little house was slowly coming together and I could not have been happier. Geisha, snuggled in her cosy fleece-lined house, positioned on the wide terracotta tiled windowsill so she could look out of the windows and watch the various comings and goings of humans, felines and sundry wildlife, opened a bleary eye, regarded me briefly and went back to sleep.

I toyed with making a proper lunch, decided against it, found some bread, local cheese and salami, threw a couple of tomatoes onto a plate with a drizzle of olive oil, added a twist or two of ground black pepper and a pinch of sea salt, grabbed one of the wonderfully useful small bottles of red wine that they sold in one of the little supermarkets and settled down on the L-shaped sofa with my loaded tray sitting sturdily on my lap. Gazing out of the window into the burgeoning spring blossom and emerging foliage of the myriad fruit trees in the orchard, I reflected how perfect this place was and how lucky I was to be living here.

The only slightly jarring note was the lack of adequate phone signal, I resolved to visit the shop in town on the morrow. Or maybe the day after!

A few hours later there was a gentle knock on the door. I manoeuvred myself off the sofa where I had sunk into a gentle reverie and warmed by the *stufa*, had no intention of doing anything much, and went to answer it. Ayesha, back from school and smiling from ear to ear was carrying a large plate. Gingerly she offered it to me. "Mi madre thought you might like some pizza for dinner? She's just taken it out of the oven." Thanking her, taking the proffered plate and telling her to make sure she thanked Farah, I looked at the foil-wrapped parcel from which were emerging mouth-watering whiffs of something which if it tasted as delicious as it smelled was truly a great and thoughtful gift.

That evening I sampled the first of Farah's pizzas, an incredible confection of vegetables, olives, peppers, capers, tuna and various herbs; the like of which I had never before or since tasted. It was as delectable as it looked and became the number one request of the friends who came to see me. What is more, Luisa and Ugo always requested it when their friends came to stay - which, for a nation of incredible cooks, is high praise indeed!

Chapter 10

History, a castle and a proposal

We settled in quickly, Geisha finding her spot on the broad south-facing windowsill by the *stufa* most congenial. She seemed to enjoy overlooking the orchard where she could survey the feline goings on and warm her old bones at the same time. She showed little interest in going out and exploring and the cats seemed to sense that she was old and frail, because when she did, they kept a respectful distance. Even Mimi who, on our lunch in the orchard had come to inspect Geisha who had been sitting snoozing on my knee. She'd sniffed her, looked at me and settled down at my feet. I was pleased - the last thing Geisha needed was feline turf wars. In fact the Hamlet's cat population seemed to have their pecking order pretty much sorted! Everyone had their place and their favourites and, despite the arrival of Geisha, the status quo had remained pretty much the same.

As for me, I'd soon got used to the daunting mountain roads but I would, I was sure, never get used to the sheer beauty of the place. People talk about the beauty of neighbouring Tuscany but, having spent considerable time in both places, I can honestly say that the landscape in this little-known corner of the world, is superior and has no equal.

At almost every turn, achingly beautiful vistas opened up, my favourite being what I had termed my "supermarket drive", the 8 kms from home to Carpineti. The views from the dizzying road which wound sinuously around the base of Monte Valestra changing hourly, according to the light, the season, the time of day and the cloud cover. On some days the panorama was like a Japanese painting, the rising layers of misty hills portraying nature as part of a mysterious cosmic realm, as if it was only half there. Slipping in and out of time like a mythological Otherworld.

Yet over these mountains were the fleshpots of the Tuscan Riviera and the more enigmatic and, to me, appealing Liguria still full of myths and legends after many centuries of relative obscurity. Nowadays the famed Cinque Terre, the chain of five picturesque seaside villages and the naval port of La Spezia as well as good motorway connections have revitalised the Tuscan/Ligurian border and many many foreigners have moved in to the area, buying second homes and holidaying there.

Admittedly the Tuscan and Ligurian hilltowns are stunning, with places such as San Gimignano and Volterra, rightly being designated UNESCO world heritage sites. But so are the northern Appenine mountains - the Parco Tosco Emiliano is a UNESCO biosphere and, with some of the darkest and most unpolluted skies in Europe, is also a haven for astronomers. In fact, one of the tiny *borghi* near Carpineti proudly hosts a small private observatory in a shed! From where the star, Tincana, was discovered and named for the *borgo*, it even appears on NASA's star registry.

However the fact remains that this area is relatively undiscovered. This puzzles me because the area from Parma south to Bologna and west to the mountains is where, according to popular consensus, the best food in Italy is to be found. I've seen it in the proud traditions of the artisan food producers in the area and the publicity for the annual *Città Slow* organic slow food festival in the neighbouring town of Felina.

From talking to Mauro and Luisa I gathered that there are many Italian gastronomic tourists coming to the area, but that to a wider international clientele there is little foreign tourism and very little investment in buying property, apart from the couple from the BBC - despite the area being so easily accessible from an international airport, Bologna, and the property prices being a fraction of what they are in Tuscany.

To many Italians however, the area is one with a rich and astonishing history, for it is here that Matilda di Canossa changed the course of Italian history and, together with Pope Gregory VII, also the Roman Catholic Church and the Papacy. Removing them, once and for all, from the feudal control of the Germanic Holy Roman Empire and effectively kick-starting the existence of the free Italian communities and the restoration of Papal authority in Rome. She was so important that she is even buried in St Peter's in the Vatican City, one of only three women.

In the interim period between meeting Signor S and moving in, I'd decided to research the area and had come across this extraordinary woman after whom the piazza in Carpineti is named, as well as having a designated motorway exit on the A1 named after her!

Happily exploring the immediate area online and having read a bit of its history, I found out that the following day was to be the 900th anniversary of Matilda and Gregory's arrival at Carpineti castle in

March 1077. I decided to visit the castle hoping that there might be some sort of ceremony to celebrate the fact. Heading to the excellent website of the *Comune* I was disappointed to see that the castle was not open to the public until Easter. But I learned that the grounds were accessible all year round and that only the church, the *Pieve* of Sant'Andrea and the castle keep itself would be closed. Oh, and the restaurant!

Perched atop Monte Atongnano, 805 metres above sea level, the castle commanded a strategic position with massive views across towards the mountains. Today the roads leading up to it climb steeply among woods of Hornbeam, as I swung round a succession of arduous hairpin bends the castle came into view, its mellow stones warm in the Spring sunshine. I parked in the tiny car park at the bottom of a perilously steep cobbled incline, relieved to see that there was a wooden handrail for me to hang on to. It proved to be somewhat rickety so I ascended slowly, stopping occasionally to pause for breath. As I rounded the last bend I saw, to my surprise an ENEL van, from the state power company, parked precariously at the top. Heaven knows how they had got the car up the slope, so great was its gradient. Two boiler-suited *technici* were methodically examining the power supply to what appeared to be the (closed) restaurant. A welcoming wooden bench beside them beckoned me and I sat down with a grateful sigh. I wished them a cheery *Buon Giorno* and, indicating the vertiginous access, complimented them on their feat of getting the van up there. *"Eh beh Signora, ci siamo abituati, ma non è facile."* We're used to it, but it's not easy. I noted that the van was a Fiat Panda 4x4 the vehicle of choice it seemed for these mountain roads, for everyone appeared to have one. Mental note to self. Might I also need one?

I concurred and sat for a while watching them work and enjoying the warmth of the sun on my back. Leaning slightly backwards and craning my neck I looked up at the great stone mass of the castle, its Keep and tower rising above me into a ridiculously blue sky. To my right was the restaurant, built in the traditional 'rustic' style, a cross between Alpine and medieval, with a loggia supported on great chestnut beams and with the ubiquitous *cotto* tiled roof. The sign for Algida ice cream swayed in a gentle breeze, somehow at temporal odds with the rest of the architecture.

The wooden shutters were firmly closed and the place had a sad air of abandonment, having been empty for the winter. I guessed that the *Technici* were there to reconnect the power prior to opening at Easter, a month hence.

To my left was a sweep of broad stone steps, guarded by a stone house on one side and a great stone wall on the other. The arched entrance was inaccessible, closed off by a solid locked wooden gate. I asked the *Technici* if there was another way up to the castle and they told me that although the Keep and the little church were closed there was a longer path which led around the back, and less steep, which was a boon.

I reflected that this made sense as it was unlikely that the animals in the Countess' retinue or those of her visitors, would be left outside the protective walls and that they certainly would not have been able to navigate the stone steps. I suspect it was also used by grateful

Technici and other workmen as lugging their equipment up and down stone steps would have been a major inconvenience.

Thanking them I started off slowly, grateful that the gradient was more gentle. I plodded up it slowly, and as it wound around the back of the complex I was able to look down on Carpineti far below, nestling at the foot of the great wood.

The path culminated in a broad level grassy area, probably once called a greensward, with the entrance from the Gatehouse steps to my left, alongside which sat the gorgeous little church, the Pieve of Sant'Andrea, with the great entrance to the castle on my right.

In front of me was a sort of walled garden with a beautifully simple arched entrance and through it I could see, literally, into the wild blue yonder. Heading towards the gated entrance to the castle, and by peering through the wooden slats, I could see a path led steeply upwards through a further series of thick walls and fortified gates to the keep itself, surmounted by its imposing tower, miraculously still seemingly intact. I later learnt that it had been restored but this did not, in any way, detract from the sheer spectacle and majesty of the castle.

What a wonderful place I thought to myself, heading towards a very welcome and conveniently located wooden picnic table with bench so I could sit entranced and look out over the lands of the Grand Contessa. Apparently Carpineti castle had been her favourite and I could see why. Almost impossible to breach, accessed in her time by a quite terrifying and vertiginous path that wound its way from Monte Valestra to what is now the little car park and with stunning views, this was a magnificent spot.

The church of Sant'Andrea with its adjacent campanile gave off an air of quiet peace, as did the enchanting little walled garden and my imagination ran riot, envisaging Matilda and Pope Gregory taking the air or just sitting and talking. Of course it would all have been very different, a hive of activity, with courtiers and soldiers scurrying to and fro, visitors arriving on foot from the gatehouse, now repurposed as the ticket office and a small B&B. But I was so enjoying the tranquility and the sparkling air that I just sat entranced trying to tune into the events of that day 900 years ago.

My peace was shattered and, I felt, somewhat rudely interrupted by a very 21st century sound, a man talking loudly into his mobile. I opened my eyes and saw a MAMIL a Lycra clad middle-aged cyclist, lovingly laying his no doubt wildly-expensive titanium bike, down on the sunlit grass. He then teetered towards me on his cycling shoes, the ones that clip in to the pedals and without so much as a nod in my direction plopped himself down on the other end of the bench and continued his phone call.

My peaceful reverie shattered, I snorted in disgust and glared at him. Poor man, he'd done nothing wrong, other than invade my personal space, but my mood vanished as suddenly as mist in the sunlight and the medieval ghosts of the castle with it.

I nodded at him and ventured a *Buon Giorno*. His call over, he responded, somewhat grudgingly I felt, looking at me through wraparound mirrored sunglasses which made him look like a large yellow beetle. I asked him how he'd made it up the steep incline with his bike. He told me that there was a path through the woods from

Carpineti which led up to the other side of the castle. I made interested noises and he suddenly became quite loquacious describing his route from near Reggio Emilia, some 30 kms distant. As he talked I looked at him, he was, in every respect, identical to all the other shaven-headed, whip-thin middle-aged male cyclists who singly or in packs inhabit each and every road I'd driven in this area. By inhabit I mean inhabit as they seem totally incapable of keeping to one side of the road, preferring to whizz along in the centre, much to the annoyance of other road users. In an area like this where the roads are so bendy and precipitous it's pretty dangerous for them to swarm in the middle of the road as the farmers in their 4x4s also tend to drive one-handed slap bang in the middle while yelling into their phones. They are brightly-coloured accidents waiting to happen.

I was also curious about the yellow jersey phenomenon. I'd understood that the *maillot jaune* , the famed 'yellow jersey', was solely reserved for the leaders of the Tour de France and not every Tom, Dick and Harry - or should that be Tommaso, Ricardo and Enrico - that chose to get on a bicycle. Does it make them feel more *sportivo* wearing the famed yellow? Or was it some sort of sympathetic magic where the donning of the legendary coloured top somehow imbued them with cycling superpowers and as soon as they got home and doffed the article they returned to normal?!

After a minute or two he seemed to get bored of talking to me, so got up and left without so much as a *Ciao, Arriverderci* or the unequivocal *Addio*. I was not sad to see him go but he'd interrupted my solitude and the moment had been lost, so I gingerly retraced my steps, clambering back down the steep cobbled path to the car parked far below, vowing that the next time I would bring a walking stick or staff with me as the wooden railing really was very rickety in places and if I had fallen I was sure that I'd have taken it down with me.

Out of the sunshine it was cold and I was hungry. I didn't feel like going home for lunch so instead I headed out of Carpineti in a different - and new - direction, looking for a Trattoria where I could eat some pasta and have a glass of wine.

The road was very different from the other side of the mountain, it even had bus stops and was the main road from Reggio Emilia to Castelnovo ne' Monti, the last major town before the mountain pass to Liguria. It wound through woodland, interspersed with alpine-type meadows, just beginning to show the first blooms of spring flowers.

Small well-tended houses, some with a horse or a goat grazing in the adjacent field were dotted about and I spotted several brown roadsigns, indicating monasteries and churches that definitely warranted further investigation as well as several homemade signs advertising firewood, organic honey, cheeses and fruit for sale in the houses and farms by the road.

As I rounded a bend, I slowed to look at a roadside shrine to a local saint, beautifully housed in a small stone construction with a faded picture of the saint safely tucked away behind an ornate iron grille and several posies of flowers and a couple of those long-burning candles crowding the small offering shelf at the front. I'd heard it said that the local saints were famous for curing all sorts of medical ailments and I was always attracted to the simple beauty of these shrines at crossroads and waysides.

Just around the corner I entered a small village, well more of a group of houses around a bar and was astonished to see a large rainbow flag, the LGBTQ+ emblem, hanging outside the main house in the group. I wonder who lived there and what was their story. Beyond the houses was a beautifully restored small medieval church together with a group of similarly refurbished houses. The brown sign proclaimed it to be 11th Century and it looked just gorgeous sitting there in the sunshine. A couple of hundred metres past it was an imposing building which proudly announced itself as the Trattoria Vasirani. A few cars were parked in the courtyard which was always a good sign. There were a couple of tables and chairs outside and despite it being chilly, they were facing into the sun and so it would be warm enough to sit outside. Apart from the smokers no Italian would dream of sitting outside in such weather, but as a Vitamin D starved northerner, I craved the opportunity to sit and, like a sunflower, turn my face to the sun. So I chose the comfiest looking chair, settling into it with a sigh of contentment. The glass door opened with a squeak and out stepped the most glorious woman.

She looked like Brigitte Bardot, dressed in tight black leggings with platform mules and a black top over which jingled and sparkled myriad necklaces. Her artfully dyed blonde hair was piled atop her head à la Bardot and her make up was a cross between the French bombshell and Cleopatra. She bade me *Buon Giorno* in a voice husky from, no doubt, many many years of smoking. She was totally magnificent and I warmed to her instantly as she gave me a huge welcoming smile upon hearing me speak Italian. She explained that lunch started at 12.00, we were a few minutes away, so would I like an *aperitivo* while I waited for a table to be made ready? We briefly debated the various merits of this and I settled on some house wine which I could then finish with my meal.

She disappeared back into the restaurant and minutes later popped out with a small plate of local salami and cheese and a small carafe of red wine. Not Lambrusco but something *fermo,* still. I sipped it appreciatively as I took in the view. More Alpine meadows billowing towards the sky, dotted with yet more small but prosperous looking houses, some in the local stone and some, like my neighbour in Valestra, looking more like a Swiss chalet but without the ornately carved gables and railings or the window boxes of geraniums and the meticulously cut logs sawed to exact lengths in identical woodpiles that so characterise the Alpine residences of Switzerland, Austria and Bavaria.

One other thing that differentiated this place from its northern counterpart was the distant double row of *Cypressi,* the ubiquitous Cypress (Cupressus Sempervirens) trees of Tuscany which have almost become their trademark. I recall having read in an edition of Italy magazine that this very durable and scented wood was famously used for the doors of St. Peter's Basilica in the Vatican City and that the poet Ovid recorded the best-known myth associated with the tree. An unfortunate boy named Cyparissus had accidentally killed one of the Greek God Apollo's beloved tame stags. His grief was so inconsolable that he asked to weep forever. Apollo transformed Cyparissus into a cypress and his endless tears became the tree's sap.

The trees are indigenous to Tuscany and they looked gorgeous winding sinuously up the hillside. A huge sigh of contentment escaped me and with that I realised that I really was extremely hungry.

Not ten minutes later I was seated at a well laid table, covered with snowy napery and a vast assortment of cutlery as the smiling proprietor whose name I had just learned was Valentina, reeled off a long list of mouthwatering antipasti. I told her that since I'd already eaten the equivalent of an antipasto with my wine outside, I'd go straight to the *primo piatto,* the pasta course. Again she launched into a veritable catalogue of homemade options. I settled for *Tortellini in Brodo,* which I knew would be rich and delicious.

Valentina then proceeded to recite the main course options, including the delicious local *Barzigole.* But she also mentioned a *frittata,* a glorious mixture of eggs mixed with vegetables, meats or cheeses or a combination of them and fried into a sort of omelette or crustless quiche. I decided I'd wait until after the Tortellini to see how hungry I was. My relationship with food had changed dramatically several years previously when I had undergone a gastric bypass. My now much-reduced stomach pouch simply couldn't take too much food without painful and pretty revolting consequences. The problem was that I often forgot about this and 'my eyes always having been bigger than my stomach' often resulted in my needing to ask for a packet of leftovers to take home with me.

I explained the basics to Valentina and she, being such a Goddess, said why don't you have a half portion of each course?

"Could I?"

"Of course" she replied as if it was the most natural thing in the world.

I realised that this was the absolute pinnacle of customer service and that this lady was not only friendly and welcoming but also very very commercially astute thus guaranteeing my loyalty and patronage for ever!

The half litre of red wine had miraculously disappeared! "It seems to have evaporated" I said, indicating the empty jug. Valentina laughed and said I obviously needed another one. I concurred and wondered vaguely whether the local police lay in wait for slightly intoxicated drivers leaving this inestimable establishment.

Judging by the amount of alcohol being consumed around me I reckoned that I and my fellow diners were either very foolhardy or that the local Police received a well-deserved case of wine from time to time, ensuring that they go and park elsewhere looking for miscreants.

It was fascinating watching the other people in the restaurant. Apart from myself the other patrons were workers. An interesting mix of what looked like manual labourers with obvious blue-collar workers, salesmen and a several couples. I'd had some cursory glances from the crowded tables when I'd come in, but not the outright and, to me, somewhat hostile stares that I'd encountered in the cities. A couple of men at the adjacent table had even smiled at me as I'd sat down and upon overhearing my exchange with Valentina about the "evaporating wine" had laughed out loud and raised their glasses to me. I liked it here. I would definitely come again.

It goes without saying that the food was delicious, the half-sized portions a perfect and thoughtful touch and the local wine from, I gathered by the somewhat vague wave Valentina gave in the direction of the cypress trees, the hill opposite.

I elected to take my coffee outside and treated myself to an '*affogato*' an espresso coffee poured over a portion of vanilla ice cream. Sitting once again at 'my' table I became the subject of friendly enquiry from the three smokers sitting at the adjacent table who had spotted my right-hand drive car and, having put two and two together, had deduced that it and I belonged to each other. Their good-natured questioning revealed a genuine desire to find out what a lone foreign woman was doing in this part of the world where tourists were rare. Especially Italian-speaking ones!

I explained what had happened and was very moved by their apparent concern at my plight. There were mutterings of outrage at my cold-blooded dismissal. There were also expressions of admiration for my bravery and "*grinta*", my True Grit! Imagine, they said, living all alone in a foreign country. Shaking their heads in bewilderment as they contemplated the unimaginable horror of living away from home without family around them.

I told them that I had spent the last 30 years travelling and working abroad and that I was not close to my family. They asked if I was married. I said I wasn't. Then they asked me about Brexit and how was I going to stay in Italy once it happened. I said I didn't know. Laughing uproariously they suggested, as Signor S had, that I find myself an Italian husband so that I could stay. I grinned and told them about my Irish passport application. Pity they said, Aurelio here is looking for another wife. Aurelio must have been in his 50's, so younger than me. A handsome dark haired man with startlingly deep black eyes under bushy eyebrows and a well-worn face with a big toothy grin and a stubbly chin. He looked solid and dependable yet slightly sad and I wondered how he had lost his wife. I didn't ask.

I told them that he'd probably die of malnutrition as I was a terrible cook at which they laughed uproariously. "He's rich, he can bring you here every day or Valentina can teach you how to cook." I thanked them and said that I had been alone for so long that I was genuinely happy and the thought of having to stay at home as a housewife - a *casalinga* - when my soul was that of a gypsy a *zingara* was anathema to me. I really liked being alone.

Of course they didn't believe me but they were so impressed with my *grinta* that they offered me a *digestivo* to go with my *affogato*. I politely declined, explaining that I wasn't yet used to these mountain roads and that I was already going to have to drive home very slowly due to the wine I'd consumed. A *digestivo* of the type they were suggesting involved a glass or two of the local firewater - usually *Nocino* or something similar. And about 90% proof!

This brought the conversation to an end as they had to return to work. Solemnly they bade me goodbye, addressing me as Signora and wishing me the best of luck with everything.

I went back into the restaurant found the Ladies lavatory, mercifully with a sit down loo and not one of those stand-up Turkish ones that necessitate absolute equilibrium in order not to fall into its noisome depths. I still cannot understand why a country as civilised as Italy uses such things and how on earth does one use them without a major mishap?!

Emerging unscathed I saw Valentina waiting for me at the till with a smile on her face: "you have made some friends?"

I told her that they had suggested I marry Aurelio and her snort of laughter told me everything I needed to know. I left, having paid a modest amount for a wonderful and fun lunch and turning the car around drove home slowly, reflecting on the day's encounters - which could not have been more different.

Chapter 11

'Be fearless in the pursuit of what sets your soul on fire...'
Jennifer Lee

It didn't take me long to settle in and, with the spring sunshine, I welcomed the opportunity to explore my area. I still had errands to do - such as sorting out the wifi and, hopefully, phone; finding a vet for Geisha as her annual booster vaccination was due. I also needed to find a slightly larger supermarket than the little ones in Carpineti - I longed for a Conad, the supermarket which had been close to the flat in Verona and with which I was familiar - I even had a loyalty card.

Standing in the forecourt, trying to hook into Farah's wifi signal, I had discovered that if I sat in a chair plonked right in the middle I could just obtain one. Thus I discovered that there was a Conad in Felina, the town of the slow food festival, Città Slow, and only a few kilometres further on from Carpineti. I also found out that I was going to have to go into Castelnuovo ne' Monti, to the phone shop as the one in Carpineti could only do top-ups and not new contracts.

So early one morning I headed off, asking Farah to ensure that the fire was lit and kept going all day so that Geisha's ageing bones would stay warm. She was now beginning to show her age and I know that she needed to be kept cozy. I would also ask the vet to give her a thorough health check when she had her jab.

My plan was to pop into the wifi shop in Carpineti, get to the Conad in Felina before the lunchtime closing and then head off to Castelnovo for lunch somewhere, before taking the scenic route home, after a drive-through recce to see what this much larger town offered; the last one before the forbidding passes of the Appenines and thus marking the boundary of my magical land.

The shop in Carpineti was run by two women - a mother and daughter apparently - from listening in to the phone conversations of the latter while I waited, it was seemingly she who provided customer assistance. With a certain amount of dramatic eye-rolling, she was patiently explaining to some poor soul that they had to find their Customer number in order for her to be able to login on her computer to see what, if anything, she could do remotely to sort out some technical problem. Her mother, a redoubtable bespectacled lady, with a big welcoming smile and a bowl of little sweets on her desk, was most helpful and it didn't take long for me to decide which wifi package would suit me - I was delighted that the recommended package even threw in a free landline - with a limited number of calls per month.

Rosanna explained that a '*tecnico*' from Castelnovo would have to come and install the '*parabola*'- dish - on the roof and that connection was not automatically guaranteed as it was dependent on whether the signal from the area's TV and phone mast could be accessed. Accessed in terms of whether there were trees obscuring the sight lines and thus the signal. I nodded solemnly, we fixed a date and I was told that the *Tecnico* would arrive any time between 07.00 and 12.00 on the given day.

My paperwork was in order, my passport perused and photocopied, my British credit card regarded with distrust, a discussion ensuing as to whether I was going to be able to pay long term with a foreign card. Luckily there were a number of foreign customers with second homes in the area so Rosanna was used to foreign credit cards - but not ones in Sterling. Once again the spectre of Brexit raised its head and she gently suggested that I paid by direct debit through my Italian bank. In Verona. Another sniff. Verona might as well have been in another country. "Why don't you open an account here in Carpineti? There are several good banks. They can handle the transfer of accounts for you as part of their service." I readily agreed but told her that for the moment she was going to have to take my deposit and first three months' fee from my British credit card. There were several worrying and tense moments as she tried to put the payment through and we both held our breath as the card machine beeped ominously. Then a green light flashed, Rosanna smiled and I exhaled. The payment had gone through and I looked at my phone half expecting an SMS or call from my British bank to check that the payment was bona fide and that I wasn't some foreign thief attempting to spend my money. No more beeping, no call or SMS - so all was well. I signed the paperwork and grinned at Rosanna and her beleaguered daughter who was still patiently dealing with what seemed to be an increasingly-irate and tech-phobic customer.

I said goodbye to them both and, as I drove through the centre of town had a quick look at the banks. One was very local, *St Geminiano e St Prospero*, one was very regional, *Credem* and one was national but owned by a big German bank - *Unicredit*. Mentally I plumped for the latter - not least because there had been a branch near the flat in

Verona and the technical sophistication of its cashpoint had impressed me! Probably not the best way of choosing a bank, but the German ownership also comforted me.

There had been a lot of scandals about small Italian banks in the couple of years that I had been in Italy and I wanted the security of knowing that my pitifully small account would be looked after properly. I'd also run into the torturous bureaucracy of a small bank with my current one in Verona. Admittedly it had improved slightly when it had been taken over by a larger Italian group, but the piles of dusty files and mountains of paperwork in my branch had not endeared me to it. The '*Bancomat*' the exterior cash machine had not always worked and the anti-terrorist automatic entrance doors had shut me in their hermetically-sealed embrace on more than one occasion - eliciting squeals of horror from the Teller who had had to leave her bullet-proofed cashiers desk to release me from the unforgiving clutches of the over-zealous doors.

The Unicredit building was an elegant patrician whitewashed house with a cash machine, car parking and no ghastly tubular anti terrorist doors… it even had flowers in window boxes outside. I plumped for it and wandered in. There was no queue and the welcoming smile from the cashier and the smart modern interior with comfy seats and colour brochures on a glass table and not a dusty file in sight, were encouraging.

I explained that I wanted to open an account and was there someone with whom I could speak? There was. A *Dottore*, who would be available shortly as he was just finishing with another customer.

Would I like to wait? I told her I would and sank gratefully into a bright red and really quite comfortable chair, reflecting on how their obvious customer service training was paying dividends. I felt welcomed and, apart from a slight narrowing of the eyes as I had first started speaking - a not unusual occurrence when my foreign accent and slightly odd grammar marked me out as a foreigner - I did not feel at all uncomfortable or unwelcome. Maximum points to Unicredit!

After a few minutes there was a flurry of goodbyes and handshakes from the direction of the office and a man, in his late 30's or early 40's approached me smiling and introduced himself as Pietro Carbonesi. I gave him my name, which for anyone who is not of Anglo-Saxon origin can be difficult to process, and, to his eternal credit he didn't blink, indicated the door of his open office and ushered me in. I explained that I was Resident in Verona, that I was moving down here and that I wanted to transfer my account. He asked a few questions - and suggested that I opened an '*Estero*'- foreign - account which would make transfers to and from the UK easier.

I agreed and he produced the requisite paperwork which he proceeded to fill in - electronically. Once I had shown him my existing bank details, my *Codice Fiscale* and my Passport as well as my *Carta d'Identità* he handed me an iPad, asked me to check the details and if I was happy with them he would deal with the whole process of closing my Verona account - without my having to ever talk to or see them again - and opening my new Unicredit account. He suggested that as it might take a week or two I might want to withdraw some money from the cashpoint outside to tide me over. Good thinking. I excused myself and popped out into the sunshine and withdrew my daily limit. Returning inside, we proceeded to begin the signature process. Which is where the whole thing nearly descended into farce.

For, being understandably cautious about fraud and money-laundering, the bank had, like all banks, instituted an electronic signature pad but here, in Italy, I had to provide about twenty-one signatures - all of which had to be identical otherwise the machine would not recognise me and lock me out…

I took a deep breath and started - the first dozen or so were ok, then fatigue set in and my somewhat eclectic signature became even more so and the pad beeped and flashed red. We looked at each other, I gulped, knowing that we were about halfway through and I had to continue concentrating and almost exactly replicating my scrawled name another nine times. Heaven knows how I did it - but I did and once Dottor Carbonesi had pressed the transmit button, we had nothing to but sit and chat while we waited for confirmation.

He had been wonderfully reserved by not asking about me and now was the time, I felt, to give him a bit of background information. To my astonishment he switched to flawless English, asking how I felt about being alone in Italy. I told him I was absolutely delighted and that I loved the country, and that having just discovered this corner of the world I was even happier. I loved its wildness.

"What is the difference between 'wildness' and 'wilderness'?" He asked me.

I nearly fell off my chair with amazement, such a question demonstrated an extremely high level of English. I explained the difference as best I could and he seemed content. I liked this man and he was so professional that he made me feel secure and safe in a way that I had not felt in my bank in Verona. Knowing that he had such an excellent command of English could also be useful in any emergency. Wow what a find!

He offered me his mobile number 'in case of necessity' picking up on my probably palpable relief, and of course he had mine as part of the registration process. We briefly discussed where I was living. It seemed that Signor S was well known in the area and that I was 'under his protection' in the sense that living on the property of a large and well-respected local landowner, I was, somehow protected. From what I had no idea, but it was a good feeling to know that I was being acknowledged as part of the local community by virtue of my association with the Hamlet.

The iPad beeped again, confirming that everything had gone through and I was presented with a smart folder of paperwork, an e-banking link and told that I could pick up my debit card as soon as the transfer had been completed - in about a fortnight. In the meantime I could use my British cards if I needed anything urgently. I was really impressed. As we left his office, I was introduced to the bank manager, a chic and vivacious woman in her fifties who shook my hand warmly and welcomed me to her branch. She regretted that she didn't have time to offer me a coffee but as soon as my account was open she would redress the balance. I replied that I would be delighted to accept her invitation. My goodness this was a LOT different to the experience

I'd had in Verona. I felt less tense already and as I left the bank, I breathed a huge sigh of relief.

Here in the middle of a relatively-unknown corner of north west Italy, I was being treated with kindness, friendliness and courtesy. I'd been told by Aurora, when I had told her where I was going, that the mountain people were known to be unfriendly, taciturn and suspicious of 'incomers' - and by incomers that meant Italians from other areas! She'd warned me that I should probably expect open hostility - thankfully she could not have been more wrong!

Looking at my watch I saw that, if I left now I had time to pop to Conad in Felina, so I climbed into the car and to the unblinking stares of the ever-present group of old men sitting in the sunshine outside the bar opposite, drove off up the street.

Passing Valentina's Trattoria on my way I saw her sweeping the area around the outside tables ready for the lunchtime influx. Today I had decided not to treat myself to lunch for although the *Pranzo di Lavoro* - the working lunch - was usually €12 - I was going to get provisions and should not get into the habit of eating out every day. Besides Conad did sandwiches, strange but delicious and slightly-damp confections called '*Tramezzini*', a sort of version of the English sandwich - two slices of bread with the crusts cut off and a filling of some sort. They were pretty unappetising but with a bottle of water and a piece of fruit more than adequate for a lunch on the go. I felt I wanted to explore a bit, find somewhere to park, eat my *tramezzino* and drink in a view or two.

Following the signs for Conad I parked, pulled out a Euro for the trolley and wandered into the small supermarket. It was smaller than my local one in Verona but stacked to the gills with the usual impressive assortment of goods. Fresh fruit and veg in abundance, great meat, cheese and fish counters, a bakery, an excellent wine section and all manner of local delicacies in amongst the more familiar items. They even had the *Tramezzini* though who, in this land of delicious and cheap lunches, apart from me wanted to eat them was beyond me! I quickly found what I needed and heading for the pet food section was delighted to see that Geisha's favourite food was there in plentiful quantities along with some other brands with which I was unfamiliar. So I stocked up for her too. My trolley was becoming full and the couple of reusable bags which I always kept in the car, were not going to be adequate. Luckily Conad does a fantastic line in extra large recycled but sturdy carriers and I loaded two onto my pile as I queued for the checkout.

The cheery and well-rounded woman behind the till welcomed me, asked me if I had a *Tessera* - the loyalty card - I said I did and produced it. At which point she looked sadly at me. "This is for a different Region, the Veneto…We are in Emilia Romagna."

The people in the queue behind me leaned forward, no doubt dying for a bit of excitement with the foreigner at the till. I laughed and said that it was ok - could I have one of theirs instead? She said she'd get the Manager who could help me, meanwhile would I like to leave my trolley over in the corner so that when I'd been set up with the card I could immediately put my purchases onto it and start earning points?

The people behind me, having listened to the conversation, generally agreed that this was an excellent idea and one woman told me that she was saving for a set of cookware, Conad's gifts being renowned for their quality. Glancing momentarily at brochure which the cashier proffered me, I must say there were several things there which looked both useful and stylish. Manoeuvring my trolley out of the way and into the custody of a handsome young trainee - who had been somewhat listlessly stacking shelves - I was ceremoniously ushered into the office of the manager. She too was friendly and welcoming - I was beginning to wonder whether it was something in the water which made everybody so nice - and in a matter of minutes I was set up with another *Tessera* and escorted back to the queue who all insisted that I shouldn't have to wait in line all over again and moved aside to let me back to the head of the queue. Brandishing my newly-acquired card I was given a cardboard folder and a very long ribbon of sticky stamps which I was informed I had to stick into the folder in order to start accumulating the necessary points for the bewildering array of goodies.

My *tramezzini* raised a few eyebrows and I felt that I needed to explain to my audience that I was going off to have a picnic lunch somewhere. Instead I told the now lengthening queue that I was new to the area and that it was so beautiful in the spring sunshine I wanted to explore.

"If you're going exploring" said the cashier whose name badge pronounced her to be Rosa, "you are going to need a freezer bag to keep your refrigerated things cool." With a flourish I pulled out my red freezer bag and waved it at her to good-natured laughter. I paid, hurriedly loaded my goodies and got out of the way so that the people who had waited patiently while the little excitement with the foreign woman had taken place (and no doubt bringing their day a bit of variety) could get home and start preparing their lunch.

Leaving the supermarket to a chorus of *"Arriverderci"* I shook my head in wonder, replaced the trolley, reclaimed my Euro, loaded the shopping into the back of the car, making sure that the *Tramezzini*, my water and a banana would be immediately to hand when I found a picnic spot.

Exiting the car park, I turned right onto the main road and, rounding the corner, stamped on the brakes in amazement. Luckily there was nothing behind me and so pulling onto the side of the road I gazed, totally awestruck, at what was before me.

For set upon the hills and starkly outlined against the blue sky was what I can only describe as an Ayers Rock or the Devils Tower in Wyoming (made famous by the film 'Close Encounters of the Third Kind'). A massive geological feature, rising majestically from the land, its sheer flanks bereft of plant life; naked rock walls sculpted over millions of years into undulating waves. The sense of raw elemental power, of something as old as time, emanating from it was, even here, kilometres away, quite giddying. I just sat and stared. I'd not heard of it, I had no idea what and where it was, but the energy of it was astonishing. What was it? Where was it? How could I get there, for I was being drawn magnetically to it. I decided to follow the road and, sure enough, as I drew closer to it,

I could see some of the brown signs indicating an area of specific interest, pointing towards it, the Pietra di Bismantova.

Turning off the main road into Castelnovo I continued to follow the signs as the lane wound upwards through wooded hillsides, hazel, from what I could tell, until sweeping around a tight hairpin bend the massive rock appeared before me in all's it magnificence. I shivered for there was something so powerfully raw and elemental about it.

Pulling into the car park I was delighted to see that not only had the municipal or regional authority laid out a spacious car park, with informative notice boards and many places to site and drink in the view, long hardwood benches and tables were set on smart decking along one edge which formed a sort of infinity deck, jutting out into a magnificent panoramic vista right over to the mountains of the west. Interspersed among the trees at the other edge of the car park were several shady free-standing picnic tables with integral benches. To the rear of the car park stood the Pietra, solid and imposing while I gazed alternately awestruck at both it and the view. What a place!

Hugging myself with delight I went to sit on one of the long benches. There was even a mounted telescope complete with an explanatory brass 'diorama' showing which of the distant peaks was which. The benches were positioned in such a way that one could sit facing either way, looking out over the 180 degrees of breathtaking countryside or leaning backwards while craning one's neck to take in all the lithic splendour of the Pietra as it rose majestically into the sky.

This place was astonishing and I was the only car there. I revelled in the joy of having the place to myself and, looking around, saw that there was a large notice board at the base of the rock, as well as a long and very steep flight of stone steps, seemingly carved out of the rock face. Surely there weren't steps all the way up to the top? I doubted whether I'd make it, both for reasons of health, mobility and the vertigo I suffer any time I go anywhere near an edge. Especially with nothing to hold onto. The thought of making it up to the top only to be unable to descend due to the debilitating effects of the vertigo decided me, I wouldn't even begin to attempt it.

Wandering over to the noticeboard, which was written in Italian and English, I read that the Pietra was a spur formed of Triassic gypsum, an outcrop or *inselberg* 300 metres high, its undulating walls reminiscent of waves of the ancient Miocene sea of Tethys, of which it was part. The noticeboard informed me that a shark's tooth had been found in the area, along with many other marine fossils. The natural bowl of the steep-sided Secchia valley was evident from the far-reaching views, the snow-covered peaks of Monte Cusna and Monte Cimone clearly visible in the bright sunshine, and, opposite, seemingly far far away to my left, yet only 30 minutes' drive, I could see Monte Valestra, smaller but no less lovely.

At the base of the Pietra stood a Hermitage, dedicated to the Madonna of the Bismantova and, on a ridge further up, directly underneath the overhanging mass, was a climbing school, complete with accommodation and a small cafe. The approach was steep and vehicles were banned so I left it and concentrated on immersing myself in the flow of energy that literally washed over the top of the Pietra, like some invisible waterfall of supernatural power. This place was extraordinary, unpublicised to all but the most dedicated seeker, yet, as the noticeboard informed me, a place of worship and pilgrimage for centuries, if not millennia. Dante had even mentioned it in The Inferno - and connected it with Matilda!

It was bisected by many trails for hiking and cycling and the climbing school was where the famous *Alpinisti*, the Italian Alpine Brigade, would come for rock-climbing training. Being almost sheer, the Pietra presented challenging ascents and, glinting in the sunshine, were the metal pitons that had been hammered into the rock face to assist the *arrampicaristi,* the climbers. I felt it sad that man's depredations into nature were so evident.

Musing on this I looked around and at one end of the car park, behind a stand of trees was a rustic-looking sign to the *Rifugio della Pietra* which was closed and another for an Inn and Trattoria, the *Foresteria di San Benedetto* which was open! Immediately forgetting my *Tramezzino* from Conad, I got back into the car and drove the short way there. Having parked by an oak tree, I approached the entrance to be greeted by a friendly young man who, upon hearing that I was hungry asked me where I would like to sit. In an oddly British fashion we then proceeded to discuss the weather. He concluded that it was far too cold for me to sit outside, I disagreed, pointing out that I was British and therefore, technically, impervious to the cold! He laughed and we compromised him showing me to a table, sheltered under an overhang and therefore out of the wind that blew in admittedly-icy gusts, down from the mountains. I sat there, trying not to shiver, until laughingly admitting defeat - after all he knew the climate of this area better than I - and headed indoors to a cosy room furnished with solid wooden furniture and tables gaily bedecked with red and white checked table cloths. In the corner, at a table adjacent to a cheery fire, sat an old man, stolidly working his way through a huge plate of pasta. He looked up upon hearing my foreign accented Italian and stared unblinkingly at me.

The young man seated me at a table looking out through the big glass doors at the sunny meadow below the Foresteria. When he brought the menu, the *posate,* crockery, glassware and cutlery, I asked him whether he had a brochure for the accommodation part.

"*Certo, lo porto subito*" he returned with a slightly dog-eared pamphlet with photographs of the rooms - all attractively decorated in what can only be described as rustic Alpine style and which looked welcoming and homely. I had a momentary pang of self-pity when I briefly fantasised that I was not physically challenged and could hike and cycle and that I could do it with someone like-minded, male and breathtakingly attractive so that we could stay in this wonderful place and spend the weekend actively exploring the area - and each other! Dream on. I sighed deeply and, almost on cue, the waiter approached with a glass of Lambrusco and a plate of nibbles, small hard biscuits and some of the without-a-doubt local salami and Parmesan. My brief episode of 'what-if' melted away and equilibrium was restored.

The pamphlet was most informative, not only about the Pietra itself but also about how the area had been sacred since the Copper, Bronze and Etruscan ages. In the 4th to 6th centuries CE, there had been a settlement on the top plateau and many artefacts both local and from far afield attested to its being a place of gathering and a necropolis with offerings from faraway lands adding to the intrigue.

The waiter, upon seeing my interest, came back with a book of the area which further intrigued me, it confirmed that it had always been a place for magic and the supernatural, which is why, I guess, that the little Hermitage had been built. In order to 'tap' the extraordinary natural energies and facilitate deeper prayer and meditation. I wasn't convinced that the energies were all benign for there had been a necropolis at the base and there was talk of human sacrifice to appease the local Gods and Genius Loci. Apparently those to be sacrificed had been thrown off the top of the plateau to be dashed to pieces at the base. No wonder there had been a Necropolis.

I read that in the times of Matilda di Canossa, there had been a small fortress on the top which also doubled as a watchtower, enabling a line of castles from Canossa onwards to act as watchtowers and to signal each other in times of crisis. Given that Matilda and Gregory VII were constantly engaged in a series of battles and standoffs with her cousin the Holy Roman Emperor, Henry IV, who was actually German and neither Holy nor Roman, this was a sensible precaution. Her lands lay on the path of the ancient route from Canterbury to Rome, the Via Francigena, which doubled as a sort of medieval motorway and the route down which marauding troops would have come. The idea of huge signal fires burning and being seen for miles reminded me of the scene in Peter Jackson's The Two Towers, the second in his highly-acclaimed Lord of the Rings trilogy, when Merry and Gandalf were in Minas Tirith and Merry lit the beacon so that

Aragorn and the rest of the army in Rohan would know to come to their aid. The beacons were all situated on mountaintops and the superb tracking shots, showing the flames rising one after the other across the mountains of New Zealand is something I will never forget. It raised goosebumps, along with the uplifting score of Howard Shore.

For a second I was back in Britain watching the film on the massive screen of the Odeon in London's Leicester Square and my heart constricted, bringing tears to my eyes, for though I was loving this beautiful corner of Italy, in my DNA I am a Brit and I longed to be in my land. I wondered whether I would ever return.

Luckily, the abundant menu, took my mind off missing Albion and I wanted to try everything. The Greeks have got it right with their Meze. Small portions of everything, so that you can have a complete meal without having to choose between so many mouth-watering options. I asked the waiter what he recommended and he unhesitatingly suggested pasta - *Cappellacci con crema di Gorgonzola e radicchio*. Then a *bistecca* cooked on charcoal, some *contorni* - vegetables - and some *patate al rosmarino*. He asked how I wanted my steak cooked and looked visibly relieved when I said medium-rare. Like the French, the Italians simply cannot understand why the Brits prefer their meat well-done, which they deem 'ruined'!

He suggested that I have a quarter litre jug of a local red - not Lambrusco this time - and returned with it and the bread basket, smelling delicious, with still-warm slices of focaccia, and white rolls which looked like they'd been baked with milk. Possibly a nod to the *Madonna del Latte* (the Holy Virgin of Milk) who had been worshipped here by the locals as La Madonnina who had walked barefooted from Castelnovo to the Sanctuary and then, having preformed their prayers and rituals, continued barefoot up to the top of the Pietra. There is even something called the '*mal di Preda*' the sickness of the Pietra in the local dialect, such is its allure and magnetism, where visitors become obsessed with and nostalgic for the place.

I could see why, for this special place was already working its magic on me and I wished that I could have rented a room and just stayed for a while, to tune into the many shades that inhabited the slopes. But there was Geisha snoozing at home who, despite the ministrations of the besotted Farah and Ayesha, would start wondering where I was if I didn't come home that evening. I promised her that I would never leave her alone - without company - overnight and I had never broken that promise.

Lunch was everything it promised to be and a second jug of the extremely good wine, accompanied by two jugs of crystal clear water, no doubt drawn from the well nearby, was lulling me into a sort of reverie - the magic of the Pietra was claiming another soul.

Hauling myself reluctantly back into some semblance of normality, I asked for the bill, paid and slowly headed into Castelnovo, bidding goodbye to the Pietra as I drove down the hill to wait outside the easily-located phone shop for a half an hour before it reopened for the late afternoon and evening. There a very bureaucratic and somewhat sobering conversation with a tech-savvy twenty-something resulted in my closing my existing phone contract (or so I thought) and opening a pay-as-you-go SIM only contract with another service provider.

I'd had a lovely day - despite three lots of bureaucracy - and I'd discovered my henceforth go-to magic place for when I needed space for contemplation and real contact with the numinous. Somewhere I could indeed eat my sandwiches!

Chapter 12

'All great discoveries are made by those whose feelings run ahead of their thinkings'

The next few weeks rushed by with a seemingly-endless amount of admin, so I spent a lot of time at home, curled up on the sofa in front of the *stufa* with Geisha by my side as I did endless amounts of paperwork. Contracts had arrived from the Bank, the wifi people and the mobile phone network. All of which had required hours of reading long-winded and boring small print, but all of which was necessary. My small printer finally gave up, after copying, to my mind, an unnecessarily long document, thus necessitating another trip into Castelnovo to find a computer shop in order to replace it.

Sitting in the driveway hooked up to Farah's wifi signal, I was ready for my own wifi to arrive. The home phone had come, along with the wifi Router and other bits of equipment, but I was still awaiting the visit of the *Tecnico* to install the dish on Farah's roof, so they all remained in their boxes with the multilingual instructions while I waited, somewhat impatiently . As I searched Castelnovo online I found a shop that did repairs, sold new equipment and provided parts, inks and paper and I knew roughly where it was and saw that it had a small dedicated parking space outside, which would be useful since parking in the town centre, like any town centre anywhere, was difficult.

I decided that I would go the next day, not having been out for over a week, my store of fresh food was dwindling and I wanted to visit the organic butcher in Valestra and get some *Barzigole* and visit Mauro and Luisa in the Forno for some cheese, *erbazzone* and maybe a naughty cake or two! Combining the two trips would be sensible since I was spending a lot on fuel, the cost being higher up in the mountains than it had been in Verona. The mountain roads were necessarily long so what seemed to be a quick journey actually ended up being a marathon of swinging the car around tight bends while trying not to drive off the edge of the road as I gazed in awe at the surrounding countryside.

As I sat and mused upon this, surrounded by the ever more curious cats who were beginning to lose their nervousness of the new person in their community, my phone rang. It was Rosanna from the wifi shop asking me whether I would be in the next day as the *Tecnico* would be in the area.

"*Certo*" I responded, putting my mooted shopping expedition into temporary suspension. She informed me that he would most likely be with me around 11.00am and did I have a ladder. I told her that I didn't and she said that she'd make sure he brought his. Thanking her I assured her that I would be ready from 10.00 am onwards just in case he was going to be early. She snorted with amusement, I laughed and told her that it was a very British trait and that it was going to take a lot of time for me to lose it.

I remembered to ask her what my new phone number would be, as she'd not yet given it to me. "Hold on, I'll check…ah yes, here it is…" slowly, as if speaking to a small child or an imbecile, she gave me the number, digit by digit, as I put her on speaker and entered it into my phonebook. I repeated it to make sure that I had got it correctly. I had. We said goodbye and she hung up. I reflected on how she had slowly given me the number and was thankful because each country has a different way of expressing numbers. For example in Britain a phone number is usually given thus. The first zero is referred to as 'O', the letter O not the numeral zero. So a number like, say 01457 679836 would be spoken like this Oh-one-four-five-seven, six-seven-nine, eight-three-six. That is, the entire area code, followed by six numbers grouped into two sets of three digits. Not in Italy!

The area code would be given in its entirety using, quite sensibly, the zero as opposed to the letter O! Then all hell breaks loose, because the subsequent numbers are referred to in three letter groups with the first letter being a multiple of one hundred, the second letter being a multiple of ten and the last being merely a unitary number. Six hundred and seventy nine, eight hundred and thirty six. Or worse… in other countries, Greece for example, the entire number is broken down into pairs.. 01-45-76-79-83-6… which when spoken rapidly in whichever language and no matter how well I speak that language, renders the number as totally incomprehensible. This lady was obviously used to dealing with foreigners and I was grateful for her foresight and consideration.

Something similar happens with names. My surname is double-barrelled, meaning that it has a first part, a hyphen and a second part. Explaining double-barrelled surnames to a country not used to them is difficult. Especially as most people have no idea what a hyphen is. So I had to learn 'hyphen' in Italian - *trattino*. Then because my name

191

is Scottish in origin it is not easily pronounceable for those who are not used to such things, especially as the 'P' in Campbell is silent! In English-speaking countries the phonetic alphabet is used - A=Alpha, B=Bravo, C=Charlie, D=Delta etc. Not so in Italy, a thorough knowledge of not only the Italian alphabet is required - but the letters j, k, w, x and y do not exist in Italian - they are 'imported' letters. So I developed my own geographical alphabet based on the towns and cities of Italy. Where the imported letters appear in a word, they are pronounced as an Italian would - lungo I (for J), Kappa for K, Doppio Voo (double V) for W, Icks for X and Eeee Greque (Greek I) for Y…

Spelling my surname thus becomes… C=Como, A=Ancona, M=Milano, P=Palermo, B=Bologna, E=Empoli, Doppio (double) L=Livorno - Trattino (hyphen) - Kappa =K, Empoli, Milano, Palermo.

Complicated enough - then you get the email address. My name is bad enough, then you have to explain that there is no hyphen in the email address and what on earth is the @ sign called in Italian…? *Chiocciola*! Literally 'snail'. (In Greek it is *Papaki* - 'little duck'). Total nightmare!

I then had to give her the road address and some instructions for the *Tecnico* because the postal address and the actual location are somewhat different and Google Maps isn't always spot on - and that's assuming that you can get a signal! How do you describe "keep driving until you pass the meadow and the clump of trees, keep straight on then, when you get to a glimpse of a lake on the right and a few rows of the vines on the left, turn into the opening in the hedge on the left…"(there is a gate but it's usually obscured by the hedge!)

I suddenly realise I don't know the Italian for hedge – it's not been a necessary word in my everyday lexicon - until now. So I use *cespuglio* instead - bush - *grande cespuglio* - big bush. They don't teach you these things when you learn a language and they should!

All the while I'm thinking if the *Tecnico* ever gets to the house with those instructions it will be a miracle!

Oh and he also needs to know the all-important "*attenzione ai gatti*" "watch out for the cats…"!

The next morning, at 9.30, I hear a noise in the driveway. Farah's doors are firmly shut so I poke my nose out of the door to see a strapping young man in a van branded with the logo of the wifi company with a huge ladder on its roof, bending down and talking to the cats who, somewhat uncharacteristically, have come to investigate the newcomer.

I love him immediately! I introduce myself and he asks which roof is mine. I point upwards and he scratches his chin and looks worried. "It's not high enough…"

"Ah. So you can't get the signal from the *Antenna*?"

"*Esatto*" he said looking around him. He spots Farah's roof which is a storey higher than mine and asks if he can put the parabola - dish - up there instead, next to Hassan's. I don't see why not, but explain that the Signora of the house, Farah, is not feeling well and is in bed. I tell him that I will call Hassan and ask if it's ok. While I do that he goes off to get the dish, his tools, several lengths of bright blue flex and several other bits and pieces.

I can't get hold of Hassan as I can't get a signal so am frantically rushing from one part of the driveway to another in order to phone him. No luck. The *Tecnico* meanwhile has, with a resounding crash, placed his ladder up against the roof that separates my house from Farah's house. If that hasn't woken her I will be amazed.

It has and she pokes her head out of the window looking anxious. I call up to her explaining that my parabola is going to have to go next to theirs, that I'm trying to call Hassan to ask if its ok and I can't get a signal.

She disappears back inside and in a few minutes comes out saying that she has spoken to him and that it's ok. I thought it would have been, since all the properties are owned by Signor S - but still best to ask. Not least if the *Tecnico* had damaged Hassan's parabola, I would have been liable.

A voice floats down from the roof. It is ok - there's a clear line of sight to the telecom Antenna on the hill above Valestra. But that there will be a problem within a year if the trees are not "*tagliati*" trimmed, as they will interfere with the signal. These problems simply never occur to people in the cities, but out here in the most rural of locations, such things are vital. I reply that Signor S who owns the woods as far as the eye can see will ensure that this is done - and done correctly.

"*Bene*. Good." He responds, climbing down and asking whether he can come in to lay the blue cable. Not for the first time I mentally thank Ugo for his foresight, for a neatly drilled and almost totally inconspicuous hole is already in the window frame, allowing easy ingress for the vital cable which is draped somewhat rakishly over my roof, falling in cerulean loops to the level of the window sill. The work is done quickly and efficiently and we chat as he works. He is curious as to why I'm living alone in the middle of nowhere. Geisha comes and sniffs at him and he gives her his hand to investigate. To my astonishment she licks him and then coquettishly collapses onto him for a stroking. He sees my face and laughs. "I love cats" my mother runs a cat sanctuary in Castelnovo. I tell him about my first time there and my visit to the Pietra. He confirms that it is indeed a very special, magical but also haunted place. That there have been weird phenomena documented over the years. Lights, sounds and apparitions. I am fascinated. He tells me that he climbs the rocks most weekends and that it is an extremely challenging climb, not least to some of the overhangs which impede upward progress.

Remembering my upcoming visit to the computer shop, I ask him if he would recommend it. "Certainly. They have good technical knowledge and if they don't stock what you're looking for, they can arrange to get it for you the next day. And they're not expensive." I thank him, grateful for some local input.

The work is soon finished, he is kind and seeing my look of panic at setting up the wifi, volunteers to help.

"Don't tell anyone, I'm just meant to put the parabola up and do the wiring…"

Within ten minutes I have working wifi - with a full strength signal AND a phone line. I try ringing the number I was given and, to my delight, it works. NOW I have a fully-functioning home - remote but connected. It feels odd, after several weeks of isolation but I shan't miss gyrating slowly around the driveway trying to get a signal.

I thank him profusely which he acknowledges and with a quick stroke of Geisha who seems to be totally enamoured with him, and packs up his equipment, heads back to his van which, previously covered with snoozing cats, is now a mass of dusty paw prints. Taking care to ensure that none are curled up in his equipment on the roof rack, he climbs in and waving goodbye heads off to another rooftop somewhere.

I am online! I celebrate by Googling vets in the area as Geisha is now due for her annual shot. I see that there is a vet's office in Cerredolo, about 20 minutes away in the other direction from my usual local trips - and decide to go and do a recce before booking her in. But first there are some phone calls to make and realising that I now have the means to choose a printer model by searching online and then calling the shop in Castelnovo, I am saving myself a lot of time and angst.

I find what I'm looking for, call the shop, no they don't have that model in stock but they can order it and if I come in on Friday they will have it ready for me to collect. I asked them if I could pay for it by giving them my card number down the phone. They were horrified! "No, Signora. Come in and see if the machine is what you are looking for, and if so you can pay then." I thanked them and we agreed that it would come with a full set of inks and that I could get paper in bulk from the *Cartoleria* up the road. Sometimes life is just so much easier with phone and internet!

Having checked the opening hours - and days - of the local vet, I decided that this afternoon was probably a good time to pop into Cerredolo using a road I'd not yet driven but which I'd seen when poring over the map I'd recently bought of the area.

Instead of taking the road down the mountain, though Levizzano and joining the main road which runs from Sassuolo along the Secchia valley and up into the hills or branches off and continues round in a broad loop to Castelnovo, I decided to take the top route, a tiny road that runs along a ridge high above the bowl of the Secchia valley.

The Secchia, known to Pliny as the Gabellus, is one of the main tributaries of the great Po river which is the longest river in Italy. The Secchia delineates the south eastern edge and the Enza the north western edge of this part of the great ancient sea of Tethys and, to me, they act as the boundary of 'my' newly-found home territory.

Both rivers rise in the mountains, in the Alpe di Succiso, close to the pass of Cerreto and both act as natural breaks between the gently bucolic Alpine landscape that I have fallen in love with and a more wooded, less spectacular and less agrarian countryside, where Cerredolo is situated, on the other side of the main road, the SP486.

Leaving the Hamlet, instead of turning left down the hill, I continued straight on at the T junction, climbing slowly among verdant fields with herds of cows munching contentedly on the delicious-looking and no doubt highly-nutritious grass of these high pastures. Old terracotta-roofed farmhouses, their Valestra stone walls shining creamily in the afternoon sun sat perched stop vertiginous hills commanding fabulous 180 degree views. The road wound ever

197

upwards and I changed gear accordingly until the last bend, where in front of me was the road that I had wanted to reach. I stopped at the T junction and got out, secure in the knowledge that there was very little traffic on this road and I was unlikely to be disturbed as I stood and gawped at the frankly incredible view. For spread out in front of me was the whole of the bowl of the valley with the Pietra glistening whitely at the far end before the hills climbed upwards to the mountain peaks. The shadows of the occasional cloud moved in a stately pavane across the green valley below me, passing over tiny red-roofed hamlets where, apart from the flashing of the TV dishes in the sun, time seemed to have stood still. The sea of Tethys was aptly named, for the Goddess Tethys was a daughter of the Titans; Ouranos the Sky God and Gaia the Earth Goddess. Here set out in front of me was a perfect example of the marriage of heaven and earth. Beautiful undulating waves of verdant countryside under the wide open skies of the area - designated as a special area for astronomy due to the dark, dark night skies and almost total lack of light pollution.

To my right was a small house, modern, well built with a massive verandah looking out over the panorama. I was envious - though I suspected in the winter when the steep roads were silver - or worse - black with ice and the land shivered in the unrelenting grip of an Alpine winter, it would be unmitigated hell. At least for someone who had little or no practise in driving on snow and ice. But now in the earliest flowering of Spring it was magical and in the stifling heat of summer, the open aspect and accompanying breezes must have been heavenly.

I drank in the view for as long as I could then, realising that I still had several kilometres to go, reluctantly tore myself away and headed down the road, through tiny hamlets, some no more than two or three houses grouped together, some medieval, some more modern - but all beautiful.

I came out onto the main road by a petrol station, opposite a John Deere agricultural showroom and narrowly avoided being squashed by a massive lorry thundering along the road totally ignoring the speed limit. I was back in reality!

Turning off the main road to follow the route into Cerredolo I noticed that though it seemed to have less shops than Carpineti there was a massive wine warehouse, the cantina, the Enoteca Il Cantinone, just visible up a side street - I'd already spotted the signs - and once I'd checked in at the vets, I resolved to go and investigate.

Easily finding the veterinary clinic, I parked close by and walked through a small narrow *vicolo* - alleyway - noticing a shop that seemed frozen in time. A wonderful array of household goods from what appeared to be several decades ago were somnolently and somewhat dustily displayed in a rickety window. I noticed that the shop opened shortly and resolved to visit it - I actually needed some twine with which to tie back my kitchen mosquito screen for it banged against the door in the wind. Usually in the middle of the night.

Entering the vet's waiting room, I saw that there were already three people sitting with their pets, all cats, which I took to be a good sign. Firstly that the vet was obviously good with felines and secondly that the solid-looking farming people cared for their animals by bringing them to the vet. As Signor S had said, our little feline colony kept rats and other vermin - as well as snakes - away. A sensible owner realised the value of their pets and looked after them accordingly. Something I became to appreciate more as time wore on and I started meeting other people. Their love and care for their animals was every bit as noticeable as that of their love and care for their land.

The veterinary clients looked somewhat askance at me, due to my conspicuous lack of an animal. I smiled at them all and explained that I was new to the area and just wanted to ask the Vet whether he or she (I wasn't sure which vet I'd see and it appeared there were two - one of each) could just answer a quick question. They all nodded sagely and one of the cats miaowed as if in agreement and we all laughed.

The door slid open and out popped a white-coated vet. A friendly-looking man in his 40's. He looked questioningly at the room and asked who was first in the queue. As one, the customers all nodded at me, explaining to him that I had only come for information and would therefore be quick.

I thanked them and responding to the vet's invitation, walked into the consulting room and sat down. It was actually better equipped than the one we had been used to in Verona and there was no house cat wandering around stressing out the patients. All good. I sat down where indicated and explained that I was the owner of an elderly Siamese who had started to lose weight, drink more and sleep a lot. He asked about Geisha and I showed him her vaccination certificate. He said that I should bring her in for a check-up and that he could do the shots at the same time. We made an appointment for the following week and then, to my astonishment, he spoke in English, with a broad American accent. I shook my head in amazement, this felt so weird, speaking to an American in the middle of nowhere. He explained that he was actually Italian, Toanesi, from nearby Toano in which Comune Cerredolo was situated. He'd studied in Wisconsin and come home after several years in the US. This explained the mystery of the T-shirt I'd seen him wearing under his white coat - something about the Irish and bars - in English.

I responded by saying that it was a relief to know that in an emergency there was an English-speaking vet with whom I could converse. I explained that as I was self-taught my Italian lacked a certain finesse, like the word for hedge and medical/veterinary terminology. He laughed loudly, gave me his card with the all-important out-of-hours number and said he looked forward to meeting Geisha the following week, but that if her condition deteriorated I was to call him immediately. He asked where we lived and I told him.

"Ah yes, I know where you are, by the big manor house. Nice place!" I agreed and we parted, once more speaking Italian. The people in the waiting room asked if all was ok and I smiled happily at them, assuring them that everything was indeed ok.

So happy was I that I decided to forego the fly-blown household goods store, the twine could wait, I even decided to forego the wine warehouse and headed home via the faster route, wanting to get back to Geisha and tell her all about her new Doctor.

Arriving home, I let myself in and immediately wondered what on earth was the incessant though thankfully-muted beeping noise. A quick investigation of my new 'communication hub' revealed a message on the phone's answerphone. It was from my best friend, to whom I had texted the number earlier, announcing that she had decided it was about time she came out to stay for a week and that she would fly to Bologna - our nearest airport - when would be convenient for us?

Excitedly I called her back, we discussed dates and agreed that she would arrive in just under 3 weeks' time. Geisha's love slave as we had christened her, for we had driven to Italy all together, was going to be our first guest. I couldn't wait and started poring over maps trying to think up interesting and fun things to do.

That night I lay in bed, Geisha snuggled up beside me, for once eschewing the *stufa*, I listened to the sounds of owls hunting and the wind in the trees. Thinking that I must talk to Hassan about trimming the wifi trees as I had named them, I drifted contentedly off to sleep.

Chapter 13

Thelma and Louise…!

Jane arrived at Bologna airport, bright and early on the appointed morning. Of course I had got there far too early - but thankfully so - because the automatic car parking barrier wasn't working properly. Because I have the ViaPass, it means I can drive straight through rather than reach across through the passenger window to push a button and retrieve a ticket. Before I obtained it going anywhere with an automatic barrier filled me with anxiety and trepidation. It was not always within my reach to lean put of the window and press an admittedly large red button, nor was I always close enough to be able to pull the resulting proffered ticket from the slot, usually much to the annoyance of drivers waiting behind me, who would hoot their horns and yell imprecations at me, something about foreign drivers being imbeciles. I'd even bought a long-handled grabber with which to reach across and, theoretically, push the button and pull out the proffered ticket. But it had only worked once and then the rubber suction pads on the ends of the grip had fallen off thus rendering it useless. So it was with an enormous sense of relief that I had discovered that my ViaPass not only got me through the motorway tolls unscathed, but was also accepted in many car parks - which was an absolute godsend.

The queue for the ViaPass parking barrier was long. It had stopped working and though this wasn't necessarily the fault of the poor couple in the BMW they had decided to reverse and try another barrier which was causing havoc. It occurred to me that they might not actually have the requisite pass. Many times I had come across this, a driver in a hurry who had entered the wrong lane and without the pass was angrily trying to get through the wilfully intransigent barrier! So it was with a lot of shouting, hooting and gesticulating that we all patiently backed up, some cars actually backing onto the roundabout from the feeder road and waited for a *Tecnico* to come and resolve the situation. After about five minutes of further yelling and hooting a man appeared, spoke to the couple in the lead car, having ascertained that all was in order and, that they DID have a functioning pass, he pressed some magic button, reset the system and the barrier gracefully opened. He then worked his way back down the queue to make absolutely sure than only those with the requisite and still valid electronic pass were waiting to go through. Coming upon me, he started momentarily as there was no-one sitting in what was, to him, the driver's seat, my passenger seat. I opened the window remotely and he peered in.

"Signora, this entrance is only for people with an electronic pass…" he said, eyes narrowing suspiciously at the sight of me.

"Yes, I know." I replied smiling, indicating the small tell-tale grey box affixed to the windscreen adjacent to the rear-view mirror.

"*Ah! Va Bene!*" He smiled too, no doubt relieved that he wouldn't have to explain to an undoubtedly idiotic foreigner that this was not a normal barrier.

Me sitting on the right-hand side had also phased him, but assured that I had a steering wheel firmly in my grasp and that I had the requisite magic box, he left me to go and yell at the Italians behind me who did NOT possess one!

Finally passing through and fortuitously finding a space near the walkway to the Terminal, I made my way slowly there, weaving in and out of seemingly randomly-placed concrete bollards, incomprehensible ribbons of red plastic tape wafting forlornly about in the breeze and badly-parked cars to find myself faced with an insurmountable barrier of concrete seperatme from the enticingly close doors to the Arrivals hall. Muttering with exasperation I looked around for an easy way through and saw that there was a shortcut through a small space, just wide enough to squeeze through, and saving me about 5 minutes of torturous navigation round the badly-signposted official route to the building.

Once inside I was assailed by the ubiquitous homage to the gods of retail, most of the shrines to which catered to the needs of the inveterate shopper; pen shops, cosmetic shops, souvenir shops (though why anyone would want to buy souvenirs in Arrivals flummoxed me - surely they would wait until departing before buying the requisite icon celebrating their stay in Bologna?). There was a smattering of banks with cashpoints, the inevitable Car Hire, Information and Lost Luggage desks and, most sensibly, situated adjacent to the seating area just outside the Arrivals Hall, a small supermarket and cafe.

I headed for the cafe and waited behind a large group of Italians who had just arrived back home and were vociferously announcing to the world at large that they desperately needed a decent coffee! I have to say that Italian coffee is excellent and I patiently waited for my turn, deciding that it was time for an Espresso and a chocolate filled brioche. The transaction was accomplished in double-quick time, the girl operating the Gaggia coffee machine a multi-tasking whirl of efficiency. Watching her put the coffee grounds into the bowl-shaped container, the 'puck', pat it down with a special device, the 'tamper' just made for this very purpose, neatly slot it into the massive red and silver machine, place two cups (one for me and one for whomever else had ordered an Espresso) under the twin spout, press a button and then wait for the whooshing, steaming alchemy to take place, while frothing milk with the steam wand in a separate jug for those who had ordered a Cappuccino and indicating the various packets of sugar and sweetener while also asking the assembled clientele who wanted cacao on their cappuccino was enlightening. My Espresso arrived, hot but not too hot, with just the right amount of 'crema' the brown froth on the top. I thanked her and, awestruck as always by the sheer technical wizardry of making a coffee, wandered off to find a seat just by the exit door from the Customs Area.

Texting Jane that I was in situ, I positioned myself in her direct line of sight - assuming that she exited from the EU aisle occasionally glimpsed through the automatic doors I watched as people trickled out to be greeted by their nearest and dearest, their driver, their tour guide or, in Jane's case, their best friend.

There was laughter, tears and all emotions in between, I love people-watching and so, apparently do others, for as one astonishingly pretty girl emerged, a good-looking young man bearing a bouquet of flowers came forward shyly. They stood face-to-face, looked deep into each other's eyes and then kissed passionately for a very long time! The Arrivals area erupted in cheers and applause - for in Italy we love nothing more than love itself! The couple, when they eventually surfaced for air, smilingly acknowledged the crowd's approbation and, hand in hand, disappeared outside and into - hopefully - a bright future filled with much happiness and many beautiful children.

In the wake of all this romance Jane emerged, pulling her trolley bag and scowling slightly as she looked around for me. I moved towards her, grinning like an idiot for she and I have known each other since we were ten and we have shared many many adventures together over the years. I refer to us as Thelma and Louise for we have driven all over Europe, down tiny unmarked roads, off-piste as it were, with sometimes a map for company and sometimes only our noses - leading us to places off the beaten track where with a rudimentary smattering of the language of whatever country we are visiting, we have soaked up the atmosphere, eaten the food, drunk the wine and chatted with the locals. I was so looking forward to showing her "my" mountains and introducing her to all the marvellous things I had discovered.

We hugged tightly and I was once again momentarily overwhelmed with longing for England when she and I could see each other whenever we wanted. She was amazing, for now that I had been working abroad for several years - she'd always turn up for a few days, sometimes longer, on her own - with the blessing of her wonderfully taciturn husband - and we would settle into our comfortable routine as if we'd seen each other just a week or so before.

This was her third trip to Italy since I'd moved. The first, she'd accompanied me as Geisha's Minder as we drove down through France and into Italy, stopping for a couple of nights here and there before we'd arrived in Verona on a blazingly hot day. Without hesitation she'd taken over organising the unloading of the car as I made sure Geisha was happily ensconced in what would be our new home, fed, watered and provided with a clean litter box.

She and her husband had also come out for my 60th birthday several months later and we had had a wonderful few days, with other friends - English and Italian - where we had eaten and drunk too much and I'd given a small party, kindly hosted by close Italian friends in their gorgeous restored house about an hour outside Verona. The day after, walking around the stunning historical centre of Verona, she had hugged me and told me that I was "a lucky lucky bitch"!

Well if she'd thought I was lucky in Verona, wait until she had seen the Hamlet and the mountains!

We chattered like sparrows as we negotiated the assault course back to the car and making a quick getaway through a thankfully now fully-operational barrier, my Via Pass beeping reassuringly as we passed through, we headed for the motorway and Modena Nord about 30 minutes away.

I was glad that it was a sunny day for as we turned off the motorway and headed down the dual carriageway into Sassuolo, the air, once we had left the motorway was less polluted and the hills could clearly be seen. I said nothing as we passed through the brutish suburbs and turned onto the road for home. We drove quickly through the outskirts of Castellarano, Muraglione and Roteglia (all of which I intended to investigate at some point) and we turned off on the road to home.

We climbed upwards and as always, I lowered my window so that the fresh clean air, scented with a hint of woodsmoke and the lingering crispness of the snow on the mountains, could blow in. Jane inhaled it in great lungfuls while gazing out over the wide open kilometres of this part of the Secchia Valley. Some of the long-exhausted and abandoned clay quarries were beginning to be covered with the fresh green shoots of spring, softening their contours and blending them into the landscape.

I'd decided to take a slightly different route up the mountain having decided that we probably needed a loo and another coffee. I'd mentally earmarked a Trattoria with bar by the side of the road that I had passed on a couple of occasions, it looked stolidly welcoming with troughs of bright red geraniums softening the appearance of the old stone building, as it snoozed somnolently in the morning sunshine. As we parked I noticed a couple of chairs, a bench and a small table to one side of the building facing the sun and decided that if it was sheltered enough from the still snowy wind, it would be a lovely place to drink our coffees.

Wandering through the front door, I noticed that the door to the restaurant was slightly ajar and at the far end a wood fire blazed merrily. From the kitchen emanated the most delicious smells accompanied by the music of pots and pans clanging gastronomically!

My mouth watered but it was too early to eat - though not for much longer.

Instead we turned left into the bar, furnished with a single table and a couple of chairs. We were courteously greeted by the barman, a man in his 40's with a shock of dark curly hair, lively brown eyes and a shy smile, who, for a minute, looked slightly concerned as he had heard us speaking English. The anxiety about English speakers does not always stem from suspicion of foreigners, rather the regret that the person concerned didn't learn more English at school. Something that Farah told me was being addressed as Ayesha and her classmates were all learning the language.

The younger generation, used to the Internet and cheap air travel, mostly speak English of varying levels. I have been told by many Italians over the years that they regret not having learnt English but that they are also very concerned about speaking it badly or making mistakes. I always respond with "if you don't make mistakes how can you learn?!"

Jane, knowing the convention about not having a cappuccino after 11.00am ostentatiously looked at her watch, saw that it was just approaching 12.00 and announced that, in London, it was an hour earlier and that she would, therefore, like a cappuccino!

I translated this and the barman grinned at her "*molto furbo*!" "Very smart!" She smiled back and asked me to ask if we could take our coffees outside. I did and the poor man looked horrified "But Signora, it's freezing" he said. "It's in the sun" I pointed out and he agreed that it was, indeed in the sun and that if we really wanted to sit out, would we please excuse him as he went out to make sure that the table and chairs were clean and not dusty. He bustled out with a roll of kitchen towel and a cloth and reappeared a minute or two later, ready to begin the alchemical process of producing Jane's cappuccino.

I, in the meantime, had decided that I'd actually prefer a glass of wine, seeing that it was almost midday. Anyway the old hunters always had a beer and a grappa mid morning so I didn't feel as if I was doing anything too terrible. I asked for his suggestion as to a suitable *aperitivo*. Having decided on red wine, we then had to decide whether to go for *fermo* or *frizzante*.

I could tell that he was proud of his wines and so asked him to give me something local and not necessarily widely known. He was delighted - as was I - for he chose me a *fermo*, a still red wine, not too strong and absolutely delicious - apparently produced nearby. I asked him to show me the bottle and, on noting down the details I enquired whether the Enoteca in Cerredolo would sell it.

"You know the Enoteca signora?" He seemed astonished that this English woman who had appeared from nowhere knew about it. I explained that I was living at the Hamlet and had been finding my way round the area. He nodded approvingly. "Signor S is a good man, very well respected."

Having established my credentials, I introduced myself. He in turn introduced himself, Gabriele, and his family's restaurant, Ca'Poggioli.

Jane having returned from the loo, joined us and I explained our conversation. "Why don't we have lunch here? After we have had an *aperitivo* in the sunshine…"

She agreed, having smelt the mouthwatering aromas emanating from the kitchen. So I asked Gabriele whether we could eat, suggesting that we did so early, at about 12.30 before the lunchtime rush. He asked if we'd like the table in the corner, which looked cozy and perfect and we headed out into the ever-so slightly chilly sunshine with Jane's cappuccino and my wine, knowing that we could soon warm ourselves by the fire.

We spent a lovely but admittedly nippy half an hour in the sunshine, Jane with her back to the stone wall of the building and her face turned towards the sun. Me shivering slightly but being brave for her sake!

Lunch was a wonder - Gabriele came and escorted us to the dining room, tastefully decorated in a rustic but extremely elegant way. The tables were covered with ecru thick cotton cloths and with proper napkins. The walls were stone, adorned with interesting old prints and paintings, there was an impressive wine cabinet filled with all manner of bottles, their labels all mostly small vineyards with some of the great - and expensive - Chiantis from neighbouring Tuscany, along with a wide selection of intriguing-looking Lambruscos and even some wine from Lunigiana. Several agricultural artefacts were displayed in well-lit niches as well as several antique farm implements dotted about. The chairs were solid and wooden with individual cushions offering comfort. The whole place exuded an air of gentle, rustic and gastronomic refinement.

As soon as were seated, Gabriele stood solemnly at the head of the table and recited a list of today's specials, all local dishes made with organic ingredients and everything hand made by his mother and sister. We asked him to give us an *'assaggio'*, taste, of a couple of dishes from each course which we could share and swap and would he please also recommend the wine. He nodded solemnly, taking the responsibility seriously of introducing us to the best that this area could offer.

We ended up having a feast - for the *Antipasti* a selection of mixed *'crostini'* little rounds of toasted bread, spread with two types of pate, olive paste and a paste made of dried tomatoes, we also shared *'sgonfiotti di grana'* literally 'deflated pieces' of Grana Padano.

For the pasta course, we were each given several different types of *tortelli,* the larger brother of the better-known tortellini, one stuffed with *zucca* - pumpkin, one with spicy cabbage, and one with meat. All dressed with olive oil, grated parmesan and, in our case, grated black pepper. The main course was meat - for Jane a plate of thinly sliced rare steak and in my case the ovine *barzigole*, accompanied by mixed vegetables and the most delicious rosemary potatoes.

There was no room for pudding - until Jane remembered that she adored *'affogato'* so we had two of those.

The wine had been sublime and again I had noted down the label, always keen to add to my knowledge of good local wines. Actually I'd never discovered a bad local wine! The Italians are rightly proud of their vinicultural heritage and would not dream of producing something deemed undrinkable, not even for cooking.

It was a weary couple of ladies, who sat in the car groaning slightly from over-full tummies as we drove slowly up the hill home to a warm house, a welcoming Geisha who recognised her love slave and head-butted Jane fondly, settling on her lap as she collapsed onto the sofa with a contented sigh. Farah popped her head in to ask whether she should get some more wood for the merrily-burning *stufa* and would we like pizza for supper!

Cognisant of the amount of food we had just eaten we looked at each other. "You've never tasted anything so good…" I said and Jane acquiesced. Farah smiled beatifically for I knew that she'd like nothing better than to welcome my friend to the Hamlet. We agreed that she'd bring it over at about 7.30 by which time, I was in no doubt whatsoever, that we'd be ready for another glass of wine or two!

Chapter 14

'Bikers Welcome'

We had spent a wonderful evening chatting and had indeed drunk another bottle of the rich, fruity red wine I'd found in the local supermarket. From an unfamiliar vineyard, it was produced at a small family concern, in a small town between the Hamlet and Bologna on the off-motorway route to the airport. A route that I'd been longing to explore as its gentle hills with the occasional glimpse of a turret or two, had been seen out of the corner of my eye on my many trips to and from Bologna. It was an area that I knew little about and if I could easily get to the airport without taking the motorway, then it was most definitely worth exploring.

So it was the next morning, we were, unsurprisingly, somewhat groggy. Jane, not known for her lark-like qualities, struggled bravely upright from the sofa bed - which she had pronounced supremely comfortable. I presented her with a coffee and sat in the easy chair by the fire. Farah had left us enough wood overnight to keep the *stufa* going and it was with a sense of pride that, upon opening the door, I saw the embers still glowing which, with a bit of air from the bellows and some nice less dense logs, would soon roar into life.

As we sipped our coffees, and I devoured a hunk of the dense local bread and some cheese, we chatted about our plans for Jane's stay. Naturally I wanted to show her everything and naturally she wanted to see everything. But where to start? Oddly I didn't want to show her the Pietra - yet. I rather wanted to explore the area to the south, close to the Tuscan border where I was told they were many villages that time had left alone. I'd looked up the road to the Passo delle Radici and it wound up and through these villages. Culminating in its apex of 1,529 metres above sea level, it formed a natural border with Tuscany and according to my Wikipedia searches was tranquil and beautiful. There was even an Albergo/Ristorante at the top which offered *cucina casalinga*, home cooked food. Perfect!

Excitement for our forthcoming adventure overcame the grogginess and we were washed, dressed and in the car within an hour. Farah came out of the house to say good morning and asked if I'd like her to tidy up a bit while we were out. I knew that she actually wanted to see that Geisha was warm and happy and Geisha loved the attention, so of course I said yes. I told her we'd be out all day and to please light the fire if it got chilly. Geisha for her part was perfectly content to snooze in her fleecy cave, not least because I'd bought her a microwaveable wheat bag, which tucked inside kept her warm for hours. Farah knew to use it if the temperature dropped and was most assiduous about catering to the wishes of the Imperial Paw!

Jane and I set off in high spirits, the late spring sunshine, warming us and the landscape, bathing the rolling fields and the newly burgeoning leaves of the trees in a golden glow. Perched precariously on the side of a steep hill was a red tractor, doggedly working its way diagonally across the field as the shining blades of its wickedly sharp-looking plough, bit purposefully into the rich earth. The ploughed seams looked like rich dark chocolate and I was reminded of a passage in one of the C.S.Lewis Narnia books where the moles had a banquet of different types of earth. His beautiful descriptions of the 'edible' earths have stayed with me and, decades later, looking at the fields, I knew exactly what he had meant.

Everything up in these high meadows seemed magical and bathed in an otherworldly light. Jane, still in her morning semi stupor, opened her window and sniffed the air, and murmured "this is perfect"... we drove in silence, savouring the smell and taste of the air, slightly tinged with woodsmoke but with a hint of blossom. The trees in the orchard outside the kitchen door had already burst into bloom - practically overnight - and the sounds of the birds and insects was, by country standards, deafening! I could see why this area was one of the major producers of milk and meat, for the pastures up here were rich and fertile.

We drove in silence for a while, descending in wide looping curves down to the main road. The energetic difference between the reality of being on the state road with its busy everyday traffic and the otherworldliness of the high pastures, where encountering another vehicle was quite a shock, was notable.

The road ran alongside the swiftly-flowing river. Its waters the icy pale blue of the spring runoff from the snow melt of the mountains. Tumbling boisterously over rocks and stones it leapt and rushed towards the sea in an aqueous frenzy of seeming excitement to be heading for the Po River and then the sea. By which time its exuberant water spirits would have been subdued by the ponderous flow of the great artery of northern Italy, the longest river in the country. But as we drove alongside the river it was still gambolling like a spring lamb.

We turned off into Cerredolo, leaving the main bulk of the traffic to continue its way along the larger *Strada Provinciale*, while we followed the road as it wound upwards alongside the hillsides, offering views of a very different landscape. It was as if the main road formed a barrier between my green hills and valleys and a harsher more wooded environment, but one that was liberally dotted with small villages comprising compact houses of forbidding dark stone, enlivened only by vast troughs and window boxes brimming with bright red geraniums. Every single house had at least one and it was a heart-warming sight to see such a display of spring-greeting floriculture.

Concentrating on the road which was becoming quite twisty and noticing that despite being a secondary road, there was a lot of traffic, a constant stream of cars, vans and tractors with the occasional truck, I wasn't able to look at the landscape but I could feel the difference. The sun barely penetrated the landscape and the trees were still bare, I imagine that in winter life here could be very harsh and uncompromising.

Not all was gloomy for as we rounded a bend in the road, we saw a pretty building, with a sun-dappled terrace and a large parking area with amazing views of the surrounding hills. A somewhat incongruous sign, in English, said 'Bikers Welcome'. That was enough to pique my curiosity and I swung across the road into the gravelled car park. "Time for a proper coffee!" I turned to Jane who was looking somewhat mulishly it has to be said, at the English sign. "I don't want to have coffee surrounded my MAMILS.."

"Mammals?" I responded somewhat bemused... "what sort of mammals? I don't see anything..."

She snorted with laughter "No, MAMILS, middle aged men in Lycra... it says Bikers Welcome.."

It was my turn to snort with laughter. "They're CYCLISTS you prat! Bikers are the cool dudes on Harleys..."

She grinned and since we didn't see a brace of Harleys - or indeed any other motorbikes - parked nearby we assumed that we were temporarily safe from the Easy Rider or Hell's Angels crowd. So we left the car and crossed the road to the welcoming terrace which looked lovely in the sunshine. Unlike most cafes, the terrace furniture wasn't the ubiquitous white plastic, but nice wooden tables with comfy-looking chairs. Jane hovered, having come from an English winter I could see that she would prefer to sit outside, but not being sure whether it was just a tad too chilly, she remained undecided. I decided to go inside and order our coffees, knowing that the proprietor probably wouldn't come outside looking for sun-worshipping tourists.

I was wrong, a businesslike lady in her 40's popped her head out of the door and seeing us bade us a hearty *"Buon Giorno"* to which we responded. I explained that if possible, we'd love to sit outside with our coffees. We both find that the Italian habit of standing at the bar and downing the coffee in as few gulps as possible, takes the pleasure out of 'having a coffee'. Which, to us, is to be taken sitting down and savoured. Preferably with something on which to nibble. She looked at us as if we were insane but acquiesced (top marks for customer service!) and rushed back inside, muttering something about getting a cloth to clean the dust from the table and chairs.

The necessary dusting and wiping accomplished we sat in lone splendour at the table, the sunlight dapping the surface as it shone through the branches of the tree. Out of the wind it was actually warm enough and we gyrated a bit so as to get the full benefit of the rays and their Vitamin D, before time moved the planet round so that the sun disappeared behind the hills opposite.

We checked our phones to see what the time was and Jane was able to safely order her cappuccino and I my more usual decaf Americano, having decided that so many espressos were definitely not doing me any good. The Americano never fails to revolt the person taking the order! Paola, having introduced herself, returned with the coffees, a plate of little homemade biscuits and two glasses of water. She was curious as to what we were doing in the area and I explained. She didn't know of the Hamlet or Signor S and I realised that this side of the Secchia was indeed a different world, a border of sorts. She decided that we must meet Fabio, the chef, who had lived in England for many years and so a minute or two later he abandoned the alchemical workshop that was his kitchen and came out to say Hello. It was weird speaking English with him, his English was excellent and he told us that he was originally from Rome but had gone to the UK twenty years earlier to work with one of the great show-jumping teams. I looked puzzled, trying to figure out how show jumping had segued into cooking. He explained that he'd always loved cooking and while living in England had taken the opportunity to learn the secrets of true, good, English cooking and not the unappetising muck most tourists used to encounter on their British holidays and for which we still had a dreadful reputation! He'd fused the best of British with the best of Italian and when he decided to return to Italy, he'd brought with him the most eclectic recipe book!

Intrigued I asked to see the menu and, sure enough, there were 'traditional' Italian dishes but with an Anglo Saxon twist - whether it be in the sauce or the accompaniments, there was a definite nod to Britain. To our amazement and delight there was also Sticky Toffee Pudding on the dessert menu. I asked him how that went down with the locals. He responded that they had loved it and I had a momentary vision of weather-beaten hunters tucking into plates of gooey British deliciousness!

Jane was equally fascinated by this and so a second menu was brought which elicited much mouth-watering discussion between us. There was no alternative but to ask Paola whether we could have lunch outside too. Of course she had agreed readily and sprung into action with plates and glasses and napkins and all the necessary paraphernalia for a good Italian lunch.

My only regret was that as I was driving I could only have one or possibly two glasses of wine and the wine list was equally as eclectic as the menu.

As we sat there, the sun got hotter and hotter so much so that we endeavoured to move the table into a patch of shade. Our fair Anglo Saxon skins starting to glow slightly. Paola emerged with the sunshade, muttering about not usually having to get it out until at least

May... then actually agreed that it WAS a bit warm. Unusual for April. Global warming we concluded and continued our delicious lunch suitably shaded. Fabio popped out to see what we thought of his fusion cooking and we reassured him that everything was absolutely delicious and that it was a very clever idea to offer something else other than the more traditional regional fare. But not so outré that it became a deterrent to the regular customers, Sticky Toffee Pudding or not!

The restaurant, a prettily decorated large room off the bar, soon started filling up and the little parking area became more crowded. It was fascinating for us, with our grandstand view, to see who was stopping. The usual mixture of businessmen, lorry drivers and some older couples. All of whom looked askance at the mad sun-worshipping foreigners as ostentatiously shuddering and clutching their puffa jackets around them they headed inside to the safety of the centrally heated dining room.

Time wore on and I realised that we'd not probably not make it to the Passo delle Radici this afternoon so I hooked into Paola's Wi-fi to look at a map of the area and decide where we were going to go instead. I recognised a couple of names from a book I'd been reading about Matilda di Canossa. She and her mother had stayed many times at the Rocca di Montefiorino - a great medieval castle in the centre of a hilltop town known for its brave Partisan stand against the Nazis and the Italian fascists towards the end of the Second World War. In fact they had declared a Partisan Republic which sadly had not lasted long but there was a fierce and proud tradition of fighting against tyranny and the partisans and their republic were rightly commemorated in the *Museo Repubblica di Montefiorino e Resistenza Italiana.*

A few kilometres further on was a small town called Frassinoro which boasted a church dedicated by Matilda's mother, so it was almost a thousand years old and still extant.

We decided that we would visit both these towns and have a wander but would probably not visit the somewhat harrowing Museum.

The lunch unhurried, passed slowly, more customers came and went and we realised that we were falling into a sort of stupor. Maybe, just maybe we should eschew more exploring and head for home for a quiet afternoon by the fire and a good chat! Again looking at the map I saw that we could actually get to the Passo via another route which passed by the Pietra. Happily hugging that thought to myself I suggested to Jane that we did this the following day or the one after. Weather permitting.

I'd forgotten how tired she was likely to be, given the stresses and strains of travelling and the fact that she'd had not one but two early starts. For my part I was also feeling a little tired. Too much mountain air! So it was with a cozy sense of complicity that we split the bill, said goodbye to Paola and Fabio and headed back down the hill towards Cerredolo.

Glancing at the clock in the car, I saw that it was nearly time for the shops to open again, and suggested that we passed by the *Enoteca* to see what goodies it had and whether we wanted to get some different wines to taste. It was a real treat to have a guest for it meant that I could drink without feeling guilty. I don't like drinking alone - especially if I open a bottle to try something and then feel duty-bound to finish it.

I think if I'd been a little more organised I would have invested in one of those ingenious Vacu Vin wine savers which pump out the air in the bottle, thus leaving the wine in good condition. I mentally put that on my list ready for my next trip to Luca the Ironmonger.

The *Enoteca* was up a side street with a gratifyingly large parking space outside. Walking into a large warehouse-like space we gasped out loud. It was literally floor to ceiling racks of wine. Great 28 litre Demijohns of wine lay in between the racks. All sorts of wine. Racks of wine - red, white, pink and fizzy, liqueurs, spirits, cognacs, whiskies and many artisan beers with an entire range named after characters from Greek mythology, differing types of mineral waters and a corner devoted to home produced cakes, breads, sweets and biscuits. All '*tipico*' to the region and something not usually seen in a bakery or supermarket. There were also many types of pasta, organic and gluten free and *cannaroli* rice for risotto, as well as balsamic vinegar and many types of *Extra Vergine* Olive Oil, both organic and not. Bottles of preserves and chutneys and sachets of dried herbs added to the cornucopia. Wherever we looked there was something we wanted to try. We were in heaven!

I asked the lady who had silently appeared from the back of the warehouse what local wines she could recommend. I didn't necessarily want just the DOCG wines of the Region, which used the indigenous varieties of grape, but I was also interested in some which were blended with 'foreign' grapes such as Merlot or Cabernet. She pointed me to some *spumante,* the word literally meaning 'foaming', *Franciacorta* from the Province of Brescia, the equivalent of the Veneto's *Prosecco* or *Spumante* from other regions. There were some sweeter white wines from the Trento region, way up in the Dolomites, there were the Amarones, Bardolinos and Valpolicellas from around Verona, the delicious Soave - from the medieval and still-extant walled town of the same name - and mixed in with some interesting DOCG Tuscan wines, there were some of the great Super Tuscans - the Tignanellos, the Sassicaias and the Ornellaias - the result of having mixed the indigenous Tuscan grapes with those of Merlot, Syrah and Cabernet Sauvignon.

There were also wines from Lunigiana, the vines apparently having been transported from Troy back in the mists of times when Aeneas and his band of defeated Trojans made landfall in the lands of the mysterious Ligurii tribesmen, just over the mountains to the west.

What I liked most about this place was not the astonishing range of products but the almost industrial approach to selling it. There was no chi chi decor, no touristy wine tastings just the very serious business of selling several of life's necessities in a down-to-earth fashion. The knowledge displayed by the *venditrice* was astonishing. She, for her own part seemed surprised that we also knew what we were looking for.

In that I was fortunate, for many years earlier I had been in a relationship with a wine producer who had taught me a lot. Add to that the fact that my parents, newly wealthy as a result of years of hard

225

work and some great good fortune, had invested a goodly proportion of their income in wine, regularly taking off through France in a Jaguar XK150S on jaunts to visit wine-producing Chateaux and to purchase, with the help of their shipper, Lovibond, the stock for the wine cellar they were assembling at home.

I'd grown up with amazing wines, despite loathing being sent down to the cellar which was spooky, I'd cherished the dark bottles with their wine labels featuring grainy black and white photographs of the Chateaux of origin. Names such as Margaux, Gevrey Chambertin and Puligny-Montrachet, Pouilly Fuisse and Aloxe Corton. There was also my favourite, Chateau d'Yquem, a dessert wine which, when sniffed with eyes closed, instantly transported me to a hot, dry terrace in the south of France where great bunches of grapes hung, ripening in the sunshine.

My parents had also visited Italy many times in the late 1950's, motoring down to spend some time in the sun-washed streets of Positano, but they had never brought back Italian wine other than some of those wonderful straw-wrapped Chianti bottles, the 'fiasco' which when emptied then became the evocative wax-draped candle holders of the 1950's and 60's.

My Italian wine knowledge was due to my very close friend and a succession of extraordinarily generous wine-loving colleagues and clients who, over the years and upon seeing my interest, had taken it upon themselves to educate me. Something for which I was immensely grateful.

Jane also knew what she liked, having like me, over the years, drunk a fair selection of good and unusual wines and so we spent a happy hour with the Signora, who it turned out was the mother of the Enoteca's owner. I liked the fact that she was no-nonsense and didn't wander around brandishing a corkscrew, ready to pounce on an unsuspecting bottle and pour us a finger or two to sample. Try as I might, I had never mastered the art of true wine tasting, sipping, swilling and spitting. Despite the exhortations of my Italian oenophile friend I just found it revolting to spit out wine into a bucket or slightly more elegant receptacle such as a spittoon!

We were in such raptures that we were in severe danger of spending way too much money on wine that we wouldn't be able to drink before Jane had to return home (3 days hence), so we resigned ourselves to being sensible. Moreover due to the restrictions of taking liquid on a plane, Jane couldn't even buy wine to take back. The Signora told us that the 'Duty Free' at Bologna airport did have some good wines but not like these, which were produced on small estates and in limited quantities.

We ended up with a mixed case of bottles of *fermo, frizzante* and *spumante* though Jane was not convinced about the Lambrusco. Fizzy red wine is not something that sits comfortably with those not used to it. I had learnt to love it and in the heat of summer a glass of chilled Lambrusco is just delicious. I had learnt that there were several kinds, ranging from the dark purplish red down to light red and that there were eight principal regions, all centred around the provinces of Modena, Parma, Reggio Emilia and Mantua. We also bought some little nibbly biscuits made with local Parmesan and jars of a wickedly indulgent spread made from Parmesan and black truffles. The Signora asked me if I'd been to the *Salumeria* just up the road which specialised in cheese and meat. I hadn't and knew that we both liked nothing better than to pick at a plate of various delicatessen meats and cheeses, so having ascertained the exact location of the shop, I realised that we could visit it, stock up on goodies and take a different route home - still without seeing the Pietra and spoiling the surprise!

Chapter 15

'Our friends are lenses through which we read our own minds'
Ralph Waldo Emerson

Jane and I never got to Montefiorino, Frassinoro or the Passo delle Radici, instead, the next day, we sat in the sunshine in the garden and sipped coffee, drank wine, nibbled salami and cheese and talked. Geisha cautiously poked her nose out of the open kitchen door and headed for the sanctuary of my lap where, upon spying Mimi half hidden in the long grass and looking hopefully at a piece of salami, hissed in a warning sort of way. As if to say, "this is my Mamma and if she chooses to stroke you when I'm not looking, I shall turn a blind eye, but try it when I'm with her and you're in trouble..."

Mimi retreated and a giveaway rustle in the grass announced the presence of one of the farm cats who was also not going to mess with Geisha in all her Siamese magnificence. Siamese are well known for being forthright when the mood takes them so I silently promised Mimi a surreptitious stroke when Geisha was asleep. The farm cats were conflicted by rampant curiosity - they knew a cat lover when they saw one - and the desire for treats and maybe, just maybe a tentative but fleeting caress.

Jane sighed deeply, a contented exhalation, rather than a worried one. I'd given up trying to get her out of bed early enough to do anything time-consuming, so we'd happily compromised. She could sleep as long as she wanted and I could get up early and go to bed early. So we swapped rooms, I took the sofa bed and gave Jane my room so she could read in her bed until the wee small hours and Geisha and I could be cozy together by the *stufa* and, more importantly, I could have my 6.30 am coffee without disturbing her.

It had worked well and we were both chilled and well-rested, nattering away as we had done for years. As she sat in the sunshine, her pale English face turned sunwards, I looked her. Really looked at her. We'd known each other since we were ten years old and had accompanied each other through many adventures. We'd also navigated each other's transformations in looks, style and sartorial leanings, through the 60's where I'd wandered around London braless and shoeless (much to her mother's horror and disapproval) to the odd decade that was the 70's with big hair and big clothes! Jane's style had emerged as somewhat eclectic which mirrored my own. We had always been into beads and scarves and earrings. Now, decades later she still travelled with a bag of the most amazing big jewellery, which suited her but no longer suited me!

I'd liked her at school because she was intelligent and different and us oddballs seemed to gravitate towards each other and stick together while the blonde bunnies did their thing. Their thing usually involved being bitchy to those of less blessed in the looks department by the Goddess Aphrodite.

I'd invited her home one exeat from our all-girls Boarding School. A very upper-class establishment housed in an ostensibly-haunted Elizabethan mansion, which, to our collective amusement featured many years later in a Hollywood movie called Wild Child! My parents had liked her immediately and she, them. She was sensible and quick-witted and had a very dry sense of humour which my father adored. In later years he was most impressed as she did, on a daily basis, the fiendishly difficult Times crossword, whereas he and I, working together simply couldn't get our heads around the cryptic clues. It needed a particular mindset and Jane had that. In bucket loads.

So I gazed upon her with enormous affection, realising how much I missed her when she was back in London or elsewhere. But now, sitting drowsily in the warm late Spring sunshine, listening to the insects busy doing their thing in the plants, the birds all frantically calling to each other - especially when a stalking feline appeared on the horizon, I really looked at her as if for the first time in decades.

A striking mobile face, which could go from happily engaged to exasperated in a nano-second! Shoulder length mid brown hair, with artfully placed lowlights, which she had taken to screwing up into a topknot and plopping on the top of her head with the aid of combs. Same height as me, not to tall not too short and a very good figure which, for some reason she chose to hide in baggy colourful clothes, in natural materials. More often than not she wore tennis shoes (sneakers) on her feet which gave her a slightly nautical air. She always had a capacious shoulder bag stuffed to the brim with all sorts of mysterious but no doubt useful things. She wore little or no make up and, in recent years, like me, had to wear glasses pretty much all of the time.

She is one of the nicest people I know and everyone who meets her would agree with me. Whereas I am like Marmite - people either love me or hate me. Her close friends are an eclectic and highly intelligent group of people and she and her husband, when they are not exploring some unusual part of the world, like nothing better than to go and listen to newly formed bands in local pubs. Whereas I'd rather be on the sofa with a good book or a good film and Geisha!

With another huge sigh, she reached for the bottle of rosé that had formed part of the case from the *Enoteca*, looked questioningly at my glass, acknowledged my nod of acquiescence, and topped it up, leaving but a dribble for herself. I got up, groaning as my knees objected, deposited Geisha on Jane's lap and staggered up the steps to get more wine.

"Can you bring out the pepper mill while you're in there?"

"Yep, anything else?"

"Some more tomatoes?"

Doing as I was bid I collected the wine, the punnet of tomatoes and the pepper mill, noticing that Geisha had followed me in and was heading for a snooze, obviously having had enough of Mimi and the other cats. Leaving her to her sunlit bedding, I returned to the orchard, and the buzzing wildlife.

Jane poured herself more wine and turning slightly in her chair, so as not to be in direct sunlight, regarded me solemnly.

"Cass this is idyllic, but are you really going to live here? Don't you think that perhaps you should think of returning home and maybe keeping this on, I know the rent is low, for the summer? Are you sure you can cope with these roads in the depths of winter? The thought of you skidding on black ice and hurtling down the mountain worries me. What happens if it snows hard and you are snowed in for weeks? You can't rely on Farah and Hassan to look after you and, despite the *stufa* and the radiators in the bathroom and bedroom it is going to be absolutely freezing here for several months."

I looked at her and something in me responded to what she was saying. I absolutely loved it here but I hadn't experienced hard mountain weather, nor was I sure I could cope being snowed in for weeks on end and, she was right, the roads would be absolutely terrifying in icy conditions. Moreover, despite the low outgoings, there was still the question of my having to pay €250 per month to the State because of my freelance status - and they didn't care if I had no income, I was still expected to pay. No wonder there was a thriving Black Economy, it was the only way people could supplement their earnings. Or even, in some cases, it being their sole source of income.

If finding work in Verona had been nigh on impossible - a city with a thriving economy - how on earth was I going to manage here? I could give English lessons but there were the terrifying icy roads to consider and would I find pupils, not being actually licensed - or qualified - to teach? The lovely ladies in the cafe were one thing, but I most certainly couldn't expect to charge them anything and if asked to help with English at student level, I was not sure I could cope, never having listened to the teacher at school when we were learning grammar! I could manage verbs, adverbs, adjectives etc. but when faced with the difference between compound nouns, concrete nouns and collective nouns, I didn't have a clue. It didn't seem to matter if one was a native speaker, we knew these things subliminally but being asked to dissect a sentence into its constituent parts was horrifying! Faced with an intelligent and inquisitive student, I would be hard put to explain the grammatical subtleties of my own language. A somewhat sobering thought.

I explained that I HAD thought of returning home, but I simply didn't have the money to finance the move, and my home was still tenanted so not only would I have to continue to store my furniture, goods and chattels but I'd also have to rent somewhere for Geisha and I to live. An outlay of quite considerable proportions. This, being inexpensive, was my only option. Anyway it was magical here. Jane snorted. "Yes magical until you can't pay your bills, or you get sick and because you haven't paid your dues for social security they won't treat you..." She was right. The feeling in my stomach told me that she was right.

I looked at her and told her that, despite this place being truly magical, I acknowledged that it was an adventure and not real life. That my ageing DNA was physically longing for Britain and the thought of never seeing it again and being stuck in a country where the merciless and never-ending bureaucracy made me feel physically sick, did worry me.

We discussed my parlous financial state. She offered to lend me money and I flatly refused. I knew she could afford it, but borrowing money - other than change for parking or a coffee - was something I simply couldn't do. I thanked her and said it would change the dynamic between us and that she was the constant in my life, my best friend, solid and dependable and sensible. She said I made her sound like a particularly unappealing piece of furniture and we both laughed.

But something had changed. I knew she was right, and mentally blessed her for bringing the subject up. Furthermore I suspected that her trip here wasn't merely to visit me and see my new abode. I asked her and she confessed that she and her husband were worried about me. I was getting on and needed to be back in my own country for at least part of the year. My health wasn't great and I would probably soon need to be near Britain's fantastic, unequalled and much-envied health service - the NHS.

We discussed what assets I had, none, but I did have a small private pension in the UK from which I believed I might be able to draw down something, but I wasn't sure, given my Italian Residency. Maybe that could finance the move home. The wine disappeared as we chatted on into the afternoon, the sun now behind us and a slight chill in the air. So we moved back inside and as I lit the *stufa*, at which I was becoming quite proficient, Jane cleared things away and, in true, British fashion, put the kettle on! Finding a kettle in Italy had been interesting - for making coffee they most sensibly used those wonderful Gaggia or Bialetti or Lavazza steel percolator coffee makers. But I wanted occasional cups of tea and long black coffees or soup in a mug so had gone in search of a kettle. Amazon Italy had had several *bollitores*, kettles, and I had found one which didn't take ages to boil and thus use up far too much electricity in the process.

We sat, sipping coffee, nibbling on biscuits from the Forno.

My tenants were due to purchase my house in England at the end of their tenancy, which was up in November. I was due to visit them before then to confirm - or not - whether I still wanted to sell.

Something had prevented me from selling the house when I had originally moved to Verona and instead I had had to resort to letting it. Phew! Suddenly my path became clear - well, clearer.

Technically I was Resident in Italy, Non-Resident in the UK and therefore subject to a different set of rules and taxes, though that would probably all change when Brexit happened. Sobering thought. At the same time I knew I had to go down to Florence - no hardship there as I loved the city - and meet with my *Commercialista*, and try to sort out how I could get away with not paying the €250 per month social security contribution, how I could relinquish my Residency status and how I could get home. A surge of visceral longing for my homeland and my cottage swept through me. I guess you can take the woman out of Britain but not Britain out of the woman!

For such an important and in-depth conversation - once again life-changing - it had actually taken very little time to decide what, deep down I had known was the right thing to do. Happily I also knew that I could do nothing until September at the earliest and this was April. So I had at least five months in which to discover and enjoy the beautiful place in which I found myself.

I was profoundly grateful to Jane and her husband for worrying about and caring about me and I told her so. She looked at me as if I was mad and said "You dopey old bag, don't think this is just for you, I miss you! I want you back in England - at least for part of the time..."

We talked long into the night, for all the reasons that I had left England - no work and thus no income - which was still valid and I honestly didn't have a clue as to what I was going to do when I got home. But I'd cross that bridge if and when I got to it.

The next morning I took Jane to the Pietra, first stopping in Felina, just outside the motorbike shop and telling her to close her eyes until I said she could open them. Pulling off the road, and making sure that we were in direct eye line of the massive rock, I told her to open them. Her reaction was most gratifying. "Bloody hell... what IS that?". I told her as we headed there, gratified that it was another beautiful sunny day and as it was midweek, the car park would be empty and we would probably have the place all to ourselves.

However, before going straight to the Pietra, we'd first headed into Castelnovo, to a small *alimentari* - food store - where a very jolly old lady made enormous sandwiches from freshly-baked loaves (she'd just taken them out of the bread oven the first time I'd visited her) using local cheeses and meats. Today the bread was not quite so fresh - a couple of hours old - but still perfect for our panini. Once we had discussed the various merits of each of the cheeses and been given a sliver to taste and then repeated the process with the salamis and prosciutto, she had set about making our huge repast, adding a couple of tomatoes and bottles of *acqua minerale* and asking if we needed plates and napkins. We did. I told her that I had a knife in the car with which to slice the tomatoes.

She wasn't having any of it and, deftly slicing them with a wicked-looking knife, wrapped them in foil, adding a drop of olive oil and some salt and pepper, before putting them into the bag. Jane and I beamed at her, recognising a like-minded picnic aficionado. The bill

237

was less than €10. "I can see why you're going to miss this place" Jane muttered as we headed up the road to the Pietra.

I was right, we did have the car park to ourselves and uttering appreciate noises and the occasional expletive Jane gazed upon the snow capped mountains before turning around to look at the Pietra itself. She too felt the power of the place and looked at me questioningly, as if to ask whether I felt anything. "Yes, but I'm not sure what it is".

We spent a happy hour or so sitting on the bench with our back to the Pietra, just gazing out over the lush countryside where thin blue columns of smoke rose lazily into the air and birds swooped and dived around the rock above us. Jane declined the trek to the top, content just to sit and admire the unspoilt aura of this little-known part of Italy. I told her I was glad it wasn't like Glastonbury or Ayers Rock, full of tourists all desperately trying to immerse themselves in the sanctity of the place and the supernatural energies before climbing back into their air- conditioned buses and heading off to the next wondrous thing.

Gazing out into the landscape I mused aloud as to whether there was a little road that would take us back the long way round, rather than having to retrace our steps and go back via Felina and Carpineti. I retrieved my enormous *Atlante Stradale* - road map - of Italy from the car and we peered at it. Of course it was way too large-scale and the tiny roads we were looking for were, at this scale, non existent, but we both have an unerring sense of direction and I knew where we needed to end up in order to connect with the main road coming back past Cerredolo. So I did as I have done many many times before and in many countries, I put Jane in charge of navigation.

I showed her where we were, where we wanted to end up and pointed away from the direct route home. She did the rest!

For the next three hours we oohed and aahed our way through tiny hamlets, down farm tracks, across rickety bridges and into people's driveways as we endeavoured to navigate our way across country. It was astounding how the landscape changed, one minute Bucolic Alpine, the next Wild and Rugged - somewhat reminiscent of the Highlands of Scotland - and lastly, Medieval Hamlet, of which there were many and each more beautiful that the last . My car looked and felt very out of place in this, the land of the 4x4 Panda or the huge Toyota Landcruisers of the richer landowners and farmers. When we did encounter anyone they looked at us incredulously as if two middle-aged ladies driving the countryside roads in a sleek Audi A4 was something out of a movie. Thelma and Louise!

It look us over three hours to get home, partly because some of the roads had petered out into nothing and I'd had to reverse back to the actual road through several farmyards, to the accompaniment of wildly-excited baying farm dogs and partly because the places indicated on the occasional signpost, were simply too small for my Atlas of Italy! But it was glorious, the scenery was stunning, the architecture of the *case coloniche* - farm houses - was suspended in local stone and terracotta-tiled time and the smells, both good and bad, added to the atmosphere of the journey. Even coming back into the surprisingly modern local big town, Villa Minozzo, which sported the usual mini market, cafes and bakery, it was as if it was another world and I knew that, while I had made the right decision, I was going to miss the simple and unpretentious life of this part of the world. Where the quality of the home made pasta, bread and local produce counted for more than the latest post on social media or what was going on in the wider world. Looking in from the outside this life seemed idyllic, yet talking to a couple of the kids that had graduated from school the previous year and who were desperately trying to find some sort of work, it was a prison. Seeing my right hand drive car they would come and talk to me, shyly practising their English and telling me about their school trip to London or Brighton or Birmingham and how lucky I was to live in England - despite the awful food!

Jane left the next day, her mission accomplished. We drove in bleary silence to the airport, I was somewhat hung over, as we had decided to finish the case from the Enoteca, and rather than taking the alluring but longer scenic route we blasted grim-faced down the motorway. Arriving at the airport I was not having any more nonsense with the automatic ticket barrier, so with Jane waving my Blue (disability) Badge at anyone who was interested we headed for the Kiss and Fly area. Only the Italians could call the Drop Off point, Kiss and Fly! Squeezing into a mercifully vacant space by a pillar, not a delineated parking space, rather a sort of parking no-mans-land, we unloaded the car and redesignated the area the Hug and Fly. Somewhat tearfully we hung onto each other for a good minute or two, Jane promised she'd be back in the summer (we had hatched plans over the wine the previous night) and then, somewhat unsteadily, it has to be said, she headed into the terminal building and the journey home to her lovely husband.

I backed out of the space, only to be sworn at by some prat in a Lancia, wound down my window, reciprocated by giving him both barrels in Italian and, sticking my Anglo-Saxon nose in the air, headed back towards the motorway, home (for now) and Geisha.

Chapter 16

"Ben tornata a casa! Welcome home!"

Jane had left me with a plan, but many more questions more answers. For the time being, I put them out of my head, determined to enjoy my remaining time in this place. So I busied myself with really exploring the area, to what end I was not sure but I was hopelessly in love with the sweeping valleys, the tiny *borghi*, the endless vistas and around each corner there was always something interesting or unusual to discover. I soon learnt that, despite their being incredibly rich in culture, art and architecture I simply was not attracted to the three cities of Parma, Reggio Emilia and Modena. More fool me with hindsight, but having lived in cities my soul yearned for country air, simple pleasures and beautiful views. I liked the people too. They were down-to-earth, hardworking and rightly proud of their area and, despite their taciturn reputation, were friendly and engaging whenever our paths crossed. Very different from the *froideur* of the city-dweller.

Off I went, heading carefully down unmade roads - *strade bianche* - tumbling apologetically into farmyards but getting the lie of the land and in so doing, finding some astonishingly beautiful old houses, farms and hidden chapels. No doubt each with its own story. There were times when I wished I had a 4x4 for my sleek once-gleaming and now muddy car was not built for such roads. More than once I had heard ominous clunks from the engine compartment as I had lurched into a dried muddy rut or worse so I had to curtail the more interesting explorations and confine myself to the local country roads.

243

Thus I had gained a pretty good knowledge of the immediate area, but only geographical knowledge. There was little information that I could find online about the location and I was sure that there were many fascinating things to discover. But how? There was a local Library in Carpineti and I decided I'd go and have a nose around there. The *Comune*, the Town Hall, might also have some information, housed as it was in an evocatively ancient building in Piazza Matilda di Canossa. I also decided I needed to find about more about her too seeing as she was pretty ubiquitous, featuring on signs and hoardings. The people were proud of their association with her and so I wanted to find out more about this famous - or was she infamous - woman. I would endeavour to find out.

Returning home one afternoon, Farah emerged not from her house, but from the Manor House, looking exhausted. I asked her why she looked so tired. She explained that Signor S had telephoned this morning and had decided, since the weather was already getting warm, that he would transfer himself up to the Hamlet a month earlier than normal, hence the flurry of activity because he wanted to come the following weekend and that was only ten days hence.

Apart from Ugo and his friends braving the cold for New Year, the house had been shut up since the previous September and was no doubt full of dust and spiders webs! Farah told me that Luisa was bringing her cleaning lady up from Reggio and that the three of them would be busy cleaning, polishing and airing the rooms. The weather was perfect and within a day the washing lines in the orchard were sagging, hung with massive linen sheets, coverlets and pillow cases.

Pillows and cushions were being plumped and put out on the patio tables to dry in the sunshine and Signor S' mattress was seen, leaning against the wall by the open windows of his bedroom.

The cantina and the kitchen were thoroughly dusted and all the crockery, china and glassware were run through the dishwasher or carefully washed by hand. The *cotto* tiled floor was burnished to a smooth patina, the oxblood colour perfectly complementing the freshly polished wooden chests and shelves, the smell of the beeswax mingling with that of the floor polish. Out came the summer napery and the hand crocheted hanging that went above the fireplace. Everything was washed and pressed and the windows cleaned with vinegar. Hassan and Suleiman brought out the massive cream and yellow striped awning from storage and Farah beat it enthusiastically with an ancient carpet beater until clouds of accumulated winter dust and dead insects dropped to the gravel - much to the interest of the curious cats who had come to watch the proceedings.

Ladders were brought from the *stalla*, the stables, and leaned up again both the house and the little *fienile*, which was the wood store for the house and which contained Mimi's cozy winter quarters.

I watched fascinated as the men started to unravel lengths of cream rope, which looked a bit like the rope used for rigging on sailboats. These were then attached to a complicated series of pulleys and then laid flat on the ground so as to facilitate the threading of the rope through a series of strategically placed steel ringed eyelets on the canvas awnings. Slowly and with a lot of patience, the sheets (which now resembled the massive canvas sheets that the Romans had had strung across their amphitheatres to provide shade) were winched into place, Hassan using a hand ratchet to crank the ropes until they were taut. It was an ingenious solution, using secondary ropes to unfurl them, they were a bit like Roman blinds on windows, except that these were horizontal and using the pulley system they could be drawn across the courtyard at a height of approximately 4 metres, to provide much-needed shade in the summer months. The brightly-coloured fabric perfectly complemented the golden brown stones of the house with its dark wooden shutters. It was ingenious and really pretty.

Luisa, standing nearby, had explained to me that her father, Signor C, whom I would be meeting in July, had invented and manufactured it. She had helped him, for when they were children he had had a sailboat on the Romagna coast and she had adored going out with him and learning how to make things. It had been time well invested, for she was an immensely practical woman who could make anything or mend anything and she was possessed of enormous strength, despite being small and blonde! I had seen her manhandling the enormous *demigiana* which they used for storing the estate wine, before decanting it into bottles. I could barely move one, but she was able to move them from the small courtyard adjacent to the cantina doors, into the dark and temperature controlled depths of the cantina. The bottling took place at a bench where, equipped with a massive corking machine they would decant wine from the *demigiana* into newly-washed bottles, cork them and then put them to the back of the shelves to age and bringing those that were ready to the front of the shelf so that anyone heading into the area knew what was drinkable and what was not - yet.

It was a different energy to the elegant and polite estate-bottled wines of my childhood and I liked the pure rustic feel of it all. This was 'real' and it was done how it had always been done, no new-fangled stainless steel tanks full of wine. There was even an ancient *fiasco* with its close-fitting woven straw base hiding away in the gloomy depths of the storage area, along with an assortment of empty bottles from a wide range of wines and spirits. Nothing was wasted here. I had agreed with Luisa that I would co-purchase some of the local wine with them and so once they had bottled my share, approximately 20 bottles, I was given my own shelf - with its own label!

Once the awnings were up and drawn back against the wall, Hassan and Suleiman headed for the herb garden and the orchard to mow the grass and prune the trees and bushes. For, being lord of the manor, Signor S would want to closely inspect every inch of his domain once he returned and it had to be perfect for him. Perfect in a wonderfully rural sort of way, because the sheer size of the place and the estate meant that it would never be impeccable, there were too many variables, such as weather, flora and fauna.

The next week shot by in a flurry of activity, I offered to help but was gently discouraged from doing so, which didn't displease me as it was now warm enough to sit outside and so rather than let me be completely useless, Luisa had put me in charge of dealing with the unripe green walnuts for this year's batch of *Nocino*. Quartering them, which was harder than it seemed due to the thickness of the husks, I had to wear latex gloves due to the brown liquid which stains everything it touches and is almost impossible to remove. These were then dropped into a large glass container and mixed with sugar, cinnamon sticks, cloves, lemon zest cut into strips and a lot of 100% alcohol.

I'd seen the bottles of pure alcohol in the supermarket and wondered what they were used for, now I knew. The resulting mixture would then be stored for approximately 6-8 weeks and shaken daily to thoroughly mix the ingredients, during which time the liquid would change colour to a very dark brown - the colour of high cocoa content chocolate. It would then be carefully decanted into bottles and stored for at least a year.

The farm cats, seeing me happily engaged with my task, grew bold and slowly and silently crept closer to investigate me. Then, deciding that I was not a threat, they came and lay down nearby, seeking out the patches of sunshine, stretching their little bodies contentedly and in one or two cases purring. I resisted the temptation to try and stroke them, I knew it would frighten them and I wanted to win their trust. So I sat and continued quartering walnuts!

At 11.00 precisely on Saturday, Alberto's car drove in through the gates, Signor S, sitting like a potentate, upright in the passenger seat looking eagerly out at his childhood home, the ever-present unlit cheroot clamped between his teeth.

We all walked over to the car to welcome him, me feeling slightly shy and a bit of an imposition, as if I had no right to be there. For this was an annual pilgrimage and his staff of Hassan, Farah and Suleiman were welcoming their *Capo* back home. I on the other hand was more like a paying guest and so I stood back and watched them greeting him obvious warmth and was delighted to see that he gave Farah a huge hug and patted her arm affectionately. He then saw me and boomed, "*Signora, come va?*" I moved forward and responded that I was well, asking after his own health and then requesting that, if he didn't find it too informal, I would prefer to be called by my name. He laughed, removing the cheroot and responded that he would also like to be called by his name, Stefano and not the more formal *Signore*.

Rules established, we processed towards the house, us carrying various bags and boxes and him slowly, leaning on his stick and looking keenly from side to side, noting the new growth of the plants, the sparkling windows and the newly assembled sunshade. He was back where his roots were and his joy was palpable.

Having deposited the things that I'd been carrying in the kitchen I headed for the door, wanting to leave him alone for his homecoming with the family, Hassan, Farah and Suleiman. "*Dove vai?*" He asked, I explained that I was heading back to the *Tavernetta* as no doubt he would want to familiarise himself with the house and rest after his journey. Not a bit of it! He waved his walking stick at me and then indicating that I should seat myself in the chair opposite his by the fire, with a great grunt of satisfaction he lowered himself into his, ensuring that I had done likewise. Fixing me with his bright blue stare he enquired how I was getting on and without waiting for my reply, asked Alberto to bring us some wine. Thus we started our friendship.

It appeared that I had been asked to join the family for lunch, which I had gleefully accepted, remembering the delicious meal we had last shared together - seemingly so long ago - yet, in reality, only six months or so. This meal was not going to disappoint either and I soon came to realise that the family - the entire family - were superb cooks. I wasn't allowed to lift a finger and so Stefano and I chatted while the others swiftly, with the minimum of fuss and a lot of good-natured banter, prepared yet another amazing meal. Once again I was seated to Stefano's right and I surreptitiously checked that the rickety chair on which I had been due to sit, was replaced with another. Slightly more robust.

Lunch passed in a succession of simple but mouthwatering dishes. Some salami, local prosciutto and lumps of Parmesan, followed by tortellini in an orchard vegetable sauce, then roast game (I didn't know what it was when I asked and resolved to look it up when I got back to the *Tavernetta*) with fresh tomatoes and a leafy salad, all washed down with copious amounts of the Hamlet's Lambrusco. Then out came the *Nocino* and I knew it was not going to be possible to do anything that afternoon other than sleep!

As we ate I was regaled with tales of the house and its occupants - going back many many generations - his ancestors and forebears. Somewhat affected by the wine, I was sure I could see their shades swaying in the golden dust motes in the beams of sunlight streaming in from the courtyard. The house was coming alive again after its long winter slumber. The ghosts were happy which boded well for the next few months.

Lunch over, Stefano reached for his stick and announced that he was heading upstairs for his *sonnellino*, nap. He looked at me and told me to come back at 7.00 that evening for a glass of Prosecco. I nodded my head and grinned at him conspiratorially, for in our brief chats it seemed that we had already got the measure of each other and in so doing recognised similar souls.

I offered to help with the clearing away and the washing up, but was waved away and decided to head back to the *Tavernetta* and Geisha. The wine had affected me too and I was ready for my snooze. Alberto accompanied me to my door, wanting to check that everything was ok with the house and, in particular, that the old water heater was still working! I assured him that it was, as was everything else and added that I was so very happy here.

He looked at me seriously and said "When we are here, you eat with us. Unless of course you want to sit at home alone and eat English Pudding...". I was really touched and thanked him laughing, realising that he meant Yorkshire Pudding for which we Brits are known for eating with Sunday lunch.

"Alberto I don't even know how to cook English Pudding, so thank you, I would love to join you all when you're here."

"My father will also expect you to join him for lunch on Sundays if we are not here. But you must watch him. He tends to cook enormous meals that are not good for his health..."

This sounded even better! Naughty lunches with Stefano ... I knew I was going to adore this wonderful man.

Chapter 17

'Getting to know you, getting to know all about you...'
Rogers and Hammerstein

My life in the Hamlet had changed with the arrival of Stefano. He was intelligent, amusing, generous and very good company, while respecting each other's need for privacy, we nonetheless wished to spend time together, so we quickly settled into a mutually beneficial routine. Before leaving to return home, Alberto had asked me if I would be able to help with monitoring Stefano's blood sugar levels, as he was diabetic - and, if left to his own devices, would ignore everything that the Doctor had told him not to do and do them anyway!

Of course I said yes, hoping that it didn't mean that I had to do anything too medical as I am ridiculously squeamish. Thankfully it only involved measuring his blood sugar every morning, by using a neat little machine to prick his finger (helpfully called a finger pricker!) and then drip a drop of blood onto a test strip which, when inserted into another machine, would read the results. So I would go over at 9.00 am where he would have already put the coffee machine on to the gas hob, knowing that as I walked in the door it would be bubbling away, ready for me. He would also have raided his totally illegal stash of biscuits so that I would sit at the big table, fortifying myself with caffeine and sugar for the task ahead.

Stefano would sit patiently beside me, his long fingers ready to be stabbed. Each day we would use a different finger for I didn't want him to be covered with bruises. I know from experience that it is not painless, yet he bore it stoically, twinkling at me from beneath his eyebrows as I positioned the spreckle and then, with an intake of breath - me, not him - I would stab it forcefully onto his finger hoping that I wasn't hurting him. Some days the blood came and some days it didn't and we would discuss whether or not to try again or to leave it for a day. Once the hole had been made I would touch the test strip to the bleeding pinprick and then insert it into the measuring device. We would solemnly regard the results but not note them down. I trusted him to inform me if they were not good. He never did, so I guess that despite his penchant for unsuitable foods, he was doing ok. After all he was in his 80's and after nine decades of eating and drinking - and smoking those noisome cheroots (which thankfully, on the advice of his Doctor he now only chewed) - he was still alive and kicking.

However he had a mountain of pills to take every day, which resided in a cunningly-concealed drawer in the dining table, with spares in the adjacent sideboard. He knew what to take and when and so I left him to sort himself out with those.

The grisly ceremony over, we would take our cups and breakfast things into the kitchen, depositing them by the huge stone sink for Farah to deal with when she came in later and he would head upstairs to make his toilette. I would head back to Geisha and plan my day.

Sometimes he would ask me to sit in the courtyard with him as he read the paper. *Il Resto del Carlino* was his newspaper of choice. It was the local edition of a regional publication which, founded in Bologna in 1885, was one of the oldest newspapers in Italy. It had several local editions covering Emilia and Romagna and Stefano read the Modena version. I had commented on the unusual name of the paper and was informed that a *'Carlino'* had been a coin minted by the Papal State from the 13th century until 1796. It had entered the language, continuing despite the cessation of the coin's production. It had subsequently formed the basis of several ironic sayings, including, according to Wikipedia, my favourite "goad the powerful and whip the bullies"... The newspaper was not considered to compete with the mainstream national press and I could tell that Stefano who, before retiring, had been well-known in the region as a respected businessman with top-level connections, enjoyed reading about the daily doings of the great, the good and the maybe not-so-good of the area whose families he had known if not personally, by reputation.

Shuffling the large broadsheet pages, he would ask me my plans for the day and I told him that I was fascinated by the area and still discovering it. He was, it seemed, amused by my adventurous leanings and suggested that I took a day to go to the ever-beckoning Passo Delle Radici and on just a few kilometres into Tuscany to visit the ancient village of San Pellegrino in Alpe.

"There's a mummified Saint in the church there, who used to be the son of a Scottish king."

I looked at him astonished, for we had discussed my Scottish surname. We had also discussed our favourite whiskies. He was delighted that I proclaimed my allegiance to a particularly delicious and premium Single Malt, Talisker, from the Isle of Skye, for he too was a lover of Talisker, although he preferred Lagavulin from the Isle of Islay, also a single malt. Not sure of the story behind Talisker, I looked it up on Wikipedia and read to him the fact that it was the favourite whisky of Robert Louis Stevenson being mentioned in his poem 'The Scotsman's Return from Abroad' - all of which seemed eminently suitable when discussing San Pellegrino - except that he hadn't returned! Laughingly I said, "But he has *acqua minerale* named after him!"

"No, that is not connected with this Saint. The water comes from San Pellegrino Terme near Bergamo in Lombardia, where it has been produced for over six centuries. Leonardo da Vinci visited the town in the sixteenth century and having sampled the water, wrote a treatise on water. The sparkling *acqua leggermente frizzante* that is sold today is created by the addition of carbon dioxide to prevent the development of bacteria as the water is exported far and wide. In fact the carbon dioxide is still taken from sources in Toscana and sent to San Pellegrino *Terme*".

I listened fascinated to this, for this was precisely the sort of information that I loved! Not vital but so very interesting. As was the information about our San Pellegrino. It was too late today to set off, and anyway we had a date to visit the supermarket in Felina that afternoon. Stefano had heard good things about the in-store butcher and decided that we needed to visit it. So we sat in the sunshine making our lists and me wandering to and from the kitchen to check whether we needed to augment the already vast store of foodstuffs.

The sun was beginning to get hot so Stefano asked me if I would help him unfurl the shades. We crossed to the wall of the *Fienile* and locating the right rope to pull, we released it grunting and heaving together, occasionally pausing for breath as the awning slowly made its colourful and majestic way across the courtyard, casting scallop-like shadows onto the gravel. The difference in temperature was immediate, thus allowing us to spend more time outside. It really was the most ingenious invention and I was looking forward to meeting Signor C.

Late that afternoon, post *sonnellino*, Stefano and I, accompanied by a goodly number of large empty bags, shoehorned ourselves into the car and headed off to Conad. He was uncharacteristically quiet for a while, then, having assured himself that I knew how to drive on the winding mountain roads, announced that I was an excellent driver. I waited "for a woman" or "for a foreigner", but neither were forthcoming! He was interested in how, driving a right hand drive car in a right hand country, did I overtake? I told him, "cautiously", adding that I was so used to driving a British car in Europe that it was actually more dangerous when I drove in the UK, because my instinct was to drive on the wrong side of the road! He chortled at this and as we drove through the countryside he proceeded to regale me with tales of his wild youth in the area which seemed to contain copious amounts of sowing his wild oats! By all accounts he had been quite the Lothario, reminiscing about the pretty girls he used to meet from the neighbouring villages at the various church and agricultural festivals.

He grew sad and reflective when he told me that his wife of many years, had only passed away a couple of years previously, Alberto being their only child. She too had loved it up here in the mountains and I said that I would very much have liked to have met her. He kept a photo of her on the sideboard in the main room of the house and I recalled that she was buried in a cemetery nearby. Now that he was no longer able to drive on account of his eyesight and taxis were hard to come by up here, I wondered whether I should offer to drive him to visit her grave, but I reckoned if he wanted that he'd ask me. So I kept quiet.

As we swung around the curves in the road, I was fascinated by the titbits of information he volunteered, having exhausted, for now, his tales of his reckless youth. At one small group of houses, intriguingly named *Casa Spadaccini*, I asked him whether the *Spadaccini* meant 'small men with swords' or 'men with small swords'... it was the latter. The Spadaccini were the non-noble swordsmen of old. A Nobleman or Knight would have carried a broadsword - a *Spadone* - for hacking and cutting, whereas the Spadaccini would have used the *Spada*, a small stabbing sword, much like the short Roman Gladius.

Stefano remarked that no-one had ever asked him that. I replied that I assumed that was because they knew the answer. Apparently not. In his eyes my question indicated that I actually looked where I was going, whereas others just drove. Knowing the propensity of the Italians to multitask when driving, I was not surprised that they didn't notice such things! Instead I told him that I loved discovering new places, that my job, when I had worked for Warner Bros, had been to find new locations for multiplex cinemas all over Europe. How could I have done that with my eyes metaphorically closed? In order to make the best selection I had needed to drive around and understand the catchment area of the potential site - and that involved trying to understand the mindset of the prospective clients; so understanding their history, their geography and their way of doing things had been important in selecting the right site.

He was fascinated and asked me if I had opened any cinemas in Italy. I replied that I had and proceeded to reel off a list of locations that I could tell impressed him, especially the one near Bologna, which he'd heard of. It was odd, driving with him on the way to the supermarket, talking about my past life as an international real estate executive! I much preferred my life now and was positively drooling at the thought of our visit to the butcher's counter.

We arrived at the supermarket and I pulled up in front of the entrance, gliding neatly into the Disabled parking space. "This is for the handicapped.." Stefano told me. "Yes I know" I replied, reaching for my Blue Disabled parking badge, with the EU logo firmly stamped on it, and displayed it in the window. He snorted with laughter. "*Brava*! But you won't be able to use that when Brexit has happened..." It was my turn to snort. "Let's not talk about that, it makes me very angry and very sad..".

Walking into the small mall that housed Conad, I accepted the €1 piece that Stefano held out to me and went to the trolley park. Inserting the money into the coin slot, I released the chain and pulling the trolley backwards out and away from its companions, executed a swift turn and followed him as he strode purposefully towards the entrance.

It transpired he'd never been there before, preferring, when he had been able to drive himself, to visit the small artisan food shops that he had known for years, where he knew the owners - now usually the children or even grandchildren of his contemporaries. But this small supermarket intrigued him and he was busy examining the excellent and tempting display of fresh vegetables, peering occasionally at his list to remind himself what he needed. I picked up a basket from the side of the entrance and popped it on top of the trolley for my own small amount of shopping.

Muttering *"melanzane, zucchini, finocchio, carote, lattuga, radicchio..."* to himself like some sort of horticultural litany, he swooped on the various vegetables in question, handing them to me to weigh, bag and label. Attached to the scales was a somewhat faded photographic sheet of the various types of fruit and vegetable sold, with a number alongside. Identifying the correct vegetable, entering the corresponding code into the weighing machine and then affixing the resulting sticky label to the bagged produce took skill, not least surreptitiously swiping away over-eager housewives who wanted to queue barge before I had finished my task. Meanwhile Stefano had spied the butcher's counter and was causing havoc by requesting, in a booming voice, that the butcher attend to him, rather than taking a numbered ticket and waiting his turn.

Recognising a potentially excellent customer, the butcher gave him his full attention and soon a bewildering array of cuts of various meats were being weighed, wrapped and deposited on the counter. What I really liked about this, my first shop with Stefano, was that he knew exactly what he wanted, having planned down to the last ingredient, what he wanted to cook and what each meal would require. While I waited, I listened to the conversation between him and the butcher, a swarthily handsome man in his mid 30's who had obviously seriously studied butchery, for he knew everything and he and Stefano were soon deep into a conversation about the best cut of meat for a specific local speciality, much to the annoyance of the women patiently waiting with their tickets!

"*Cara*, why don't you go and get these?" I was handed the list and peered at it, hoping that I would be able to read his writing. I could and headed happily off to the aisle that sold about a million types of pasta, thankful that he had specified which versions to get - for there is a type of individual pasta that goes with specific sauces and woe betide the foreigner that buys the wrong type! We were also on the hunt for reduced sugar biscuits as his blood sugar level had been a bit on the high side recently and rather than give up biscuits altogether, which he liked to dunk into milky coffee for his *prima colazione* we decided we would investigate the less dangerous ones. Interestingly, alongside the national and international brands, there were some locally-produced ones - *prodotto artiginale* - which, having thoroughly checked the labels I deemed suitable.

My own small basket quickly filled up - mostly with expensive cat food and treats for Geisha who, as she aged, was becoming more and more picky. Still, the more I spent, the more points I earned on my Conad card and this month there were some really nice things to get with them!

Stefano met me in the queue for the till and proudly showed me an enormous bag of differing meats, he was going to eat like an Emperor for the next few days! We arrived at the till and I arranged our purchases into two piles, his and mine. Mine first so I could pay for them, stow them at the bottom of the trolley, leaving the majority of the space for his comestibles. I explained to the cashier that we would be paying separately and I offered her my points card for my shopping.

"No! Signora! Metta tutto insieme.." Stefano was insisting on paying for everything. I started to protest, embarrassed, I didn't want him to pay for my shopping, generous though that was.

I was stopped by a glare from those blue eyes and shut up, meekly putting the shopping, his and mine, into the trolley. The cashier was now confused as to what to do with the points card. He told her to put all of the purchases on his card and give me the points, I nearly died when I saw the amount of the total. He had spent a fortune on the meat alone.

We left the supermarket in silence. I had of course thanked him as he had handed over his card to pay.

"Vieni..." he indicated the bar opposite and held the door open as I manoeuvred the laden trolley inside. Waving me to a nearby table he strode up to the bar and ordered two Aperol Spritzes. Returning to me, he saw my still confused and embarrassed face. I was mortified. I had not expected nor anticipated that he would pay for my shopping. I hated having my independence taken away and simply didn't know how to thank him for this extraordinarily kind act without appearing sulky! Not a good look for a woman in her 60's!

So I quickly found a smile and thanked him once more but told him that it was unnecessary though very generous. He looked at me and told me that when we went to the supermarket together, he would pay. And that was that, he would brook no argument. I acquiesced and silently swore to myself that I would reduce my part of our weekly shop to a bare minimum, leaving the bulk of what I wanted to get for Geisha and I on my lone forays into Carpineti.

So we sat and drank our Aperol Spritzes and nibbled on the crostini and *patatine* that had come with the drinks and chatted about life, the universe and everything. I was still reeling from his extraordinary kindness while admitting it to myself, very very grateful for the financial assistance.

We returned home to delicious smells wafting from the kitchen for Farah was already sweating the onions and garlic for that night's pasta sauce, to which Stefano would add some fresh ingredients and perform his culinary magic. She came out when she heard the car draw up and exclaimed when she saw the enormous number of bags stuffed to the gills. She looked at me and smiled happily, knowing that between us, Stefano would be enjoying his summer up the mountain - even without the freedom of having his car.

Helping her with the bags I followed her into the kitchen and we chatted quietly as Stefano poured himself a glass of wine and sat in front of the fire, which Farah had just lit, for the evenings were cold up here - even in May. I said I must head home and feed Geisha and I also wanted to spend some time alone. I loved being part of the life of the Hamlet but there were times when my Anglo-Saxon genes reminded me that I needed some time alone - and after an interesting few hours I was ready for my own glass or two of wine and time with

Geisha. True to form dear Farah had already lit the *stufa* and the little house was warm and cosy. Even better, I had managed to figure out how to watch the latest episode of a series I had been watching. I found it sad that the excellent programmes that the BBC put out on its iPlayer, were not available outside the UK, but there was still plenty to watch without having to switch on the Italian terrestrial channels with their seemingly endless current affairs programmes or, worse, game shows hosted by improbably tanned hosts, ably assisted by pneumatically-enhanced hostesses! Stefano had told me of a channel that showed old black and white films from the heyday of Italian cinema but I'd forgotten what it was and I was too tired to go and ask.

Chapter 18

Meeting Pink Floyd and Steve McQueen

One morning a couple of weeks later when we were sitting under the yellow awnings having our coffee and chat, Stefano asked me what I was going to do now that I was settled into the *Tavernetta*. Surely I wasn't just going to spend my days exploring? He was curious as to what I'd done in my professional life, apart from the job with Warner Bros. so I told him and I could see the wheels in his brain engaging as he took on board my skills - skills that were not remotely useful or relevant halfway up a mountain in rural Italy!

"You must meet Geometra Bonini" he announced after a brief pause. "You understand real estate, you can bring foreign buyers to this area, you know a lot about it - and you know that it is as beautiful as Toscana which you English seem to love so much..."

I asked about *Geometra* Bonini and Stefano was quietly complimentary about him, calling him a good and honest man who had done work for Stefano and the family for several years. A *Geometra* is the Italian equivalent of a British Chartered Surveyor, a property professional who as well as dealing with the technical aspects of real estate, such as planning and project management is also able to transact property - not unlike an estate agent but much more professional and thus generally more well-respected. The *Geometras* I'd met throughout my working life in Italy had indeed been very professional and respectable and not at all like some of the estate agents I'd met who didn't seem to work to any form of code of practice and about whom I'd heard many horror stories of unscrupulous dealings.

We agreed that Stefano would call *Geometra* Bonini and that we would endeavour to meet him the following week as he had an office in Carpineti. I liked the idea of doing something which would enable me to introduce this beautiful part of the world to 'outsiders'. I'd been an estate agent myself, in my early 20's in central London and had been quite successful, earning myself a reputation for honesty and straight talking. I knew enough about the Italian property market, including the oft-confusing laws and taxes, to be able to provide a metaphorical bridge - a liaison - between a foreign buyer and an Italian *Geometra*. Often the two simply didn't understand each other - not only from a linguistic but also from a practical viewpoint. I knew what foreign buyers were looking for, I knew what Italian law allowed and something was needed to marry the two. A local *Geometra* would be a mine of information and knowledge as to the technical aspects of buying and converting property but they would be most unlikely to understand the mindset of middle-class European buyers, looking for their dream holiday home. This was where I came in. How astute of Stefano to spot that - and the potential gap in the market!

The more I thought about it the more I liked the idea. I was good at selling property, I enjoyed finding properties and matching them to buyers. I enjoyed meeting people and my languages meant that I could work with other nationalities and not just the Brits who could, at times, be extremely querulous, demanding and unrealistic!

A conviction underscored by having watched various international property relocation programmes when I'd been living back in the UK! I knew that there was a Dutch family, a Polish family, the couple who worked for the BBC and an English lady all owning properties in the area so it appealed to many. It was certainly one of the most beautiful places I'd ever seen and looking at the houses dotted around the countryside, each with a spectacular view, I could see the potential. I just hoped that *Geometra* Bonini and I got on.

I thanked Stefano and our discussion moved on to Sunday lunch that weekend. Having arrived only a week or before, Stefano was keen to go to the bar in the village, see his old friends and have a beer. Would I mind driving him? Not at all, I would be delighted. So it was that we arranged to go to the bar for an aperitivo, followed by a visit to the Hamlet's lake where there was a regional fishing competition taking place the following weekend. As the landowner and effective lord of the manor, Stefano was duty bound to attend. I'd seen the lake and very much wanted to visit but had been deterred by the *Privato* signs I'd seen erected at the end of the road leading to it. Its position was in a natural bowl of the surrounding hills and it had a lovely rustic cabin at one end and a wildflower strewn path around the edge, with strategically placed large boulders at intervals. Perfect places on which to perch and just chill. But I'd not wanted to be chased off by irate gentlemen for trespassing so was delighted when Stefano suggested we visit. He asked me if I'd been and told him I hadn't and why. He laughed, almost spitting out his revolting half-chewed and ever-present cigar in the process. "But this is my land, you are my tenant, you can go anywhere you want. Come, it's almost lunchtime, we will walk down to the *circolo,* club, and I will introduce you to Enzo who runs it. The *Circolo* was a long low stone building down by the crossroads. It was used mainly as a bar and clubhouse for the farmers and visiting fishermen in the area, as well as being the home of the local football club, whose training sessions on a Wednesday evening, had provided a noisy and fun acoustic backdrop to my somewhat quiet evenings. It also hosted the many *Feste* of the summer, and a semi-permanent marquee leant somewhat haphazardly to one side of the main building. I could only imagine how hellishly hot it must have been inside during the summer months when it was used for a series of communal events.

Despite being in a tiny hamlet, the area was well known, I was informed, for hosting the annual farmer's fair, complete with barbecues, hog roasts and disco. It also hosted the annual tractor festival where the farmers in the area would compete in agility and speed trials in their tractors, having first processed through the countryside, their gleaming machines bedecked with flowers and adorned with their wives, girlfriends and daughters, all in their best clothes. Telling me about these, Stefano had gazed reflectively into the middle distance, seeing the ghosts of his childhood when he had participated in these events but when the ploughs had been horse drawn and the carriages great wheeled carts which had seated up to twenty happy garlanded festival goers. He happily informed me that once he'd manage to steal a kiss from ALL of the girls in the cart "Even the *brutte,* the ugly ones"!

We walked slowly to the *Circolo*, and as we passed the original entrance to the great house he explained that with the advent of the motor car, the entrance archway had become too narrow and so a second driveway had been constructed, the one which we still used. Over the years part of the huge family had moved away and so the rear portion of the great house had been sold to the forebears of the man who now ran the *Circolo*, Enzo. Stefano remembered him as a baby, apparently his now ancient and almost totally blind and deaf father still lived in the other part, together with his immediate family and several cousins. Whereas in Stefano's part it was empty for most of the year, though Alberto, Ugo and Luisa came form time to time with their friends while Stefano was still down in the city. He loved that they loved and used the house when he was absent. I remarked that maybe the ghosts got lonely without company and he chuckled knowingly, looking at me sideways from beneath his eyebrows.

We reached the verandah of the *Circolo* and I hovered outside a little unsure whether to go in or not. Stefano beckoned me in and introduced me to the man behind the bar, Enzo.

"This is the Signora *Inglese* I told you about. She is to be an honorary member of the *Circolo*..." his declaration brooked no disagreement, even though it transpired that he himself wasn't actually a member!

I introduced myself properly and shook hands with Enzo, a solidly built man with dark curly hair, raisin-dark eyes and a wide happy smile. He was, to my mind, somewhat incongruously dressed in cut-off cargo pants and a very smart pair of trendy hiking sandals.

Somehow in this place, redolent with the history of his ancestors, I didn't expect him to be quite so modern, imaging him instead in nondescript day clothes, topped by a long white apron and sturdy boots. How wrong was I?! He didn't stand on ceremony and told me to call him Enzo, but I noticed that he used the formal "*Lei*" so I followed suit, not wanting to offend or worse, to embarrass Stefano with my foreign ways! Not for the first time I thought I was so glad that I had learned the social nuances of interacting with the Italians for despite the seeming informality there is a minefield of customs and manners to be negotiated. I have seen Italians wince imperceptibly when a well-meaning tourist greets them with a "*Ciao*" as opposed to a more formal "*Buon Giorno*"or "*Buona Sera*" depending on the time of day, or, if they have made the effort to learn some Italian, but just use the informal '*Tu*' which is regarded as impolite. In fact as little as a couple of decades previously people were still addressing their grandparents and the older generation as '*Voi*' the ultra formal version of 'You', like the French '*Vous*', but in Italian now only used as 'You' plural.

Inside the *Circolo* the bar was a large wood panelled room with an intriguing mural on one wall, featuring Matilda di Canossa but painted in a most eclectic, almost impressionist, style. Stefano told me he had commissioned it years earlier from a Russian painter who had turned up out of the blue. But that in true Russian fashion, or at least the cliche that is the general perception, the artist had turned out to be rather too fond of trying to find his muse through the almost continuous consumption of alcohol, the local *Grappa* being his particular choice and had spent most of his time bemoaning his lack of inspiration into a seemingly bottomless glass. The mural had taken far longer than anticipated and since Stefano was footing the bill for board and lodging - and no doubt *Grappa* - he soon outstayed his welcome and was told to finish the mural and then look for pastures new.

With the telling of this story I realised that while Stefano was incredibly generous and philanthropic he was no fool and would not allow anyone to take advantage of his generosity. I knew that my role in his life apart from being his tenant, was to provide companionship and conversation - something which I gladly accepted.

I loved hearing his stories and what better than to sit on the *Circolo's* verandah, with a cold beer looking at the great house, his great house, and hearing about times past. He told me that his ancestor came from Florence looking for land where he could build a substantial house for his family and extended family. He had found the lush and fertile Hamlet, complete with springs and an aquifer and thus well suited for his family's needs. Wells were sunk, stone quarried from nearby Monte Valestra and fruit trees planted. Slowly the great house took shape, accessed via a narrow driveway leading to an impressive entrance archway, just wide enough to admit a coach and horses. Various agricultural buildings were constructed around the huge central house, its three stories augmented with voluminous full-height attics to house an army of servants. Wood stores, hay barns, stables, a pigsty, a great barn for the ploughs and other agricultural machinery lay grouped around a huge central *cortile*, together with various smaller buildings to house the farm workers.

It was elegant without being grand, homely and welcoming yet with an air of genteel refinement, set in grounds abundant with vegetable and herb gardens, orchards and paddocks. The land surrounding the Hamlet was substantial, great green swathes of verdant grassland, mixed woodland chock full of boar and even wolves, the vineyards and hayfields stretched as far as the eye could see, and life in the area had revolved around the great house with its multi-generational family all living in impressive manorial style.

I loved the house and the area and the thought that I might be able to earn something from selling property filled me with hope. I was looking forward to meeting *Geometra* Bonini. Ugo had told me that he was extremely efficient and well-respected by the whole community and I knew that Stefano would enjoy hearing about my meeting with him and I looked forward to telling him all about it.

What I hadn't realised was that he had every intention of accompanying me!

So it was that two days later we drove into Carpineti, Stefano dressed up in his beautifully laundered Sunday shirt and trousers and me having dug something suitable out of the wardrobe that I'd worn for work in those seemingly long ago days in Verona. Was it really only a few months ago? I knew I scrubbed up well, Stefano eyed me appraisingly noting the light make up, the smart casual linen skirt and blouse, proper shoes as opposed to my usual purple Crocs and the fact that I'd swapped my usual small backpack for a smart Schiaparelli pink leather handbag from Furla. I felt as if I was going for an interview - which in a way I was.

We parked outside my bank and walked across the road to *Geometra* Bonini's studio. It was modern and welcoming and uncluttered. It looked extremely professional and I was interested to note that in the small reception area was an assortment of technical equipment, neatly stowed in black zipped bags. The lady who had showed us in, told us that the *Geometra* was on the phone and would we mind waiting. So we sat chatting quietly while I looked around. High vaulted wooden ceilings, more Scandinavian in style than rural Italian, smart grey tiled floors, light wood furniture and two surprisingly comfortable modern chairs on which to sit. A large multi-tasking photocopier and scanner stood in the corner next to a small fridge and a water cooler.

A voice emanated from the half open office door bidding us to come in, as we stood the *Geometra* appeared in the doorway apologising that he didn't speak English! I laughed and replied in Italian that it was not necessary. He was about 1.80 metres tall, muscular in a sporty sort of way with shaved head and some chic glasses perched on his forehead, laughing brown eyes regarded me and his open friendly face broke into a huge smile of relief as he heard me speak.

We were ushered into his office and I noted with amazement and absolute delight that on the wall was a large poster advertising Pink Floyd Live at Pompeii (from the 1970's) next to a smaller one of Steve McQueen on the motorbike in the famous shot from the film The

Great Escape. My favourite band and one of my favourite films, this was surely someone I could do business with!

We sat and Stefano explained who and what I was, getting wildly confused about my previous career and bigging me up shamelessly to the *Geometra,* who looked mystified. There are times when hyperbole is not necessary and Stefano's glowing account of my professional life while gratifying, was somewhat embarrassing in its effusiveness! I also didn't want to give the impression that some highfaluting international real estate executive was trying to muscle in to the *Geometra's* patch.

As Stefano spoke I appraised him. He wore jeans with a Polo shirt and expensive sports shoes. Casual yet elegant and business like. I felt overdressed. Looking around his office I saw that he was an Apple aficionado (as was I) and that a smart iMac took up most of his desk, alongside which lay the requisite iPhone and other Apple paraphernalia. At least we would be able to communicate via FaceTime as I also had an iPhone! I was intrigued to see that he sat not on a chair but on one of those fiendishly-uncomfortable Scandinavian stools which are apparently good for posture. He was fit looking and tanned and obviously worked out. He listened to Stefano attentively, looking at me from time to time with a half smile on his face as he saw me trying hard not to grimace at yet another superlative about my experience and abilities.

I grinned back at him and at the first opportunity, assured him that I had come to the Hamlet as a result of wanting to live somewhere peaceful and that my high-powered career was well and truly over!

However, if he was interested I would be delighted to discuss how we might be able to work together, me by bringing my knowledge of international real estate and the requirements of potential foreign clients and he by identifying suitable properties for them. I explained that this beautiful part of the world was almost entirely unknown to those outside it and that while neighbouring Tuscany was known worldwide, it seemed a little unfair that this area had been passed by and that the less stunning and seismically more vulnerable Umbria and Le Marche had succeeded Tuscany as the expats' regions of choice.

The *Geometra*, "please call me Paolo", agreed, looking surprised at my reference to earthquakes, and said that the local Mayor was more than keen to attract investment into the region. I was delighted to hear that and asked about the success of the existing estate agent in town. I made it very clear that I understood the difference between an Estate Agent who was not required to have professional qualifications and a *Geometra* who was. I realised that my time working in the Italian commercial real estate sector had served me well for I still had a pretty good idea of the Byzantine laws and regulations governing it. Not least the seismic codes!

Paolo looked thoughtful for a moment and answered most diplomatically to the effect that the local estate agent had a certain amount of success but that he had not had many dealings with foreign clients.

As we chatted, Stefano looked at me appraisingly, he'd never heard me talking business and I could see that he was a little surprised that I could hold my own in a discussion about earthquake regulations!

I had a good feeling about Paolo, he asked intelligent questions about the types of properties that foreign buyers were likely to find interesting. I suggested that perhaps we spent a morning together looking at some things that he had for sale and then I could tell him what might - and what might not - appeal to foreign, mostly British, purchasers.

He looked pleased and we agreed to meet at the end of the week. He asked what sort of properties I had in mind. I told him a mixture of properties ready to move into, both rustic and more modern, properties that required renovation and redevelopment (respecting the planning and seismic regulations) and anything else, quirky, like an abandoned village perhaps. He raised an eyebrow. "Abandoned village?"

"Yes. There are several examples in Tuscany and Umbria of foreigners buying and restoring dilapidated *borghi* and then selling the properties either off plan or completely redeveloped."

He was intrigued by this and asked me if I might be free all day on the Friday as there were several things that he thought might be suitable, including three abandoned villages! I was absolutely delighted and told him that anyone who had a Pink Floyd poster in his office was someone I could do business with. He laughed and at that moment the seeds of a productive collaboration and a good friendship were sown.

Stefano, sensing this, suggested we head to the bar next door for an *aperitivo*. Paolo demurred explaining that, regrettably, he had an appointment at the Planning Office in Castelnovo but that we would definitely reconvene to toast the introduction soon. He thanked Stefano for introducing me and as he walked us to the door he asked me which was my favourite Pink Floyd album! I told him and he laughed delightedly, saying that it was also one of his favourites. I liked this man and I was looking forward to discovering what he had for sale in this enchanting area.

Chapter 19

'an Englishman's house is his castle…'

As agreed, at 8.30am on the following Friday, Paolo came to pick me up. I was excited and looking forward to seeing what type of properties he was going to show me. What I was not prepared for was that I couldn't actually get into his 4x4, it was too high for my poor old knees to propel me into the passenger seat.

Paolo looked embarrassed and started to apologise for not having asked me whether getting in and out of his vehicle might be difficult. I told him not to worry and to hang on a minute as I disappeared back inside the *Tavernetta* and emerged triumphantly, brandishing one of those IKEA plastic step stools and a length of string. Now he looked perplexed as I hurriedly knotted the string and looped it through the extremely useful finger holes on one side of the stool. His perplexity turned to comprehension as I placed it firmly by the open door and, grasping the string tightly in one hand, stepped onto the stool and manoeuvred myself up and into the seat, still clutching the string. A huge grin split his face as I then, triumphantly, with a look that unequivocally said "Don't judge a book by its somewhat dilapidated cover" hauled the stool up into the car by the string, smiling smugly to myself!

"*Brava! Molto Saggia!*" Well done, very wise" he complimented me wholeheartedly while breathing a huge sigh of relief as I could see he had been dreading having to hoist me up into his vehicle by manhandling me by my somewhat voluminous backside - reminiscent of Benny Hill 'assisting' the large lady into the tram in the film 'The Italian Job'- except that Paolo didn't look like the sort of person that would have enjoyed it as much as Benny Hill's character had!

Equilibrium restored we set off. He explained that first we were going to Pantano, a small village between Carpineti and Casina to see a recently restored traditional stone house, then a modern purpose-built house and two other, older properties. I wasn't too sure about the second one as I was pretty sure that Brits looking to buy their dream holiday home, would dismiss a modern house but I kept an open mind.

The drive only took 20 minutes and I knew the road but had never made it as far as Pantano so was curious to see the lie of the land. I was not disappointed, it was every bit as beautiful as the area around the Hamlet with wide sweeping views of open meadows, woodlands and little groups of houses dotting the landscape. While time seemed to have stood still with regard to the look and the 'feel' of the place, each old house boasted a satellite dish and, more often than not, had a shiny car parked outside. The combination of the ancient with the modern always left me feeling slightly disconnected as if I was in a time-slip movie.

We turned off the main road by a wayside shrine and followed the winding lane down into what looked like cul de sacs, but which turned out to be an ancient and narrow road winding its way through a tiny piazza with a gorgeous little church and an incongruous and somewhat ugly modern set of swings, through a farmyard, much to the excitement of a dog who, thankfully, wasn't chained up and who leapt joyfully at the car, his great tongue lolling excitedly as Paolo cursed good-naturedly while skilfully avoiding squashing him. The road curved round to the left and I gasped with delight for, in front of me, was a view to die for. A group of ancient stone buildings, which seemed abandoned, sat at the edge of a wide meadow full of wildflowers with magnificent wide-ranging views and sitting portentously at the end of a long valley, just visible through the heat haze, was the Pietra di Bismantova.

I would have paid thousands on top of any house price just for that view and told Paolo so. He looked quizzically at me, enquiring whether people really took notice of such things. I knew that he was local, having been born in Valestra - Stefano had filled me in on his family history - so I wondered whether he was inured to the beauty of his surroundings and simply took them for granted. I explained that the sort of people who bought a second home, a holiday home, were buying a dream - and that dream encompassed many things not least the opportunity to sit on their verandah/terrace/loggia in the evenings sipping a glass of something cool and literally drinking in the view. Which is why Tuscany appealed to so many people on so many levels. The views were astonishing and the wine to die for! Add to that the appeal of a sensitively restored stone house (cool in summer and warm in winter), together with an acceptable price, and you were on to a winner!

"Ah, capisco. La panorama vale qualcosa…" Ah I understand, the view is worth something he said, nodding his head slowly. I realised that as he spoke no English, it was unlikely that he had come into contact with many Brits and therefore had absolutely no idea as to

281

what their likes and dislikes might be. I could see he was intrigued and eager to learn what was the magic formula for attracting foreign buyers. It was going to be an interesting day!

He slowed the Jeep and pointed at a building almost dead ahead. Shining softly in the sunshine was a creamy golden stone house. Three storeys high and nestling on the edge of a meadow it looked stunning. The doors, shutters and window frames were painted a smart greeny grey - very chic and modern but also totally in keeping with the stonework. A parking place alongside a very functional but attractive retaining wall of wire netted stone, was paved with slabs which matched the stonework. He pulled over and leapt out, I followed more slowly, having first to carefully lower the stool by the string, ensuring that it landed right side up and didn't tip over. Once it was in place I gingerly descended onto it and thence onto terra firma. Paolo had been talking to me when he realised that I wasn't actually behind him and that I was occupied elsewhere. He was mortified that he had forgotten his manners and not been there to assist me! I was charmed but assured him that I was perfectly capable and would ask for help if needed.

I turned my attention to the house, Paolo explained that while it had been constructed from the stones of an ancient chapel that had fallen into ruin nearby, it had been restored using cutting-edge eco technology and that he had Project Managed the job also ensuring that the state-of-the-art controls for heating and lighting and air circulation did what they were supposed to do. I was extremely impressed - even more so when he pressed a hidden button and the garage door (reclaimed and restored chestnut planks) opened noiselessly to reveal what I can only describe as a high tech control room! Like something out of a Bond movie.

Walking in he showed me the master controls for the house and explained that inside, there were individual controls not just for each floor but also for each room. All incorporated and juxtaposed into a beautiful traditional house with original features sitting elegantly alongside edgy modern touches such as the strikingly contemporary fireplace with eco woodburner, the steel staircase with tensioned steel-roped banisters and the stylish bathrooms. As in most new European houses the kitchen was plumbed and wired in, ready to welcome the units and islands which were conspicuous by their absence - leaving the final design to the buyer. A sensible solution I felt, not least because kitchens, like bathrooms, are an intensely personal choice.

Small windows set deep into the thick stone walls acted as focal points while larger windows and doors with capacious shutters opened the house up to the vistas and the air. The middle floor led out to a slate-paved terrace overlooking the stupendous view while the flooring inside was reclaimed polished hardwood throughout. The place was absolutely stunning and, even better, came with a large amount of land including some vines and an orchard.

The price was a fraction of what it would have been in Tuscany and I told Paolo this. He looked genuinely shocked at the amount that someone would have paid for this had it been on the other side of the mountains!

"If you can find more of these types of houses, you will be inundated with enquiries."

"Finished houses?"

"Yes, some, but there are also people who like a project - the opportunity to put their stamp on it and if they can deal with a reputable Surveyor/Project Manager like you then they will feel that their investment - and their dream - is safe"

"I understand."

Leaving me to wander around the house again, he disappeared into the control room to check the temperature and humidity levels and that everything was working properly. He'd told me that the owner lived in the very north of Italy, almost on the Austrian border, and he had retained Paolo's services to look after the property while it was for sale. He was also instructed to sell it, along with an agent from Reggio Emilia.

I was really impressed not only at the quality of the finishing on the house but also on the professionalism of Paolo. He took his duties seriously and, when he identified an anomaly in the humidity sensor, was on the phone immediately to the *Tecnico* to come and fix it. Not only a beautiful eco house but also a great 4G phone signal.

This reminded me to ask him about Wi-fi and broadband in this area. Of course there was the Eolo option but here there didn't appear to be a radio mast from which they could bounce the signal, so how could one get connected here? He explained to me that the Italian Government had a rural broadband initiative and that the Mayor of Carpineti, Tiziano Borghi, had recently attended a seminar and applied for funding as a result of what he had learned. It seems that the cabling for superfast wifi was to be laid in the roads of the entire municipality within a matter of a couple of months so that everyone, including the poor beleaguered farmers, could get properly online to submit their data and work - and students study - from home. Eolo would still be the service provider but there would no longer be the need to be within uninterrupted sight of a radio mast. How incredibly forward-thinking of the Mayor and I told Paolo that in England, which apparently he considered to be the zenith of civilisation, we were still waiting for decent rural broadband.

Yet again, Italy had done something so innovative that it would change people's lives. The people who lived in this Italy of olden times, tiny hamlets and groups of ancient-looking houses in this gentle beautiful region worked hard on the land from dawn to dusk yet due to this forward-thinking were be able to stream Game of Thrones (which Ugo told me had an avid Italian audience) or their programme of choice when they got home after a hard day's work without the need for the ubiquitous and ugly satellite dish and tonsured trees!

I remarked upon the foresight of the Dottor Borghi and was told that he and only one other Mayor from a municipality down in the south had attended the original seminar and applied for the grants. I imagined that there would soon be many many rural municipalities doing the same and wondered whether it was a case of 'first come first served' and that the grants were limited. I asked whether the initiative included my Hamlet. "Unfortunately not, you are in a different municipality, though by only a matter of metres...: he looked rueful. I muttered something about hoping that the Mayor of our municipality would be similarly far-sighted and got a non-committal grunt by way of reply. It seemed that I would have to continue to hope that the tree surgeon kept the sight lines clear to the radio mast for my antenna!

We left the property having greeted a farmer and his wife, neighbours, who had come to see what was going on. I remarked that it would be great for the owners of the house to have such vigilant neighbours - while knowing full well that many purchasers would actually see this advantage as a disadvantage. I explained this mentality to Paolo.

"There is a saying, that an Englishman's home is his castle" this means that we tend to like to keep to ourselves and often prefer not to interact with those who live nearby. He looked astonished, for in Italy it was the complete opposite. Everyone preferred being together, in families, in village communities and the like where they looked out for each other and came together for high days and holidays, proud to share their heritage and connection. As evidenced by events such as the farmer's annual parade and picnic. Of course there were exceptions - in both countries. I told him that I thought that part of the psychology of selling properties in this area was that in the absence of the owners, during the off-season months for example, they would be delighted to have a rapport with their neighbours who would keep an eye on their place and deal with any emergencies that might arise - without the need for hiring an expensive property management service - if such a thing existed in this area. He agreed, looking thoughtful.

"Of course, and there is always the potential for the 'foreigner' to endear himself to the neighbours by offering to teach their children or grandchildren English! Just a few words and phrases, nothing formal."

286

I thought that an excellent idea and told him so. I knew from my own experiences when I'd lived abroad before - alone - that interaction with the local community had been incredibly rewarding and that I had learnt so much from the association. Including some very choice phrases from the Greek fisherman I'd befriended in a tiny little village! That and a gift of fresh fish from time to time.

Having repeated the stool ritual (much to the amusement of the farmer's wife) and once again installed myself in the passenger seat, we drove back down the lane. I looked out over the stunning view and reckoned that anyone who had the foresight to buy this property would be very very happy in it. Especially at the price I'd been quoted.

We saw four other houses in the area - each completely different. The first one was relatively modern, occupied by a charming man and wife who, if the purchase price was acceptable, offered to teach the prospective purchaser some Italian and, even better, some local recipes! The *Signora* was an accomplished cook apparently - who wasn't in this area?! But what really stood out about her, for me, was how incredibly neat and tidy their house was. And how she'd managed to store absolutely everything in vast cupboards, so that upon opening them to show me, I was presented with row upon row of vacuum bagged linens, clothing, boxes of shoes, storage boxes of cleaning materials, an incredible walk-in larder with floor to ceiling shelving loaded with categorised items and a walk-in laundry room. Her husband, a jolly man who wanted to practise his English on me, was a businessman and had converted the lower floor into a massive office with views out over the surrounding countryside - enabled by its having been built on a small escarpment. I liked the house but knew that there were unlikely to be any English buyers interested in it as being modern and pretty featureless - in massive contrast to the previous property - it simply would not fit in with their dream of an Italian holiday home. However I wanted to talk to Paolo about the potential for other nationalities who perhaps valued function over form but also of the domestic market, Italians from the great hot plains of the Padana who wanted a lock and leave *seconda casa* in the cool hills of the area. This was surely a perfect property for them?

The third property was different again - owned by an eccentric artist and used as his summer home cum studio - it was chock full of his latest work - quirky, interesting and sometimes quite macabre artworks featuring birds' skulls, leaves, feathers, horns, different types of fabric and an extremely eclectic life-sized sculpture which resembled a cross between the Tin Man from the Wizard of Oz and some terrifying automaton from an American horror movie! The house itself was somewhat dilapidated but had great potential though it needed a lot of work and I was pretty sure that it would not appeal to most of the Brits - furthermore it would definitely have to have the artwork removed before considered fit for public viewing! Having said that, it did have a wonderful view and a small garden, just big enough for a south-facing swimming pool. So there were possibilities.

Our last stop before lunch was a two-storey older property, currently divided into two reasonably good-sized apartments, the top one reached by a somewhat rickety wooden outer staircase. Both of which were let during the summer months. Solidly built and with a massive storage room at lower ground floor level, it stood in an immaculate and beautiful garden, one in which the owner, who, to my mind, resembled the singer Tom Jones, took obvious pride. As we walked around it he proudly pointed out various species of trees and plants, which though beautiful sadly left me somewhat confused, not least because I didn't speak horticultural Italian nor knew the Latin names when he tried them on me. Gardening was obviously one of his passions and I could envisage him sitting in the garden enjoying the far-ranging views and the adjacent flower-filled meadow - once again an ideal spot for a pool.

We said our goodbyes and as we drove off I reflected how different each of the properties had been and all within 3 kilometres of each other. I asked whether the area had anything like a shop or bar and was told that we'd stop off at the small bar on our way to Marola for lunch. At the top of the hill, opposite a tiny ancient chapel nestling in the shade of some cypress trees, was a large bar with small area set up as a shop selling local produce - reminiscent of the shop that Rebecca and her brother ran in Levizzano. Surrounded by a shady verandah and with a restaurant at the rear, it was a perfect place to stop for a coffee, a drink, a meal, a *panino* or even an ice cream. It even had a bus stop on the route to Carpineti from Reggio Emilia - frequency once a day. The owner, Luca was all smiles and very welcoming - smiling even more broadly when Paolo told him that I was possibly going to help him find English people to buy some of the properties in the area.

"My son is learning English, in fact he's flying to London tomorrow to go to summer school. Federico, come here and meet the *Signora*." Federico, a good-looking boy of about 15 came forward and shyly said hello in English. I replied in English and he looked uncomfortable.

"Dai, parla Inglese con la Signora…" his father told him to reply to me in English. He muttered that he hadn't understood what I'd said and that I had a strange accent! I laughed and asked him, in Italian, where his English teacher came from. He said that she was Italian - I explained in that case that she was the one who probably had a strange accent! I repeated myself very slowly again in English, asking him where he was going to summer school. This time he understood me and somewhat haltingly told me, at which point I nearly fell off the bar stool, for he was going to be studying English in the very school that both my Grandfathers had, quite coincidentally attended at the same time, in the ancient and historic market town of Oundle, a couple of hours from London!

I told him I knew the town and the school and told him of my family connection. His father said "this is an omen" and offered Paolo and I an *aperitivo* to toast the coincidence. I felt a bit like Humphrey Bogart in Casablanca when he said " of all the gin joints in all the world, she has to walk into mine…" of all the summer schools in England Federico is going to the one closely connected with my grandfathers and great uncles… coincidence and a spooky one! Was this a sign that my endeavours in Italy would be looked upon favourably by my male ancestors?!

Paolo exclaimed *"ma dai"* which basically means "goodness me..." and we toasted each other and Federico's English summer. I hoped he would enjoy his time there and return to Pantano with some happy memories.

We clambered back into the Jeep and drove the short distance to the *Enoteca dal Portico* in Marola, where my descent from the 4x4 was observed with astonishment and some quite loud comments in the local dialect which made Paolo blush! I resisted the urge to enquire further. Little did I know that this place was famed far and wide for its excellent homemade cooking. It looked really nice and comprised a largish shop to one side and the restaurant part to the other, complete with a small *terrazza* for alfresco eating.

Run by a family, with mother and grandmother in the kitchen and brother and sister front-of-house, the *Enoteca* was already full and buzzing. They obviously knew Paolo well and found us a table - the last one - in the corner overlooking yet another gorgeous view. Bringing us the menu, I looked at Paolo, knowing that he would absolutely not allow me to pay so I suggested that we went for the *Pranzo di Lavoro* and not the a la carte menu. I had guessed by the apparent quality of the food on the tables as we had passed, that the latter could be expensive and that was before I'd even seen the range of wine bottles in the cabinet to one side!

A pretty girl who looked to be in her early 20's came and recited to us the list of the day's specials and we both chose the same; no antipasto, we would start with penne with local sausage sauce (*ragu al salsiccia*) , followed by *vitello tonnato*, a mixed salad for me and *patate fritte* for Paolo who informed me that he loathed vegetables! A litre carafe of light *frizzante* wine magically appeared, together with two half litre bottles of mineral water, one still, one sparkling, and an '*assaggio*' a little taster of some smoked fish, which was delicious, to whet our appetites.

We talked like old friends. Non stop. The courses came and went, all were the epitome of traditional cooking at its very best - I could see why this place was held in such high esteem - the wine flowed and we decided on a second carafe. We discussed many things, including the wants and needs of foreign buyers so I explained my concept of the psychology of selling. I explained that when I'd been an estate agent in London by using a little psychology I'd been fortunate to match properties to buyers.

Paolo was fascinated as I explained my modus operandi and we agreed that there were many more properties to see. Including the hidden villages. Mentally I thanked Stefano for the introduction, I really hoped that I could work with Paolo on what looked to be becoming some sort of thoroughly enjoyable joint initiative.

Chapter 20

'Degustibook' Luisa's ladies

I returned home full of excitement. Meeting Paolo, spending the day with him and seeing the properties had given me back a sense of purpose. Over lunch we had discussed other properties he knew of, ranging from a small castle, to *case coloniche*, old farmhouses. Some done up, some in need of total redevelopment and all within the 'bowl' bounded by the roads and the mountains I'd come to know pretty well. I could see that he too was enthusiastic about the possibilities of working together and interested in learning what sort of properties the Brits - and other nationalities - might like. We left agreeing to meet again the following week to visit more houses, but that I would go into the office on Tuesday and we'd discuss the mechanics of our collaboration.

Driving into the courtyard I was astonished to see several cars parked, objects of much curiosity for the cats, who were lying draped across bonnets and roofs taking the evening sun. Little dusty paw prints marked their passage from one formerly spotless car to another. Looking at them somewhat bewildered, wondering why there were suddenly so many cars, I remembered that Stefano had told me that Luisa and her book group, *Degustibook*, came up to the Hamlet for a literary weekend every summer and that he returned to his flat in Reggio for a couple of days as he found 'the old chickens' as he called them, too much to cope with.

I parked outside the *Tavernetta* and paused briefly in the loggia wondering whether I should go and introduce myself when Luisa appeared.

"Cass, come and meet my friends"

I followed her to find a large group of smiling ladies of all shapes and sizes, seated around the inner courtyard, chairs and cushions had materialised from the depths of the house and the *stalla* and I saw that glasses of wine were already on the glass table. Luisa introduced me and I replied in Italian drawing gasps of amazement from the group.

"But you speak Italian really well" said one magnificent looking lady, already suntanned to the colour of walnut and wearing a wonderful voluminous kaftan. I thanked her and took the proffered seat. Looking around the group I could see their friendly curiosity and I was subjected to a barrage of questions. "Where was I from? Did I like it here? How come I spoke such good Italian? How did I get on with Stefano? Was I alone?" I answered all their questions and explained about Geisha who, no doubt, was waiting impatiently inside for her supper, having been alone all day. I excused myself saying that I had to see to her and was told by Luisa to return later as I was invited to join them all for dinner at the huge table under the loggia.

Two ladies, Tiziana and Maria, asked if they could come and see Geisha and the *Tavernetta*. Of course they'd known it as an empty storage space before my arrival and were no doubt keen to see how it had translated into a home. Of course I said yes and they accompanied me, oohing and aahing at the visible signs of my occupation, from the chairs and little table in the little portico where Farah and I would sit in the afternoons and talk, to the gaily patterned fly curtain that I'd installed over the door and the cat gate which in theory prevented the cats from invading Geisha's space when the door was open. Once inside they headed for Geisha, murmuring endearments to her, which she seemed to enjoy. She didn't stop purring and allowed them to stroke her, rubbing her head affectionately against their bejewelled hands.

They chattered away to her, and me, intrigued as to how I found life here in the mountains, how I liked being alone, what did I do, talking all the time while wandering through the building, exclaiming at the amount of books, the family silver and other pictures that were displayed in the huge oak cabinet that Ugo had rightly insisted stay in situ. It had become one of the most useful pieces of furniture I had, for it held so much, in a pleasing arrangement of drawers and glass-fronted cupboards. My family photos in their silver frames became the object of much curiosity, as did my somewhat eclectic taste in DVDs, CDs and books, all of which filled the IKEA bookcases we'd bought in Bologna.

Heading off to inspect the *zona notturna*, bedroom and bathroom, they seemed delighted by my walnut sleigh bed and my choice of bedding, lamps and bathroom furnishings.

I was enchanted by their friendliness and interest and really warmed to them. Explorations over, they returned to where I had given Geisha her supper and suggested that she might like to be introduced to the others? Her beauty would amaze them all, not least her cerulean blue eyes, her perfectly symmetrical markings and her unmistakably imperial air of hauteur! So as to keep her safe in case the farm cats decided to investigate too closely, I put her into a wide basket, with a folded pillowcase to protect her arthritic hips and, grabbing a bottle of Prosecco to contribute to the evening, we went to join the others.

Rounding the corner I stopped in amazement, for all the ladies had disappeared. Following the sounds of laughter, we found them crowded into the kitchen where, en masse, they were preparing and cooking the dinner, for 20, without so much as batting an eyelid. Geisha was briefly introduced to everyone, to much cooing and petting, accompanied by little words of endearment which she received as was her due, then turning a weary eye on me, basically asked to be returned home as if all this adoration was too much for her.

Obeying, I took her back and left her to settle while I returned to the kitchen, wondering how I could help. Encountering the force of nature that is Italian women in a kitchen, I felt woefully inadequate and knew that even if I was given the simplest task, I would not perform it to their rightly exacting standards. So I volunteered to lay the long table. My offer was accepted and accompanied by two more friendly and inquisitive ladies, we repaired to the shaded loggia, where the cane blinds hung down the open side, swinging gently in the evening breeze. The scent from the climbing roses was heady and almost overpowering, the old table, cut from a trunk of some very old and very heavy oak tree, had already been brushed. The heavy benches, also oak, were softened by the addition of long cushions in the striped yellow fabric that seemed to be the 'look' for the Hamlet's outdoor furnishings, scatter cushions had been placed in the four chairs, two at each end, and the side tables were already groaning under the weight of heavy ceramic plates, robust serving bowls, napery and cruet. Woven rush placemats were on the table and great jugs of water, with weighted crocheted covers protecting them from the flies and assorted flying pests, stood next to upturned wine and water glasses. I found the cutlery and laid the places, briefly wondering whether the way I had been taught by my mother was the same way here in Italy. One never thinks of these things, but getting them wrong would only serve to highlight the differences between us and I badly wanted to integrate.

Luckily I'd got it right and no one kindly but surreptitiously altered the place settings! I even managed to find the napkins and put them beside the *sotto piatti*, the large decorative plates that go underneath the actual eating plates at an Italian table.

Returning to the kitchen for large salad bowls, I was greeted by the most amazing sight, the ladies were in groups of two and three, each group occupied with a specific task. One was chopping tomatoes and red onions and tearing lettuce for the huge salad bowls. Another was actually hand making tortellini and I knew that the filling would also have been '*fatto a mano*'. Yet another group were washing and rinsing additional glassware for the table, drying it with great white dishcloths completed the operation so that everything was clear and sparkling. Two ladies stood over each of the two stoves stirring delicious-smelling things in the vast and ancient copper saucepans. The same copper saucepans that had been hanging in the kitchen for decades if not centuries probably. All the accoutrements for this huge meal alfresco, had appeared from the bowels of the massive oak and chestnut chests that lined the *cantina*. The *cantina* door was open and the sound of the prosciutto slicer rebounded off the curved ceiling. Great plates of mouthwatering prosciutto, protected by more huge white cloths, were being prepared and in a corner, another lady was busy with one of the fierce-looking Parmesan knives, hacking a massive cheese into edible chunks. Olives, small and black, appeared from a massive kilner jar, onions in vinegar and tiny pickled cucumbers from others.

Not being able to infiltrate any of the work groups, I fetched and carried, feeling completely in awe of the scenes of perfectly coordinated domestic harmony and teamwork. Being a loner I'd never really participated in anything like this and watching these ladies do something so completely natural to them, all the while laughing and chatting, each group perfectly in sync with the next, I was conscious of my own shortcomings. If asked, I simply could not have done anything like this and I felt useless and self conscious, my almost total lack of domestic skills for the first time in my life causing me real consternation. So I retreated to the loggia and made myself useful there, ensuring that everything was perfectly in order, that there were enough salad servers and serving spoons, that the bowls for the freshly grated Parmesan were full and covered with those little crocheted covers and their serving spoons laid to one side. I checked the salt and pepper, knowing that it was probably a huge insult to want or need to add condiments to the food as it would already have been perfectly seasoned.

I fetched straw baskets full of wine bottles, noting that my paltry offering of a bottle of not bad Prosecco had been politely stowed in the cantina. I left the group to its time-honoured and finely honed practises knowing that I could add nothing.

But I could! All was not lost, I'd noticed that the mosquitoes were beginning to become troublesome as the weather warmed. So I'd bought several of the huge citronella candles that one lit when eating outside and although their scent was a bit overpowering I knew that even the Italians suffered from mosquito bites, so I could actually be useful after all! I hurried back to the *Tavernetta*, found four large candles and took them back where I placed them strategically, having first checked the direction of the breeze so that their smoke didn't overpower the delicious food and ruin the dinner, or set the hanging bamboo blinds alight.

My foresight was appreciated by one lady who had introduced herself as Carla. She told me that the tiger mosquitoes which had infiltrated Italy in the late 1990's were now a huge pest, not only did they fly during the day, but they didn't need to be near water as did their less invasive counterparts. They were also responsible for carrying the Zika virus and, due to global warming had proliferated in Europe. I'd always been a target for mosquitoes and for years had carried bottles of a wonderful but DEET-filled product called Mosquito Milk which had proved hugely effective against them. However prolonged use of anything containing DEET was not good for one and might actually have explained certain aspects of my poor health. So I had started investigating and investing in portable electronic ultra violet devices, which could be charged via USB and which had actually proved to be pretty effective.

Not everything about life in the Hamlet was totally wonderful and the proliferation of mosquitoes was the main negative. But one that could be controlled! Even Stefano had been complaining about them a few days earlier. So my foresight was appreciated by one and all, even though the smell from the candles somewhat overpowered the perfume of the roses.

Dinner was ready, the ladies arrived in groups; those who had elected to do the serving came carrying huge plates of prosciutto, Parmesan, *coppa* and other cold meats. Great loaves of bread had materialised too and the wine was unstopped. We all sat, I was put on a chair at one end of the table, opposite Luisa at the other end and close to a lovely lady called Anna. I can honestly say that this was one of the best meals I'd ever had. Delicious home made food, twenty fun and interesting ladies whose mutual affection was palpable and the sounds of a Hamlet evening. As the sun went down, fireflies, *'lucciole'* appeared and the orchard took on an even more magical aspect. The cats, attracted by the smell of prosciutto and then the meat, formed a semi circle just outside the candlelight, their eyes gleaming and their tails twitching. They seemed to know that at the end of the meal there would be treats so they sat and waited patiently, which was pretty impressive for a bunch of semi feral cats!

In my relief at being accepted into the group and the object of many good-natured questions, I had a couple of glasses too many of wine, but managed to lose my shyness though thankfully not my manners. One of the questioners asked what I had been doing in the months I'd been in the area and I told them about my excursions and adventures and how intrigued I was about Matilda di Canossa. I realised that I actually knew a lot about her and the ladies seemed impressed. They of course knew about her, but possibly not in the way that I did. She had always been an historical figure to them but to me she was something more, her achievements 900 years earlier were nothing sort of astonishing and she had a sort of mystical quality to her. I was astounded when Luisa and two of the other ladies, Anna among them, asked me if I'd lead a group of them to Matilda sites sometime, as they'd like to know her better and maybe even see her through my eyes. I asked whether they wouldn't find it odd being told about one of their major historical figures by a foreigner. They told me that they would be interested in my objectivity and viewpoint on her and they admitted that they actually knew very little about her, other than what they'd been taught at school. So I gracefully accepted the challenge, wondering how on earth I was going to manage to produce something interesting and worthwhile. Taking another sip of wine I mulled over the prospect.

Dessert and fruit followed and then Prosecco and *Nocino* and I realised that the ladies were probably going to party all night and that, after my day with Paolo, I was actually very tired. I didn't want to seem to be a *guastafeste* - spoilsport - so I slipped away, pretending that I was needed the bathroom and crept off to my bed and Geisha, feeling guilty that I wasn't there to help clear up and hoping that this lapse would be forgiven.

The next morning, despite a very late night - I had woken periodically to the sound of gales of laughter and good-natured banter - the ladies were none the worse for wear, the place was spotless and they were awaiting the arrival of a meditation and mindfulness instructor for the day. Following which they were going to walk into Valestra and back (about 6 kilometres in searing heat) and then no doubt start preparing another huge meal. Not wanting to be in the way of these indefatigable women I decided that I would strike while the iron was hot and head for the castle of Canossa in search of Matilda and her story.

Chapter 21

'The Woman who changed the course of history'

The drive to Canossa was stunning, if a little confusing at times. The road necessitated a short stretch on the SS63 *superstrada* which ran between Castelnovo and Reggio and which, being dual carriageway, was fast. Far faster than I had become used to on the country roads. A torturous and somewhat badly-signposted looped feeder road fed into the fast-moving traffic and, being a right hand drive car, my wing mirrors were badly positioned to see in my blind spot, the place where the rear view mirror and the wing mirror were supposed to overlap. Gunning the engine I shot into slow lane and almost immediately into the cavernous black maw of a tunnel under the steep hill. My SatNav had told me to exit at the end of the subsequent tunnel, but I was disquieted by the signpost which pointed me towards Casina, the road I wanted to take. So I took the exit despite the admonition of Ben Whishaw, the voice of my SatNav. My mistake was immediately obvious and Ben's somewhat hectoring tone underscored this, not least because getting back onto the road was going to prove difficult. Italian road planners seem to have the most extraordinary habit of designing on and off ramps to be as torturous and incomprehensible as possible. I have driven all over Europe for many years and nothing like these has ever been encountered elsewhere. I can only assume that the planners are not motorists, but cyclists or even pedestrians, for trying to get back onto the road to continue my journey was nigh near impossible.

In fact so difficult was it that I ended up going back, via a twisty road, to my original on ramp, through another pitch black tunnel, following an elegant but nonetheless mystifying series of loops to retrace my steps and start again. This time I stayed firmly in the slow lane and was not lured by the siren song of Casina and its undoubted many attractions. Stoically I continued for another few kilometres until the correct exit, placed literally at the end of a second tunnel, hove into view giving me no time to brake and offering me no alternative but to swing dramatically onto the feeder road, screaming to a halt at a massive crossroads by a supermarket car park and looking frantically for the signs to Canossa, which were conspicuous by their absence.

Ben quietly informed me that I should turn left and, with a sigh of relief, I found myself on familiar terrain, a quiet country road with steep bends and breathtaking views. For twenty minutes or so I swung up around corners, occasionally meeting a 4x4 Panda or van coming in the other direction. The landscape was different, softer and more wooded and more open. Beautifully restored old houses and little groups of stone houses perched on either side of the road and I noticed several interesting-looking cafes, bars and Trattorias. In one village, with a stunning view of the distant Pietra di Bismantova, I parked the car in a small gravelled lay-by and crossed the road to the bar outside which stood several aluminium tables and white garden chairs. Since smoking wasn't permitted indoors anywhere in Italy, smokers would smoke outside and watch the world go by. Entering through the squeaky door I walked over to the bar, a bright modern Gaggia coffee machine and a display case of delicious-looking homemade pastries waiting for me. I ordered my usual *caffe* Americano, much to the disgust of the barista who snorted with disgust at my request. I explained that if I had too much caffeine I could become '*isterica*', hysterical, at which point he guffawed and said that it might be worth the risk! I laughed with him and reckoned that my small joke had now enrolled me into the club of 'ok foreigners'. Looking around the bar, I saw that it was clean and spacious and reckoned that it might actually be a good stop for coffee if the ladies and I ever made it to Canossa.

My other litmus test was the loo. Thankfully it was ok and smelt pleasantly of beeswax.

Behind the bar was a dining room, which would comfortably seat 50, useful to know for possible future sorties. I wondered what the cooking was like. Then told myself not to be so silly, the cook would be the wife or mother of the bar owner, so of course the food would be *cucina casalinga* and no doubt superb.

I took my coffee and brioche (delicious and freshly baked) out to the table and sat there alternately admiring the stunning flowers and plants of the house opposite and checking my emails on my phone for there was a strong signal. I loved the juxtaposition of the intensely rural location and the high tech advantages of 4G. There was an email from my *Commercialista* in Florence, suggesting that I needed to contact him. I ignored it, it was, after all the weekend and what on earth was he doing emailing me on a Saturday morning?! He needed to get a life!

The barman came out for a chat, having seen my car he, like everyone else, was curious about it and me. Having satisfied his curiosity I asked him if he'd always lived here. He had, or rather his family had - for generations. I looked somewhat askance at the beautiful big modern house opposite and, seeing my look, he explained that it had been built on the site of the former family house. I asked him if planning had been difficult and although surprised at my question, he said that it had all been done "*secondo le norme*" according to the planning laws, and that there had been no problem whatsoever. Useful to know for potential house buyers, though it was in a different *Comune*, the law was the law. I asked him if there were *terremoti* here and he said no, only the occasional *frana* - landslide. And that only usually after extremely heavy rain. He explained, as had Paolo, that the seismic laws made a lot of sense. He asked me where I was going and I told him, Canossa. "Well there you will see the remains of the great castle. The major part of it fell down as the result of an earthquake, after the angry people of Reggio had dismantled a large part of it and its church following the death of Matilda. Mario in the small museum there knows the story."

I thanked him, grateful for the information and reflected how generous with their knowledge these people were and how justifiably proud of their heritage. I finished my coffee, bade him goodbye and climbed back into the car for the last twenty minutes or so before I arrived in Canossa. I wasn't sure what to expect but I was intrigued.

Canossa castle, or the ruins thereof, was perched precariously atop a steeply-sided rocky scree-covered hill dominating the skyscape for miles around. In its heyday it had been one of the most impregnable castles in Italy, protected by a triple line of walls, a barracks and housing for servants. It had also included a small Benedictine monastery and the church of Sant'Apollonio. It looked dark and forbidding, not at all like the beautiful and much more serene castle at Carpineti. However it had played an important part in the history of Europe, the centre of the almost continuous war between the German Holy Roman Empire and the Pope in Rome.

Matilda had played a pivotal role in the events of several decades as well as founding or restoring Abbeys, Hermitages and places of sanctuary on the *Sentiere,* the pathways or routes that offered safe travels for pilgrims and others throughout her lands. She had also assisted in the foundation of the Law School at the fledgling university of Bologna, Europe's first. By all accounts she had been an impressive woman, and I wanted to know more about her.

While there were the hugely informative Wikipedia entries - both Italian and International - what had really intrigued me were several excellent books on her written by three foreign females. Michele K Spike, an American academic who had lived in Florence, had written a scholarly and fascinating biography of Matilda, a book on the Hundred Churches built or endowed by Matilda and her mother, Beatrice of Lorraine and she had also curated a stunning exhibition in Florence about Matilda and her life, entitled 'The Woman Who Changed the Course of History'.

Selma Sevenhuijsen, a Dutch Academic, had written a book - Queen of the Vatican - which contained a much more esoteric but nonetheless fascinating portrait of Matilda which intrigued me.

There was also Kathleen McGowan's popular fiction book, The Book of Love which was a romanticised version of the life of Matilda which focused on the esoteric and spiritual sides of this enigmatic woman, suggesting that she was part of a secret society originating with Mary Magdalene and The Holy Grail. The more I had investigated this side of her, the more intriguing things became. I found works alluding to her esotericism not only by these three foreign women, but also by Italians who lived and worked in Matilda's lands and still wrote about her, almost a thousand years after her death. It was this side that I wanted to show Luisa and her friends for I felt that they might be tantalised by the numinous side of her personality.

I'd done quite a lot of research and I now wanted to see if I could get a hint of her in the castle that had been her family seat.

Driving up to the forecourt below the castle, I parked the car and walked in the hot sunshine to the little shop that stood open at the bottom of the steep steps climbing up to the castle. It was cool inside and, to my absolute delight, stuffed full of books in Italian, English, Dutch and German by the authors I'd come across as well as others; there were posters, reproductions of paintings and medieval weaponry and bottles of wine - the labels proclaiming them to be Matilda and Enrico IV, the German Holy Roman Emperor who had come to Canossa literally on his knees to beg forgiveness from Pope Gregory

VII and with the intercession of Matilda, to ask for his excommunication from the church to be lifted.

The man behind the till introduced himself as Mario, in English. I replied in Italian and with a big smile he launched into the story of Matilda and Enrico IV. I listened for a couple of minutes then told him that I was actually interested in the more esoteric side of Matilda which elicited much more interesting and exciting information from him! He showed me several books which might fit the bill and also insisted that I go and have a look at the Labyrinth which had been created at the foot of the hill, by Selma, the Dutch academic who was very much a champion of Matilda. The labyrinth was a nod to that of Chartres inasmuch as it follows the shape but also, more prosaically, it mirrors the finger labyrinth carved into a pillar of the Duomo of San Martino in Lucca. Something that was done in the time of Matilda.

Walking the labyrinth, any labyrinth, is a mystical experience and I thought that the one in Canossa would be ideal for the ladies in September. It didn't seem too esoteric a pursuit for them and would fit neatly with their meditation and mindfulness experience.

Mario introduced me to his partner, Federica, who had designed the most wonderful Tarot pack based on Matilda and who was welcoming and enthusiastic about my project and my interest. They were both incredibly generous with their information and suggested more books and pamphlets that might be useful. If I was going to put together a proper tour I wanted to make sure that it was at least correct in as much detail as possible. Luisa's ladies didn't strike me as people who would accept anything less than well-documented facts!

Talking to Mario and Federica I told them where I'd already been and wondered if there was anything else that I should see? They mentioned a church, founded by Matilda in Neviano degli Arduini where, according to legend, she had fulfilled the conditions set down by Gregory VII when she had, somewhat scandalously, asked to lead a Mass. Such was the depth of her faith that he had acquiesced, but only if she had restored or dedicated one hundred churches. This was to be the hundredth and legend has it that she was indeed allowed to lead the Mass but that there had been an 'incident' which means she had been unable to complete it. This I had to see. After the labyrinth and the castle.

The climb to the castle was long and hot, many many steps rose inexorably upwards, the stark outlines of the ruined ramparts silhouetted against the vivid blue of an unpolluted summer sky. My vertigo caused me to stop often and I made slow progress upwards, hanging on to the stone sides of the walls as the path wound ever higher. Finally exiting onto the plateau that had been the keep, I sank gratefully onto a bench and, having recovered my breath, peered somewhat gingerly over each edge to take in the view. The castle was in an impressive location and across the valley I saw another, the castle of Rossena and the more distant tower of Rossenella all part of Matilda's strongholds in the lands that came to be named after her, the *Terre Matildiche*.

To my surprise I felt strangely uncomfortable at Canossa, I couldn't tune into Matilda or resonate with the energy and when I was asked if I'd like to walk the Labyrinth, I politely declined, saying that

I needed to get on as I had other places to visit that day, but that I would return and discuss with Mario and Federica the details of the forthcoming visit. We said goodbye, as I and the several books I had bought, headed back down the hill and across country to try to find the Hundreth Church.

Ben Whishaw was tested to his limits as his voice led me through tiny farmyards, barely wide enough for my car, into an impenetrable village piazza which was too small for the car to manoeuvre, to the amusement of the group of walkers resting in the shade. Between them shouting instructions at me and several multi-point turns, I managed to extricate myself and found the right road to the church. Situated in a dense pine wood, it had proved to be quite hard to find, but a signpost to a Seminary (full of fresh-faced youth) and a smaller one to the church led me to the right place and there standing in the afternoon sunshine was a beautiful little Romanesque *pieve*. The Pieve di Sasso, Matilda's hundreth church. Nestling in a clearing it was surrounded by pine trees through which a cooling breeze whispered. A most welcome and strategically placed bench leant somewhat haphazardly against the base of a tree. Insects buzzed, birds sang and yet the air was filled with a deep and profound sense of peace. Why this little church had been built in the middle of wood, miles from the nearest settlement was not lost on me, for this was a place of sanctity. The energy was palpable and I felt close to tears. I also felt close to Matilda, something which, despite my interest in her, I'd not, heretofore, experienced.

My feeling was that this place was somewhere special to her and walking to the big oak door, I was disappointed but unsurprised to find it was locked and a yellowing notice, barely protected from the elements, announced that the key was available from a Signora, the *Custode*, in the village. There was also a phone number. While I would have liked to have gone inside and spent time in the beautifully simple church, I didn't fancy meeting the key holder and all that could entail so I contented myself with wandering around the outside. A steep scramble up the hill along one side brought me to a somewhat curious stone, a monolith, carved with the representation of a woman's face. Could this be Matilda? A glass jar of nearly dead flowers lay at its base alongside a couple of those votive candles that shine a light in the darkness at gravesides. It was obviously a place of pilgrimage to someone or several someones and I paused briefly. The carving didn't look ancient so I guessed that it must be more modern - but surely it WAS a representation of Matilda? Or the Earth Mother? Whatever it was, it meant a lot to some people and I found that moving.

Turning away from the spot I passed the bell tower just as the bell clanged, frightening the life out of me and making me jump. Of course it was only marking the half hour - or was it - for my phone told me it was twenty to the hour. I took it as a welcome and went and laid my hands on the worn stonework, still warm from the sunshine. I liked this place and wanted to just sit and absorb its energy, but time was moving on and I needed to get home - not least to Geisha who although supportive of my days out, really preferred it when I was at home, spoiling her and watching a film or reading a book with her purring on my knee. I was also getting hungry.

Reluctantly I took my leave, having first noted down the name and number of the *Custode*, and picking up a couple of pine cones and a small stone as a souvenir of the place I headed for home, noting two interesting looking bars which definitely needed further investigation on my next trip. I knew I would return before September and I was looking forward to it, for the place had really affected me and I wanted to spend more time there.

Arriving home I was greeted with enthusiasm by several of the ladies who had moved their sun loungers into the outer courtyard by the *Tavernetta* to catch the last rays of the sun. I was tired and had a headache coming on and simply didn't feel as if I could cope with another exuberant evening, so I made my excuses and headed into the cool interior hoping that Luisa and her ladies would understand the somewhat odd foreigner who liked being alone - an anathema to most of the Italians I've spoken to! Solitude, to me, is a luxury to be fiercely preserved and solitude with my cat and some relaxing music was what I needed.

Chapter 22

Of house hunting and shiny things

Tranquility had returned to the Hamlet, Stefano had returned and he and I had firmly settled back into our coffee and blood-letting routine. That morning, once this had been achieved I headed into Carpineti for a meeting with Paolo. It felt good for my days to have purpose once again, rather than just drifting - albeit happily so - and as I swung the car round the curves in the road below the steep stone cliff of Monte Valestra I mentally went through what we needed to discuss. There was so much - where to start?

I parked outside his office and climbed slowly up the steep stone steps, thankful for the hand rail. My knees were getting worse and now that I was probably heading back home to Britain at some point in the not-too-distant future, I knew I'd have to wait for them to be seen to there. The Italian health system is amazing, but now that I was effectively without work there is no guarantee that I would have been treated - my Tessera Sanitaria had just expired so all I had was my E111 European Health Card which technically entitled me to treatment but that was no guarantee given the vagaries of the looming Brexit!

I pressed the buzzer and the door clicked. Pushing it open I walked into Paolo's office, my cheery *Buon Giorno* dying on my lips as I saw that he was in a meeting. I sat down in the reception area and got out my phone to see if I could find his Wi-fi and once he was free, ask for the password so that we could work efficiently as and when required.

As I sat, I prepared a mental review of the properties we'd seen the previous Friday. A sort of SWOT analysis as to the pros and cons from the viewpoint of a potential foreign purchaser, which I knew he'd find useful.

Half listening to his conversation with the somewhat grizzled elderly man in his office, I realised I didn't understand a word! They were speaking in Dialect, which to my ears, sounded more like French than Italian. I wondered why. I knew from my conversations with Stefano that the area had had many incomers and invaders throughout history who had strayed and settled, but I couldn't place French ones. I was, however, absolutely sure that he would know the answer.

Paolo's meeting was coming to an end, he had risen from his desk and was attempting to politely shepherd the somewhat garrulous old man out of his office, but he wasn't having any of it and stood in the doorway angrily gesticulating about something. Paolo looked at me and smiled, obviously explaining to his agitated friend that he had a foreign visitor, I heard a word that sounded like '*etrangere*' stranger or foreigner in French. The man stopped and looked closely at me, seemed to recognise me and transformed into a charming smiling version of his other self!

He turned and asked Paolo a question, the answer was a nod, which elicited a big grin and a gruff "*Buon Giorno Signora*". I responded and smiled as he moved past me towards the open door, directing a knowing look back at Paolo as he left.

Paolo laughed and ushered me into his office, explaining that I was becoming well-known in town and that no one quite seemed to know the extent of my relationship with Stefano! I chortled and exclaimed that Stefano was almost old enough to be my father! *"Eh Beh"* he responded looking amused. 'Eh Beh' is a wonderful expression, it is pretty much untranslatable but used properly can convey many meanings, something along the lines of 'whatever' would probably have best described it in this instance. I raised an eyebrow at him, amused.

He headed back around his desk and settled himself elegantly onto his Swedish stool, I grimaced and sat on the chair the angry farmer had just vacated. We went through the technical formalities of my hooking up to his Wi-fi and also remotely controlling the printer. Leafing through a pile of stuff on his desk, Paolo pounced upon a bulging folder, telling me that there were several properties that he'd like to show me; firstly to get my opinion as to whether they were *appetibile* and secondly to keep the owners happy. I asked him what he meant and he explained that people had seen us together and, putting two and two together had deluged Paolo with properties that they wanted to sell. If I liked them, he could put together quite a portfolio for us to market to potential buyers.

For the next hour we pored over a map of the area, Paolo seemed impressed at how well I already knew it and even more so when I asked him about a particularly pretty old *Casa Colonica*, farmhouse, that I'd seen the other side of Valestra. We decided that we'd visit ten or so properties as soon as his schedule allowed following which we could narrow down those I liked and he'd then talk to the owner about their expectations - and price. I agreed that was the right approach as I suspected that the moment there was a whiff of foreign interest, the price would rise exponentially and this was something he was very clear he did not want. He was adamant that 'our' properties were not only going to be saleable from an aesthetic viewpoint but also from a technical and financial one too. Technical as in all the necessary permissions up to date and financial as in no outstanding debts on any of the properties and a sensible, market-rate price.

We didn't stop talking for several hours; it was so good to work with someone again who was enthusiastic and organised. Paolo's phone rang on a regular basis and while he spoke with his clients I pored over the maps and cadastral plans that he had already produced. I knew that there was a programme on my iPad that I could use to put together sets of details which he could then put on his website - or I could send to my contacts. I'd not been in residential real estate for decades but I had a pretty good network of friends and former colleagues who I knew would be interested in my latest venture. Suddenly there was so much to think about - not least the legal aspects of our working together.

The doorbell ringing shattered my thoughts, Paolo, while still talking on the phone, pushed a button which opened the outer and inner doors and an important-looking silver haired man let himself in. Seeing me and hearing Paolo, he mouthed a "*Buon Giorno*" to me and sat down in the reception area.

Finishing his call, Paolo peered round the doorframe and seeing who it was, invited the visitor in to meet me. "Signora Campbell, *la presento Il Sindaco do Carpineti*". He was introducing me to the

Mayor! Remembering my manners, I stood and shook his hand, murmuring pleasantries and telling him how pleased I was to meet the man whose forward-thinking had resulted in the rural broadband initiative coming to the area. The Mayor was astonished and absolutely delighted and we started chatting immediately, much to Paolo's amusement. The conversation then naturally turned to our proposed venture and I was asked my honest opinion as to whether foreigners would or could be interested in buying in this part of the world. I explained that with the right marketing, absolutely. I reiterated everything I'd said to Paolo about the area's beauty, its accessibility and the fact that the prices were likely to be much more reasonable than those in Tuscany. He was gratified and said that I must go and meet with the *Assessore* in the *Comune* to discuss how they may be able to assist foreign buyers and once again I was struck by his forward-thinking.

The three of us chatted for a while longer, then realising that the Mayor had actually come for a meeting, I hurriedly made my excuses, asked Paolo if I could borrow the map onto which he'd marked several properties, and turned to leave. He said he'd call me the next day and if I was free we could go and see some of them. I told him I would indeed be free and said I'd have my IKEA step at the ready. He laughed, somewhat to the Mayor's astonishment, and we agreed that he would call me later and arrange when and where to meet the following day.

I decided to drive home another way, up the hill behind Paolo's office, the steep road winding inexplicably upwards through the

Hornbeam woods to the castle then down the other side, swinging round tight hairpin bends and then passing an abandoned *Caseificio* - a dairy and cheese factory - to turn left at a beautiful ancient homestead, another *Borgo*, but much older than mine, passing a tiny stone chapel dedicated to Santa Caterina and on through pastoral countryside to an area called Fola. I knew that this eventually led to the road around Monte Valestra and I wanted to explore the area a bit, as it was one of the missing pieces in my mental jigsaw of the map of the area.

Sloping down to my right, were fields and woodland and at the bottom a pretty group of stone buildings and one larger modern house with magnificent views out over open countryside. As I drove, something flashed by the side of the road, surely not a speed camera? There must have been barely 20 cars a week down this road, so why a speed camera? Anyway there was always a warning sign with the required speed limit, well in advance of the actual camera and I'd seen nothing. Nevertheless I slowed down and having done so, realised what had flashed at me. Beside the road was a most odd but somehow artistically inclined pile of stones. Each had been painted a different colour and was interspersed with bits of broken mirror that had been glued to, of all things, an old plastic plate. A child's blue plastic plate. This was a sort of art installation! Intrigued I stopped and got out of the car to take a photo then saw that a few metres further down the road was another, equally bright and bold and this time with a small plastic replica of the Virgin Mary lovingly surrounded by bits of broken jewellery and other disused domestic artefacts. That had to the photographed too.

Getting back into the car I drove very slowly along the road, secure in the knowledge that there was unlikely to be any traffic, so I could stop and start at my leisure. The 'installations' continued for about 5 kilometres with the main one, being cleverly inserted into a natural cleft of the rocky overhang and brightly festooned with coloured stones, ribbons, pieces of fantastically-shaped aluminium foil and other tasteful bits of household detritus. All of them were artistic and quirky and, it has to be said, fabulous!

I wondered who on earth had done them. Was it some sort of rural art exhibition? Perhaps organised by the forward-thinking Mayor? Whatever it was I loved it and spent some time photographing everything.

Returning home I was greeted by Farah who had heard the car and come out of the house to tell me that Signor C, Ugo and Luisa's father was due to arrive this evening for his annual summer holiday with Stefano. I'd known that he was coming but had forgotten that it was today, Ugo had told me that he would be bringing him and would I be at home, because it would be great to have an aperitivo together before he returned to the stifling heat of Bologna.

It would be lovely to see Ugo again and I was dying to tell him of my introduction to Paolo and our plans. I knew he would be pleased that I had something to do again - and something which might actually bring in a Euro or two. Maybe enough to get home? For I knew I had to go home and had told Paolo so, but we had discussed the possibility of my working from the UK with the occasional trip back and he on the ground in Italy. There were many potential problems to iron out but it might work and I was looking forward to Ugo's thoughts on the matter, for he was always very pragmatic and had my best interests at heart. Something for which I was eternally grateful.

So grateful that I raided my Prosecco store and put a bottle in the fridge for his arrival, rooting around in my cupboard I found some "*Tarrallacci*" small nibbly biscuits that went really well with chunks of Parmigiano. Thus prepared I had a somewhat late lunch and a snooze, for it had been quite a morning!

I was sitting in the courtyard under the awning when they arrived. Stefano had just gone inside to use the bathroom so it was sort of left to me to welcome them, a somewhat odd feeling. However before I could say anything a small furry bullet erupted from the car and started dancing excitedly around me, tail wagging so hard that I thought the lovely little dog to whom it belonged would do itself an injury.

"*Ciao Cara*! This is Asi" Ugo said indicating the now happily wriggling canine, "and this is my father, Carlo". Signor C looked, unsurprisingly, like a cross between Ugo and Luisa and smiled at me in a taciturn sort of way. I guessed he wasn't expecting to be greeted by a foreign woman!

At that point a voice boomed from the house, Stefano had heard the commotion and was shouting a welcome to them. Asi dashed off to say hello to him while Ugo and Carlo followed at a less frenetic page.

From that moment on the summer took on a different energy. Carlo and Stefano had known each other for decades and though very different in temperament seemed to enjoy each other's company. Asi, who had not been before, was a new equation and I noticed that the cats and Mimi had made themselves scarce as soon as they had seen her. She dashed around sniffing everything frantically, her long tongue lolling out of her permanently smiling face. She was gorgeous, a little Jack Russell, barely a year old and when I bent down to pat her, she leapt into my arms and started licking me. I adored her immediately.

Having settled Carlo inside with Stefano, Ugo returned to unload the car, Farah and Ayesha had appeared to help, though once Ayesha clapped eyes on Asi, help flew out of the window and the two disappeared together into the orchard where cries of "Asi, *Asi...*" could be heard. Well it seemed that the little girl and the little dog were going to have a very happy, if somewhat frenetic summer together!

Carlo reappeared and asked Ugo where he'd put the gift to Stefano. Ugo showed him something in the back of the car and he emerged with a massive box absolutely overflowing with fresh produce. Vegetables of every size, shape and colour and all, we were proudly told, grown in Carlo's garden. Stefano was delighted and made sure that they were stowed in the cool of the cantina. He loved cooking and I was sure he was mentally matching meats and fish with the various vegetables and they would eat very well for a week or so judging by the amount in the box.

I suggested to Ugo that once he'd installed Carlo, we all should have some Prosecco together. "Good idea. Dad is curious about you so I'm sure he'd enjoy getting to know you." I fervently hoped that the curiosity wasn't the same as that of the locals!

I returned to the *Tavernetta* and got the Prosecco and the *Tarrallaci*, I put another bottle in the fridge, just in case and quickly chopped some chunks of Parmesan. As I somewhat gingerly carried everything into the loggia I saw that Stefano has eschewed the usual spot with the glass table and had instead set up a tray with glasses and a plate of salami and prosciutto on the big oak table under a more conventional and unstriped awning which was strung between three trees and which formed a sort of tented roof over our heads. Placing my tray on the great table - hewed from a single tree trunk and too heavy to move - I saw that the mosquitoes were putting in an appearance and hurried back inside to find my Mosquito Milk.

Asi, who had appeared from nowhere, followed me inside and immediately located Geisha's food bowl where she greedily gobbled the entire contents while Geisha looked on in some surprise. Asi, realising that she was being scrutinised, looked up at her and seeing a potential playmate tried jumping up to say hello. An outraged hiss and arching of the back from Geisha put paid to that and from that moment on, Asi was tolerated, but in danger of receiving a scratched nose if she overstepped the bounds of what Geisha considered to be acceptable behaviour.

Making sure that Asi followed me, I shut the door and returned to the table brandishing my mosquito repellent. Carlo snorted. I ignored him and proceeded to cover myself in it. Unlike other brands it had a really nice smell and soon all three men were swatting away at the mosquitoes which, they remarked, were worse than they had ever seen them. I however, was left alone, my juju juice obviously working! They lasted about half an hour before one after the other they reached for the bottle and began covering themselves.

Carlo firstly asked me, formally, if we could address each other as *Tu*. Of course I said yes and asked him to also call me Cass, thus began a mutual respect and affection for I found Carlo to be absolutely fascinating and as interesting, albeit in a different way, from Stefano. As he talked I looked at him, seeing Ugo's nose and Luisa's bright blue eyes. He had a square face and wore gold wire rimmed glasses. When his face was resting he looked taciturn and somewhat grumpy but as soon as he smiled he was transformed, his eyes dancing merrily. Stefano was fascinated watching this interaction and I had a pretty good feeling that the three of us were going to have a good time together, once their children had departed!

Carlo had severe renal problems and Luisa had arranged that three times a week, a car from the hospital in Castelnovo would come and collect him to take him for dialysis. I was impressed with the efficiency of the system, for Carlo lived in a different *Comune*, over two and a half hours away and organising such a thing across the *Regione* was not for the faint-hearted. But Luisa was one of the most indefatigable people I had ever met and the more I knew of both families, the more I realised how amazing they were. They simply never stopped. Even when relaxing, like last weekend with her ladies,

Luisa was always on the go. Ugo too. For even now, sitting in the Hamlet sipping a glass of chilled Prosecco lightly tinged with the aroma of Mosquito repellent, he was on the phone to his British boss, discussing the finer points of a contract that was to be signed the following week.

Stefano and Carlo were chatting, Ugo was on the phone, Farah was in her house preparing the family's dinner and Ayesha and Asi were becoming inseparable. I sighed happily, picked up my glass, took a sip and reflected on my day. Mayors, Mad Artists and a Jack Russell puppy. What more could I ask for?

Chapter 23

Magic is afoot...

The next day, I woke late, feeling slightly delicate for, immersed in bonhomie, I had, once again overdone the Prosecco and of course, yet more had arrived from Stefano's *cantina*. Ugo had gone into the kitchen and rustled up a huge bowl of spaghetti with a delicious spicy tomato sauce, a true *al'arrabiata*, which we had hoovered down accompanied by liberal coverings of grated Parmigiano. Asi, exhausted by all the excitement had fallen noisily asleep at Carlo's feet and as she snored, several sets of illuminated eyes, cat's eyes, appeared all around us. Driven by curiosity they had crept to the edges of our tented enclosure and regarded their slumbering nemesis in an oddly dispassionate way. Perhaps fixing her image firmly in their minds eye, so that when she reappeared they knew how to react. She'd shifted noisily, in the throes of some wildly exciting dream, her little legs pedalling frantically as no doubt she chased them round the garden; as one they'd hissed, arching their backs, tails like brushes and shot up one of the trees, secure in the knowledge that for the time being they were safe from the vibrating behemoth below.

Taking my morning coffee out into the portico, I sat musing upon my plans for the day. It was a Saturday, Ugo had returned back down the mountain late last night and the two gentlemen, Stefano and Carlo, were no doubt up to no good in the kitchen! Savouring the tranquility I watched as, slowly and stealthily, small wary felines appeared from various bushes and one of the barns and crept towards me. Geisha and

I seemed to be an endless source of fascination to them, for they would sit for hours watching me and sniffing for her at the open door. Unable to decide whether I was friend or foe they would watch me unblinkingly until something more interesting happened. Then they would retire to sit on the car, once again covering it with their dusty paw prints. I'd given up trying to clean it and wore their approbation as a badge of honour!

Remembering that I'd seen a flyer for a concert in the small church in Valestra, I quickly scanned my phone, for I remembered taking a photo of it. Yes, there was a performance this time next week, three choirs singing a selection of folk songs from the region. I was also intrigued to look inside the church as it was tiny and white, sitting alone on the edge of the village, adjacent to the football pitch and municipal recycling bins. Its steeple leaned slightly to one side as if emulating the Leaning Tower of Pisa, although the angle of its slant was considerably less marked than that of the world famous landmark - but no doubt caused by the same seismic conditions.

I resolved to go and would check at The Forno if I needed a ticket. I love music and the thought of a serene couple of hours to myself away from the Hamlet, an opportunity to just sit and relax was too good to miss. Thinking about 'sitting and being' I decided I'd go on a short walk to the beautiful and oddly compelling grove of trees which stood in one of the wheat fields, about a kilometre from home. The wheat had been cut recently which meant that getting to the trees without stepping on an adder or worse, viper, was possible. I'd been warned about the vipers in the fields and told not to go into them without boots on.

Since I couldn't wear boots I'd avoided the field until one of the three local tractors - red tractor, blue tractor and green tractor - had reaped the seemingly ever-bountiful wheat.

The grove looked magical and mysterious and cool. A group of about 20 oak trees, young enough to have been planted around a hundred years earlier, yet mature enough to provide considerable shade stood on the edge of a field with the denser broadleaved woodland behind and open views down over the wheat fields. Since the road carried very little traffic it looked to be a peaceful spot.

In true Freya Stark mode I planned what I would take with me. I have a phobia about sitting on grass so had purchased, years earlier and which had long been stowed in the boot of the car, a fold-out camping stool, sturdy enough to bear my weight. It came with its own carry bag complete with a most convenient pocket for a water bottle. Even now, in the early part of the day, the sun was hot and I knew that the two kilometres there and back would seriously dehydrate me, so I planned accordingly, including finding my hat - a somewhat eccentric floppy version of a Pith Helmet, the headgear of choice for indefatigable adventurers and much beloved by 19th century Explorers (with a capital E). I also looked out my staff. A sturdy wooden pole, with leather loop at the top into which one inserted one's hand, so that striding purposefully through difficult terrain (who was I kidding?!) one could keep one's balance and not lose the staff in a quagmire or some other ghastly natural hazard faced by intrepid explorers.

I returned inside, hurriedly showered and dressed, not wanting to get embroiled in the matutinal doings of the big house and suitably equipped and loaded with the paraphernalia for my peregrinations, stomped off looking, I have to say, wildly eccentric and regarded with open-mouthed astonishment by the cats. Geisha, in her usual place, opened an eye, looked at me balefully, sighed deeply and went back to sleep, well used to my idiosyncratic ways.

I marched out into the road, my equipment banging somewhat annoyingly against my side, followed by the posse of pussies who had decided that this was a great adventure and who seemingly wanted to accompany me - albeit at a distance, as if to safely remove themselves from the taint of the mad English woman, but driven onwards by their natural and insatiable curiosity. I was glad the wheat had been harvested because the thought of one or more of them falling foul of a slumbering viper, was horrendous. Having said that, I had seen them harrying and eventually killing a huge and, to me, terrifying, slowworm that had inadvisedly made inroads into their territory. Briefly I pitied any poor viper.

Despite their initial enthusiasm by the roadside shrine to Santa Lucia, the Saint of clear sightedness, and protector of eyes, my feline escort left me and instead headed towards the meadow by the lake which no doubt contained much more interesting things. I carried on and was puffing and sweating by the time I reached the grove which looked gorgeously cool and inviting. More so because there didn't seem to be the ubiquitous cloud of insects usually associated with a wooded grove, for which I was grateful.

A lone driver passed me as I hesitated by the side of the road, his incredulous stare at the vision I must have presented reducing me to incontrollable giggles. Recovering my poise I somewhat shakily poked my staff long grass at the wayside, checking for reptilian presence. A scurry in the dry stalks alerted me to a small field mouse who shot off in terror. Which it wouldn't have done had there been snakes lying in wait. Encouraged I clambered over the small ditch, glad of the reassurance of my staff, for my equilibrium and balance were not great and I didn't fancy toppling into it.

A few purposeful strides took me into the circle of trees where I stood for a minute or two, savouring the cool of the leafy canopy above and trying to decide where to place my stool. I didn't fancy sitting at an angle, not least because it would ruin the mental

picture I had built of myself, sitting serenely under the trees. I found a wonderful spot, close to the roots of one of the bigger trees and, extricating the folded stool from its carrying bag, easily unfolded it, noting that it had reassuringly broad feet meaning I would not sink inexorably into the earth the moment I sat down.

It was easily set up and with the water bottle placed within arm's reach. I gingerly lowered myself onto the thankfully strong and capacious nylon seat and surveyed the grove. It reminded me of an older grove of oak trees in Cumbria in the north west of England. There, magnificent ancient oaks stood in a circle, close to a tiny chapel said to have been built on the site of the hermitage of Saint Bega near

Bassenthwaite. They looked so magical and so Druidical and so redolent of extraordinary energy. I felt that this place was a sort of younger cousin for the oaks were also planted in a circle and the atmosphere within was definitely somewhat magical. I shut my eyes and let it wash over me. A feeling of deep calm descended on me and I realised that this was probably the first time in many many months that I had felt truly calm. I loved being in the Hamlet but there was always the underlying concern of my situation and the decisions I knew I was going to have to soon make.

So I let the spirit of this place wash over me as through half closed eyes I watched great coloured butterflies dancing under the trees. I felt that if I sat there long enough, woodland creatures would join me and maybe even the Genius Loci - the spirit of place. Whatever I was feeling, the energy was very ancient and I wondered whether the shrine to Santa Lucia had somehow tapped into this. I remembered reading that when Pope Gregory the Great (not Matilda's Pope Gregory who was the seventh of his name) had sent Saint Augustine to christianise Britain, he had told him "by no means to destroy the temples of the gods but rather the idols within those temples, and to build the churches on the places where people go…" acknowledging the very real connection with the land and supernatural energy. I felt that this gorgeous peaceful grove was one such place. Whatever it was, it was working on me and I felt huge waves of tension release from my body as I sat there listening to the birdsong and the sawing of the crickets in the wheat. A gentle breeze rustled the leaves and in a Narnia-type moment, I felt they were saying hello.

Time disappeared and I just sat, then the tears started. Not knowing why I was crying I let them flow, big fat tears rolled down my face and plopped onto the ground below me. Sobs replaced the tears and before in knew it I was sobbing my heart out while the intrepid explorer part of me hoped I'd got some tissues in my pocket. I cried long and somewhat noisily for quite a while and in so doing felt the cathartic release of some of the tension and fear of the previous months. I realised that I'd been on edge ever since Geisha and I had come to Italy two years earlier I was gripped with a longing for the land of my ancestors. I really wanted to go home. sniffling mournfully and wondering how on earth I was going to manage it.

It felt good giving my problems to the trees and they seemed to accept them for I got no feeling of discomfort or censure, just a solid and reassuring presence, the spirit of the oaks - my favourite and oh-so-British trees - and the significance of this grove being oak, was not lost on me.

Feeling much better than I had in a long time, I wandered back via the lake and saw that Carlo and Asi were walking slowly around the shoreline. Carlo was throwing a stick and Asi raced around the shoreline, tail wagging furiously as she ran off with it, completely forgetting that she was supposed to be taking it back to him to throw again. I laughed delightedly at her sheer youthful exuberance, my sobbing moment forgotten. She heard me and changing direction charged towards me to show me her new toy. She careered into me, her firm warm body positively wriggling with joy at seeing her new friend. I patted her, briefly caressed her silky ears and then she was off again, heading back to Carlo who had just seen me and was waving for me to join him.

I was glad of my sunglasses as they hid the ravages of my tear-stained interlude as Carlo walked towards me, smiling. Asi was in a delirium of delight as she realised that she now had not one but two stick-throwing slaves to serve her every whim and she raced between us undecided as to who to favour with the all-important task. Carlo won. Rightfully, for he was her master and she knew that. He took the stick and with a powerful throw, especially for someone in their eighties, chucked it into the centre of the lake! Without hesitation Asi shot into the water and, swimming strongly, somehow with her tail still wagging furiously underwater and possibly acting as a propellor, headed unerringly for the stick. Retrieving it she manoeuvred her way back to the bank, falling over it as she climbed out onto the grass whereupon she shook crystalline droplets of water over the both of us, her lovely little face positive grinning with delight.

This time she placed her stick at my feet, showing her non partisan nature and I obliged by hurling it back into the lake. She almost ran over the surface of the water, such was her hurry to retrieve it. This time it had gone quite far out and I was momentarily concerned in case it was too far for her and she got into difficulties. I need not have worried, she was fine and quickly returned to repeat this wonderful new game over and over again. Carlo and I, after a decent interval of playtime, retired to two somewhat incongruously placed plastic picnic chairs, grateful that they were partially shaded by the trees. We were at the far end of the lake, where I'd not been before, always preferring to stay near the porticoed shade of the fishing club. Actually it was more of a fishing hut, club implying something grandiose which it wasn't, but it was welcoming and had the most glorious views out over the lake to the wooded hills beyond. Occasionally Green Tractor would chuff its way up the hillside and the driver, whom I actually never saw properly, would wave at me and I would wave back.

Today Carlo and I sat in our shaded splendour at what I termed to be the feeder end of the lake, for there was a small stream feeding into it, which kept the waters "alive" and no doubt teeming with fish. For what does a fishing club do, other than catch fish? I knew that there was a big regional tournament coming up soon - Stefano had been asked, as the Signor and landowner, to attend and he had asked me to accompany him. I had, of course, accepted, wondering what the whole thing entailed and I was looking forward to it. The summer was in full swing now and despite the sweltering heat - in the low 30's centigrade - down in the plains, up here it was a still bearable 26 degrees. Pretty good weather for fishing I was told, and the even cooler evenings were perfect for the myriad *Feste* planned for the forthcoming weeks.

Carlo and I chatted as we took turns to throw Asi's sticks. He was curious about me and how I knew Ugo. I explained that I'd been seconded to his office in Milan from my employers in London in the mid 90's and we'd been friends ever since. "Ah you're THAT Englishwoman" he said and I wondered what on earth Ugo had said to him! I was about to ask when Asi erupted from the water like a torpedo and flopped down beside us, but not before once again spraying us with sunlight-infused droplets which sparkled and threw mini rainbows onto the white bits of her coat.

She lay there panting slightly, worn out from all the exercise and happy to be with us. I felt a rush of love for this gregarious and enchanting little soul and leaned towards her to pat her. With a rush of slippery seal-like muscle she sprang up on my lap, covering me with her wet body and settling down with a contended sigh. Carlo looked astonished! I patted her and told her, in English, what a beautiful girl she was, she looked at me through long lashed deep brown eyes and thumped her tail enthusiastically. I laughed and replied that I adored animals and Carlo told me that Stefano had remarked on my being a huge hit with the farm cats who had taken to following me around like a feline version of the Pied Piper of Hamlin.

Our chat was interrupted by a loud hooting, at which Asi jumped off my lap and raced off in the direction of the sound, barking loudly. I looked to where she was heading and saw that Stefano was sitting in Hassan's car, having been driven out to find us. We hurried over to him. It's almost lunchtime he said and, having spotted my intrepid explorer paraphernalia in a pile by the portico, indicated to me to get in. Carlo and Asi headed back on foot and accepting the invitation I climbed in, grinning at Hassan who had raised an eyebrow at my accoutrements. Another gargantuan lunch beckoned, which would then necessitate a siesta, how on earth was I going to cope with six weeks of convivial meals?!

Chapter 24

Chocolate, trout and goosebumps

The following Saturday I was up early for it was the day of the Fishing Competition AND the concert. Stefano was also up, seemingly looking forward to playing his role as, Il Signor. Carlo decided to stay at home quietly with Asi; reading between the lines and looking at his slightly grey pallor, I saw that the previous days' dialysis in Castelnovo had taken its toll. Asi had been almost hysterical when he had disappeared into the community ambulance to be taken for his treatment and had tried to get onto his lap whining pitifully, so I had taken her into the *Tavernetta* where, with one eye fixed firmly on the snoozing Geisha (who had seemed to sense her anguish had accordingly ignored her) Asi had wriggled happily onto my lap and proceeded to snore loudly for the next couple of hours as I'd stroked her silky ears and absentmindedly patted her rotund little belly.

I had been working, wrestling with the Pages app on my iPad which, when I mastered it, would hopefully enable me to produce professional-looking real estate flyers for the properties Paolo had shown me. It had felt good, after so long, to have been able to sit down and re-engage that part of my brain. Frustratingly it had not proved as intuitive or easy as I'd hoped and the air had turned blue with my swearing as the App had resolutely refused to do what I had wanted it to do and I had lost great blocks of text while photos would randomly pop up in in the wrong place and then disappear altogether. However I'd persevered and gradually something resembling a coherent document had appeared. It had become easier - despite the snoring impediment on my lap - and I had begun to enjoy it, choosing different colourways, fonts and borders until, satisfied with the end result I had sent the demo document to the printer on my desk, closed down the iPad and gone out to look for Ayesha to take over Asi duties.

The morning of the Fishing Tournament already contained the promise of a very hot day and seeing Stefano sitting under the awning, looking resplendent in his smart clothes I'd dived into my wardrobe and brought out another of my long linen skirts and top which I hope would not let the side down.

His appraisal and silent nod of approval when I appeared told me that I had chosen well and getting carefully into the somewhat dusty car we drove the short distance to the lake, nodding *Buon Giorno* to the picture of Santa Lucia in her roadside shrine.

The car park and adjacent field were packed and I slowed down looking for somewhere to park that wasn't too far for Stefano to walk. He told me not to be so English and to drive up as close as possible to the Clubhouse and park bang in the middle of the pathway! I did as I was told and, upon seeing my car approaching, a steward hurried towards us, gesticulating and shouting for me to back up and find somewhere else to park. Stefano opened his window and leant out to greet him. Immediately recognising *Il Signor*, the official did an elegant volte face and guided me into the shade of a convenient tree, right beside the clubhouse and solicitously asked if this was convenient for us.

It met with Stefano's approval, so we got out and I followed him as he set off at a brisk pace down to the Lakeside where he took up his place beside the table full of trophies. He was immediately surrounded by a crowd of elderly men all of whom, obviously as hard of hearing as he was, were bellowing at each other in Dialect. I hung back and watched his interaction with them, realising that he had probably grown up with many of them and it was lovely to see the affection - and respect - in which they held him.

Seeing that he was happily settled, I moved off to find myself somewhere unobtrusive to sit where I could watch the proceedings. I found a perfect me-sized spot on the stone wall, with a good view of the lake. Our normally tranquil lake was besieged by two opposing lines of gaily-clad fishermen - each with an astonishing and impressive array of equipment - rods, aprons, baskets and other pescatorial paraphernalia. Each man was clad in skin tight lycra, much like their cycling brethren and I couldn't help but reflect on the differences between them and a British fishing tournament where I imagined that the protagonists would be clad in sensible tweeds and thigh length waders. I wondered why they needed to look like cyclists. Did their quarry, upon being hooked, drag them into the water and lead them a merry dance - or water ski - along the surface until exhausted they gave in to the inevitable and allowed themselves to be caught.

A man with a megaphone was busily shouting instructions and counting down on a timer. " *Tre, Due, Uno, Via...!*" He would yell and, as one, in a beautifully fluid and coordinated movement, twenty to thirty rods would simultaneously be cast into the lake with a satisfying whoosh and plop, while on the opposite bank, the equivalent number of participants would lift their rods and start packing up their gear. For a set number of minutes the fishermen would fish and then a bell rang signalling the end of the period and lines, some bearing fish and some not, would be withdrawn from the water their poor gasping prey flashing rainbow-like in the sunshine as they frantically contorted in an effort to breathe. Being English and loathing what I perceive as cruelty to animals I felt sorry for the fish, which were unceremoniously removed from the wicked-looking hooks and chucked into large buckets where they mercifully died quickly.

I was surprised for I imagined that they would be held in buckets of water to be judged for size and magnificence and then thrown back. I turned to the lady sitting next to me, busy on her phone, and asked why the fish weren't returned to the lake. She stopped her messaging and looked at me, telling me that it was illegal to do so. I asked what happened to the fish and she said that they were all taken home at the end of the day, indicating the great containers of ice that were emerging from the Clubhouse. Evidently the catch were recorded and then stored in ice for each fisherman to take with him when the tournament was over. I wondered what on earth they would do with such a vast quantity of fish.

Another bell rang and in a somewhat surreal almost choreographed movement the fishermen, who had packed up now rose as one and walked in procession to the opposite ends of the lake. It was quite a sight, fishermen looking like so many brightly-coloured birds, impenetrable reflective sunglasses firmly attached to their tanned and for the most part chiselled faces, walked purposefully and silently to their next fishing spot. I intuited that the change of venue was necessary in order to take full advantage of the fish stocks in all part of the lake. Again, almost as one they unfolded their fishing stools, set up their rods, nets and buckets and settled down to await the next bell. Those who had just landed their catches proceeded to the judging and weighing area where a small group of very serious-looking men set about with scales and tape to record and judge the catch. This was then loaded into enormous ice-filled cool boxes and in some cases waterproof bags, to be put into the back of the vehicles ready for the *padella,* the frying pan or the *congelatore,* the freezer, when they got home.

My neighbour bade me goodbye and headed off to the clubhouse and her place was immediately taken by a small tousle-haired boy absolutely caked with chocolate from a rapidly melting bar. His grandmother hobbled up, her feet obviously painful and I moved up so that she could sit with us. She thanked me and proceeded to berate the small boy for not controlling his chocolate bar! He gave her a sticky grin and turning to me proceeded to chatter away. I didn't understand a word he said but he was so happy and so passionate about whatever it was he was telling me that I didn't want to appear unfriendly so I smiled and nodded. Whenever he wanted to make a point, he happily patted me with a gooey hand, managing to get chocolate all over me. His Nonna was horrified and started to apologise profusely. I laughed and told her not to worry as it was so good to see his obvious delight in his chocolate, his day out and, it seemed, life in general. I guess I had become used to the sight of spoiled and querulous children getting bored and fractious and generally being badly - behaved. But the joyful mien of this wee boy was lovely. So we chatted. His Nonna and I in Italian, he and I in something that only we understood - and me only barely, having intuited bits of his conversation it seemed I'd managed to respond appropriately. In a very short space of time Nonna had managed to elicit from me all she wanted to know, nodding her head in approval at my Italian and looking shocked that I was unmarried and living here alone. I told her I had a cat and lived at the Hamlet, which somehow reassured her.

From time to time, the wee boy, whose name turned out to be Piero and who had been seriously studying the current phase of the fishing competition, would turn to me, point to someone or something, say something unintelligible and laugh delightedly. His mood was infectious and soon the three of us were giggling conspiratorially about I know-not-what, but it felt good.

I looked over to where Stefano was and saw that he has fine, still surrounded by his old friends, and no doubt swapping naughty reminiscences with each other. He saw me looking and waved me over. I said goodbye to my two companions, narrowly avoiding a chocolatey hug. As I left I was told by Nonna that Piero's behaviour was most uncharacteristic and he'd obviously taken a shine to me! I was enchanted for he really was the most charming little boy, his love of life infectious.

Walking over to Stefano I was presented to the Club President, a seriously dapper dark-haired man in, I suppose his 70's. He had the most amazing green eyes - emerald-coloured and sparkling with fun - somehow at odds with the formality of his clothing, the effect of which made him look like a Pixie dressed up in its best clothes. With old-fashioned courtesy he took my hand and bowed over it. Stefano informed him that I was living at the Hamlet and would he be kind and allow me to sit on the Clubhouse's terrace out of the sun on the days when I wanted to come down to sit and look at the lake. Of course he said and I was grateful for there were days when just sitting looking at the sunlight dancing on the water, hearing the plop of a leaping fish and seeing the ripples spreading slowly and lazily across the mirrored surface was almost like a meditation. The cool of the terrace would be very welcome and I spotted a couple of very comfy looking but rustic chairs - much nicer than the plastic picnic chairs Carlo and I had sat on at the other end of the lake.

Again I was grateful for Stefano's generosity in introducing me to the area. We chatted briefly and then both men were called to attend to more serious matters, the first of the day's prize giving ceremonies.

The winners were lined up, their tackle having been put away and their catches now lying inert in the great boxes of ice which was no doubt beginning to melt in the strong sunshine. The rosettes were awarded along with vouchers for new equipment and very shiny cups festooned with the red, white and green ribbons of the *Tricolore,* the

Italian flag, were presented with very and somewhat uncharacteristically short speeches. Stefano graciously bestowed the cups upon the winners, each pausing to smile into the camera lens of the local photographer.

Meanwhile at the end of the lake the serious business of denuding it of its trout continued apace.

Stefano now having performed his Signorial duties beckoned to me that it was time to go and retrieve the car - and turn on the air-conditioning for it had suddenly become very hot and I was thirsty.

We progressed slowly between trout-filled cars and I noted the happiness of the occupants. A lovely day in a beautiful place, in the sunshine and a boot full of food is not a bad way to spend a Saturday morning.

As soon as we got back, Stefano disappeared into the kitchen and, donning a huge apron, proceeded to conjure up yet another gargantuan and gourmet lunch. Carlo had perked up and bit and managed to eat well, all three of us dropping surreptitious morsels onto the floor for Asi and, at the other end of the table, the marauding Mimi. We told Stefano about Asi's joyful swimming and stick retrieval and he looked sober. "She must not go into the lake " he said, Carlo started to object, thinking that Stefano was prohibiting her. On the contrary, it appeared that there was an ancient and apparently enormous '*Silure*' a giant fish that lived on the bottom of the lake, which had been known to take swimming dogs. Dogs bigger than Asi. Carlo and I looked each other and blanched. What a lucky escape she had had.

After lunch I headed to the *Tavernetta* for a siesta before setting out in the early evening for the church in Valestra for the much-anticipated concert. Not only was I looking forward to actually seeing inside, I was looking forward to hearing Mauro sing.

In true British fashion I arrived early. The church car park was pretty empty so I managed to find a good space and, although there several people milling about outside the entrance I was able to go inside without feeling too exposed. There are times when I find it hard being stared at more or less constantly and while I know that the stares are out of curiosity and not aggressive there are times when I really wished I was invisible. This was one of them. I half hoped I'd see someone I knew, but since I didn't really know that many people it was unlikely. What was very obvious was that everyone knew everyone else which only served to heighten my shyness. So I scuttled inside, acknowledging the welcome from a nice lady who handed me a programme and headed for a cool shady corner, where I could sit hopefully unnoticed, but where I would have a good view of the central area, the apse beneath the domed ceiling. A domed ceiling which, along with the rest of the church, was gorgeously painted with murals - in bright and vibrant colours yet very tastefully done; as was the detailing on the gracefully arched ceiling and some gorgeously moulded stucco wall panels. What a surprise! This church, which from the outside, apart from its skewed bell tower, looked so innocuous and uninteresting, was a lovely discovery. It was cool inside and I was glad that I'd thought of bringing not only a cardigan but also a large pashmina. I was going to need them.

Looking down at the pamphlet I saw that there were going to be three choirs performing. Mauro's choir, the local Parish choir and a visiting choir from a neighbouring area out of our *Comune*.

One of them, I think the visiting choir, were vocally limbering up - obviously unused to the acoustics of the place they wanted to make sure that they took advantage of the time remaining before the start of the concert to hone their performance accordingly. They started singing, a Capella and I was immediately engulfed in a wave of the most sublime music so powerful that goosebumps sprang up along both arms and I felt as if my heart was about to burst out of my chest as the voices soared into the curve of the dome. Unaccompanied, these men sang with such beauty and such power that it left me literally breathless. I was stunned. I'd never heard anything like this. And this was only a warm-up.

They stopped, obviously satisfied with the effect and wandered off outside. Slowly the church started filling up as the audience took their seats, happily greeting each other across the pews with the noisy exuberance that characterises the best of Italian gatherings! I was still alone at the end of my pew when I felt a tap on my shoulder. It was the Mayor, with his wife, a lovely-looking and very pretty lady who smiled warmly at me. I could feel everyone looking at us, wondering who the strange lady was - me - as he chatted away happily and sat down beside me, indicating for his wife to sit on his other side. We were exchanging pleasantries when a very efficient-looking lady came dashing up from the performance area and almost dragged him to the seat of honour in the front row. As befitted his role in the community.

348

His wife however elected to stay with me and moved up to sit next to me, quietly introducing herself as Arianna, said she had heard a lot about me! I liked her immediately, not least for her kindness in staying with me. Maybe she preferred to shun the limelight of being the Mayor's wife, but maybe she'd picked up on my slight discomfort at being the object of somewhat noisy whispered conjecture. Whatever the reason, I was grateful.

The noise died down and everyone looked expectantly to the Apse. The choirs had taken their seats on the south side of the church and the Priest had appeared. I was, once again, amazed and scolded myself for my preconceptions. He could not have looked less like a country village priest, which I had imagined as something like Don Camillo the priest from Giovanni Guareschi's charming stories of 1950's Italy, The Little World of Don Camillo.

He was very handsome and very cool. Dressed in a polo shirt and chinos the only sign of his calling was a small hand-carved wooden cross on a leather thong around his neck. His beard was salt and pepper, his hair long at the neck and his eyes deep brown and, I have to say, somewhat gorgeous! The Mayor's wife who introduced herself as Arianna, told me that he was called Don William. William being a very popular name in this area of Italy - and not *Guglielmo* as was prevalent elsewhere in the country. He welcomed us to the church and said how happy he was to see it full. The slightly rueful look on his face made me feel for him; if I was Catholic I'd be there like a shot every Sunday! Not because he was great to look at but also because he looked to be really interesting and not at all dogmatic. He made me sad though for he said that at the morning's communion there had only been three people; I felt that such a charismatic man and such a beautiful place deserved better.

Having said his piece he handed over to the Master of Ceremonies, whom he described as 'indefatigable' and who turned out to be the efficient-looking lady. She was wonderful in her role, engaging, funny and very professional and as well as introducing the evening's concert she also took the opportunity to introduce the couple who had taken upon themselves to paint the beautiful murals. They had, she said, done it for the love of the church and the love of God. I was very impressed by their expression of faith and what a wonderful way to demonstrate it.

Without further ado the singing began. The first choir, the Parish choir, was delightful. It was a mixed choir of all ages with three guitarists and a brilliant and spirited female conductor. They sang a lively and fun repertoire beautifully, the acoustics of the cupola really picking up their voices. It was gorgeous. Arianna and I smiled at each other in delight as did the others in the audience and I felt a wonderful sense of peace and camaraderie. Having finished their set, to sustained and noisy applause, the choir took their bows and returned to their seats, faces shining with happiness.

The second choir, was our local one - but Mauro was nowhere to be seen. I wondered what had happened and hoped that he was ok. No doubt I would hear from Luisa at some point. Dressed in matching red polo shirts the choir looked relaxed and when the choir leader announced that they would be singing a repertoire of traditional music

- from various regions of Italy - I was excited. For I had heard some national songs and even some of the drinking and marching songs of the elite *Alpini* corps during my time in Italy, but I knew nothing of regional or even local music so I was intrigued. They sang about love and loss, they sang about the wartime Partisan fighters in the mountains which reminded me of Stefano's stories and the book by the English author Eric Newby, Love and War in the Appenines. Our Appenines. Here. But my favourite song was the Shepherd's Song from Abruzzo which had me stifling sobs, so beautiful were the voices and so poignant was the music.

I didn't think it could get much better - but I was wrong! The final choir, the one from another Province and composed entirely of previous members of other choirs, took the whole thing to another level. They too sang a mixture of regional and historical songs, but it was their religious pieces that reduced me to tears - and Arianna too. We sat there side by side, handing each other tissues, tears rolling down our cheeks as we tried to keep our sobs under control. My goosebumps grew to the size of ostrich eggs as the voices rolled over and around me in waves, soaring, plunging, barely audible one minute and rising to crescendoes of such power and beauty the next that I was left breathless with wonder. Magic was afoot, the energy of the whole church shifted and when the last note died away, the audience sat there momentarily shocked into awed silence and immobility. I'd never experienced anything like it.

When the spell broke, the applause was thunderous, Father William was on his feet, as were many others, myself and Arianna included.

When the three choirs came together for the final encore I gave up trying to control my emotions and just let the tears flow. Something powerful had happened to me in that wonderful place and having bade a warm farewell to Arianna, promising her that we'd meet again soon, I left hurriedly - not wanting to ruin the moment by having to interact with anyone else. I needed to be alone to assimilate what I'd just experienced which was undoubtedly one of the most enjoyable and uplifting experiences of my life. Driving home into the late evening sunset, the first stars visible in the darkening sky, I felt I needed to stop by my grove of trees and ground myself in order to regain my equilibrium. This captivating place was beginning to get to me and I was going to find it very very hard to leave.

Chapter 25

Priests, Partisans and Oratories

Life started to get busy. I spent the days diligently exploring the areas that Paolo considered *attraente* - literally 'appealing' to foreigners. Most of the locations he proposed were charming and most with incredible views, but a couple, were absolute no-no's.

One of the abandoned villages, an absolutely stunning tiny *Borgo* with its own Oratorio, was situated slap bang next to a dairy farm where the barn, the yard and the water tank often ran with slurry. Not only would this be a breeding ground for the voracious mosquitoes, but also horse flies and heaven knows what else. The smell alone could be enough to put off any prospective purchaser or maybe even developer. I had a notion that someone with vision, foresight and a large cheque book could renovate and redevelop some of the villages into tasteful holiday complexes, complete with swimming pool. It had been done with considerable success in several areas in neighbouring Tuscany and was a wonderful way of preserving the tradition and architectural heritage of the buildings. Paolo had been intrigued by this when I'd shown him the various websites and asked whether I really thought that this was a possibility here. I'd said yes, but not next to a slurry pit.

He also asked why the English wanted swimming pools so much! I explained that it wasn't just the English, but also the Northern Europeans; we found the Italian summers extremely hot and that the potential for a cooling swim amidst stunning countryside was vital.

He looked thoughtful and acknowledged that I had a valid point. He and his fiancée loathed the Italian seaside with its regimented rows of often expensive deckchairs, crowds and pricey restaurants and in fact this year, they had booked a restored 13th century tower with swimming pool in Tuscany for their holiday. I'd looked at him in incredulity and told him how English he was becoming! For a second he looked horrified, then laughed. He was beginning to understand me and that I was teasing him. I pointed out that his paradise of a hideaway would not be nice with herds of lowing and defecating cows on the other side of the lane. "*Eh, già*" he agreed with me and looked thoughtful, nodding his head towards the little hamlet snoozing quietly in the hot sunshine. "This farm is in the same ownership as the *Borgo*, maybe he'd sell the land, there are enough square metres of the existing agricultural buildings to be demolished and to get planning for them to be redeveloped...obviously they'd have to go for change of use from agricultural to residential but it could work."

I'd turned and looked at the land, it was actually a perfect place for a pool, restaurant with loggia and rooms overlooking the view. There was also room for parking. This would leave the historically and architecturally sensitive restoration of the original *Borgo* unsullied. It was a very special place and in my mind's eye I conjured up something like the impressive *Albergo diffuso* - scattered hotels - which had been perfected in Tuscany by Giancarlo Dall'Ara an hotel marketing consultant.

Having finally emerged from the economic crisis of the past years, Italy was beginning to realise the value of its built heritage and the repurposing and redevelopment of these beautiful places, which were often abandoned, was something that I passionately hoped we could make work in this area. Paolo needed little convincing and we chattered excitedly about the potential and how best to attract a developer or investor as I doubted that a group of individuals would be interested in jointly redeveloping these abandoned villages, even if we could find such a group.

I mentioned the lawyer I knew down in Firenze who specialised in working with such clients and who was keen to expand out of Tuscany into neighbouring Regions. I told him that I'd already been offered a loose form of collaboration with him and so there should be no problem. We agreed that I would set up a meeting and that we'd head down to their offices where I could also meet with my *Commercialista* and try and sort out my residence and tax matters.

Paolo was enthusiastic about the idea and we agreed that we'd put together some details of what he had so that we would be able to present some opportunities when we met. "Then I must take you to *Valmezzana*... but we will need to go in the 4x4". For most of the properties, bouncing uncomfortably down unmade roads wasn't an issue and we drove in Paolo's normal car; he resolutely refused to let me drive him, having once ridden with me for a short distance and telling me that I drove much too fast - especially when my car had the wheel on the wrong side and I couldn't see the oncoming traffic. There was no point telling him that I'd driven in a right hand drive car in Europe for years, to him it was counter-intuitive and that was that!

We agreed that we'd meet for our visit to Valmezzana - and other interesting propositions while he'd obviously got the bit between his teeth - the following day. Dropping me off outside his office and telling me that he would have a surprise for me the next day, he bounded up the stone steps and back to his day job, leaving me to wonder what on earth the surprise would be.

I decided to have a quick lunch at Da Gianni, a family-run Trattoria, outside Montefaraone on the road between Carpineti and Baiso and then spend the afternoon looking at the areas that Paolo had suggested, photographing the landscape and metaphorically wearing my British tourist hat. I'd heard that there were several foreign visitors who regularly spent time in this area and so I wanted to look at it from a visitor's viewpoint.

Pulling into the small car park I parked the car beneath a huge shady plane tree and crossed the road into the refreshingly cool but slightly gloomy interior of the Trattoria. Run by two sisters, one in the kitchen and one front of house, they'd not batted an eyelid when I'd first turned up unaccompanied. Today I was greeted like an old friend and offered my favourite table, the one in the corner facing into the restaurant so that I could observe the other customers. And they me!

The food was always wonderful, the best of Italian *cucina casalinga.* As always at lunchtime the place was packed and I was covertly and not so covertly inspected by many pairs of eyes. Obviously, unlike Valentina in the other Trattoria, there were less lone female customers in this part of the world, but being in an establishment run by females, maybe I didn't warrant such close scrutiny! Every time I opened my mouth to say something, a hush fell over the room and I wanted so much to stand up and introduce myself - and ask if anyone had anything they wanted to sell to foreign tourists!

After lunch I took my coffee outside to one of the little tables and gratefully hooking into the restaurant's Wi-fi, started looking at a map of the area. Baiso and beyond were places I didn't really know well, the landscape and the energy were different - the views were still stunning but not AS stunning at those with which I had fallen deeply in love. Situated on the main road to the town of Scandiano, Baiso was overlooked by a magnificently imposing castle, half hidden behind columns of Cypress trees. I'd been told that it was now occupied by a rich widow who welcomed visitors! Maybe Stefano knew her and if so, perhaps we could go and visit. It looked intriguing and welcoming. Not as large or impressive as that of Carpineti or Canossa but impressive nevertheless and, of course, it had been one of Matilda's castles, having been built in the Tenth Century by her Grandfather, Adalberto Atto.

My head full of ideas for projects and how Paolo and I were going to get our collaboration up and running, I looked at my watch. Still too early to ring the *Avvocato* in Firenze, they'd be back in the office around 4pm so I had enough time to go home and have a siesta with Geisha. I was beginning to get a bit worried about her, she was getting very thin and starting to look older and more tired than usual. I knew she didn't like the heat and luckily the *Tavernetta* was cool most of the time in the summer - and when it wasn't I had a small portable air conditioner and fan for our use. When she wasn't sleeping she would, with me in attendance, poke her nose

outside for a few minutes, sniff the flowers and then head for the sanctuary of my lap. She loved it when I came home for a siesta and would abandon her window sill for my bed where she'd lie alongside one thigh purring like a small diesel engine and when she'd had enough she'd climb onto her bed on the adjacent footstool and snooze once more. It was time to take her to the vet and to see what he could do, for somehow, I was going to have to get her home and soon. She was loyal and brave but I felt that she wanted to be back in her house, in England - and so did I - but how on earth was I going to manage working with Paolo on the new venture AND be resident in the UK? I needed to discuss this with the gentlemen in Florence, hey were used to dealing with expats and no doubt would come up with excellent advice.

I was looking forward to seeing them, I liked and respected them enormously and they most certainly knew what they were doing. They had been introduced to me by a business acquaintance, a high-powered Englishman who divided his time between Florence and the UK. He had praised them highly which reassured me and concerned me in equal measure - maybe this meant that they were expensive...! I pushed the thought away, went back into the Trattoria, paid my bill and headed for home, taking another route which round wound the back of Monte Valestra and which came into the village by the church, reminding me that Mauro and Luisa had invited me to their home for lunch that Sunday. Something to which I was looking forward immensely.

The phone rang as I drove past the church, it was Paolo asking whether I was free this afternoon as he now had the 4x4 and wondered whether I'd like to see Valmezzana today. He asked me where I was and I told him. He laughed and said, "Slow down. See the little lane to your right? Turn down there and you will see me!"

I did as I was told and, sure enough, in a pretty little piazza surrounded by old porticoed houses in various states of repair, there was Paolo, standing by his Toyota and grinning at me.

"What a coincidence, you calling just as I am driving by, but I don't have the step for getting in."

He looked perplexed for a moment and then said "Why don't I follow you back to the Hamlet, it's only five minutes, you can leave the car there, get the step and I'll drop you home when we've finished."

"Ok" I reversed the car, not easy in the middle of a small medieval village square, and headed for home. Ten minutes later we had swapped cars, I had safely ascended into the Toyota and we were on our way to Valmezzana.

Taking the road I had just driven, we wound around the back of the mountain and then plunged off road down a small country lane - one of the many white - unmade - roads that crisscrossed the area. The surface left me wincing and yelping as the ruts in the dried mud, though easily navigated by the Toyota, were not doing my lower back much good. Paolo stopped at a pretty but closed church, set back from the road and surrounded by fields of wheat, stained red by a sea of poppies, my favourite flower, waving in the breeze. He gestured towards a marble plaque set into the wall of the church and I could just make out the chiselled inscription, to a Don Domenico 'Carlo' Orlandini.

Paolo explained that Don Domenico, Carlo being his code name, had been a priest and a great Partisan and Resistance Fighter of the Second World War, based in this part of the world. He and his battalion of the lyrically named *Fiamme Verdi del Cusna'* - the Green Flames of Cusna - had worked with the British and American forces in fighting the Fascists and the Nazis and rescuing, hiding and repatriating more than three thousand Allied troops. Don Carlo had also been a member of the British Secret Service and had received the highest military honour, the Victoria Cross, for his work. I was astonished and felt somewhat emotional at the thought of frightened and hunted allied soldiers being looked after and helped by Don Carlo and his network of local people. I recalled that Eric Newby's book had referred to this part of the world and to the extraordinarily brave acts of heroism by the locals in hiding him - and others like him - from the enemy and ensuring that they returned safely home. A lump came into my throat and I said that I wished I could have met him. Paolo saw that I was moved - *commossa* - and told me that his father had known Don Carlo before he had died, in the late 1970's. He also suggested that I should talk to Stefano as he had been a boy in his early teens at the time of the Nazi occupation who would have a lot of information - and stories to tell. I wondered how Don Carlo managed to be both parish priest and resistance commander. On reflection, his spiritual calling was a perfect cover for his more dangerous activities, enabling him to be in many places and situations without drawing suspicion.

I thanked Paolo for showing me this and, at the little crossroads by the church, we turned right and slowly bounced our way down another rutted road, through a farmyard filled with noisily exuberant dogs and across the ridge of a field, with glorious countryside views in every direction.

Driving through an archway of trees, Paolo pulled up and I stared in astonishment, for there, sitting somnolently in the sunshine was a perfect little - but mostly ruined - village, complete with tower which, for the moment, was still standing. In the bushes to our right was the remains of another tiny Oratorio, which I was told was scheduled for renovation, dedicated as it was to Saint Francis of Paola. This meant that the much-needed electricity would be provided by the State or Region or Church and would not therefore be an expense for any prospective purchaser of the village. Dating from 1696 the *Borgo* had been inhabited until the 1970's and now, 50 years later, the stone houses, although in disrepair and roofless, stood clustered around the three storey tower - probably originally used as a watchtower but now sadly more of a decorative dovecote.

It was a gorgeous little locale, hiding away under the growth of decades of brambles and trees. Peering into the tangle of bushes and foliage, I could see that there were the skeletons of even more buildings in a more advanced state of disrepair. On closer inspection Valmezzana looked to be quite substantial and therefore potentially viable in planning terms for it had the necessary volume with which to work. I clambered down and started taking photos while Paolo disappeared towards the rear of the van, and muttering to himself, somewhat mysteriously it has to be said, unloaded a black case.

I left him to whatever it was and gingerly picked my way through the piles of stones and the somewhat wobbly walls to have a closer look at the houses. Some still looked quite sturdy, their wooden shutters closed since the last villager departed, while others were about to topple over completely. I could see that the village had actually been very pretty and the beautiful stone of the houses was complemented by the stunning handmade *cotto* tiled roofs. It would be an incredible project for a visionary and sensitive developer and I imagined that it could be bought very cheaply. The place had the most wonderful feeling of peace and tranquility about it, as if the ghosts of the inhabitants were still sitting outside their houses snoozing in the late afternoon sunshine.

An alarmed squawk and flurry of many beating wings brought me sharply out of my reverie, a veritable cloud of doves and pigeons had shot into the air from the top of the tower and I wondered why. I looked upwards and saw, to my amazement, a drone buzzing its way around the turret. In my peripheral vision I saw Paolo focusing intently on his iPhone from which he was operating the drone! That's exactly what we needed, aerial views of properties. This was obviously the surprise to which he had alluded. I didn't want to disturb him in case he lost concentration, so wandered off in the opposite direction, my mind full of ideas for redeveloping this wonderful place.

Actually I liked it more than Saccheggiana, the place we'd visited that morning. While the latter was more 'noble' and private, being walled and with its buildings almost all extant with some and the Oratorio already restored, this was something else but I couldn't put my finger on it. Obviously economic hardship and emigration would have played a large part in denuding it of its families, but I felt that this had been a happy place and it must have been heartbreaking to leave it.

I turned my attention to the well-hidden Oratorio. Who was San Francesco di Paola? I knew who San Francesco was - Assisi - Zeffirelli's stunning film Brother Sun, Sister Moon had made me aware of Saint Francis, over and above his role as protector of animals. But not this Saint Francis. Astonishingly there was an excellent 4G signal where I stood, which also would have explained why Paolo was whooping with delight, focused as he was on operating the drone! So I Googled this Saint Francis and found out that he had been born in Calabria in 1416 in the eponymous Paola and that he had become the instigator of a movement known as the Hermits of Saint Francis of Assisi. Originally a mendicant friar, he and his brother Friars had sought out sparsely populated places in which to live a life of extraordinary hardship and quiet contemplation. As well as the three traditional vows of the Franciscan way of life - poverty, chastity and obedience - they had added a fourth, abstinence from meat and other animal products. 15th century vegans in effect. Revered as a mystic he was noted for several prophecies as well as for founding a couple of monasteries and a nunnery.

I wondered who had decided that this secluded place was an ideal spot for an Oratorio dedicated to him.

Another uncharacteristic whoop from Paolo signalled the end of my reverie. It seemed that the drone, which I immediately named Daedalus (after the Ancient Greek/Cretan inventor, architect and craftsmen who had fashioned wings for himself and his son, with which to escape imprisonment by King Minos on Crete) had performed admirably. Paolo liked the name and told me that the Etruscans had named him *Taitale*. I also gave Paolo a nickname - Biggles - after the fictional World War I British flying ace and hero of the books by Captain W.E. Johns. Googling again I quickly found a photo of a book jacket and showed him the helmeted and goggled Biggles, his white silk scarf flying behind him in the slipstream of his plane. After the Don Carlo connection it seemed appropriate to name Paolo after another brave man! He seemed suitably pleased, if a little nonplussed by my obvious eccentricity, and we bumped our way back home via another white road. As we turned onto the main road I looked back and, there, sitting half hidden by the trees, its creamy walls gilded by the late afternoon sunshine, was the watchtower doing its job. Watching over its valley.

Chapter 26

Lunch, laughter and an unexpected gift

Sunday morning dawned bright and, thankfully a bit cooler than recently. Even though I'd now been in Italy for a couple of years I still found the heat, especially humid heat, oppressive. Up here the air was usually fresh but there had been a notable heat wave down in the Padana and the heat was starting to invade our area. Looking down into the valley, I could see the dark brown smudge of the A1 its pollution hanging in the stifling air so thickly that it looked almost solid. Once again I was thankful for the clean clear air of the Hamlet.

I was a little nervous about my upcoming lunch. Mauro and Luisa and their two children, Valentino and Martina lived, along with Mauro's brother and nephew in a stunning and architecturally significant Villa, that had once been the domain of a very rich and successful family which had been extremely prominent in the seventeenth and eighteenth centuries. The buildings had been lovingly restored and comprised the main villa, a tiny Oratorio and several outbuildings. Being stuccoed and painted white, not faced with local stone, it looked very elegant and stylish in a different way from the natural elegance of Stefano's house. We had arranged that I would park on the corner of the main road and ping Luisa when I was there so that Valentino could guide me in as the entrance was apparently quite hard to find. As I pondered the contents of my wardrobe that morning I wondered what to wear. The house seemed to suggest Sunday Best, but having got to know Mauro and Luisa a little, I didn't think that they would expect me to arrive looking overly formal. So I settled for informal but with, hopefully, a nodding acquaintance to chic. The dilemma of what small gift to take them had been solved a couple of weeks earlier when I'd received a delivery from the wonderful British Corner Shop. I had stocked up on gift tins of shortbread and decorative tins of tea from Fortnum & Mason to give to friends - ideal for use in such circumstances and, for myself, an almost industrial amount of Marmite, Peanut Butter and English Marmalade! I hoped that, as bakers and pâtissiers, they would find the shortbread to their liking, the large tin looked impressive and very Scottish!

An hour or so later, I was being directed down a small and very well-hidden lane to park in the spacious forecourt of the villa. A couple of cats were snoozing on the stone steps of the main doorway above which was carved an impressive coat of arms. The door opened and out popped Luisa, her face wreathed in smiles and her glorious curls, normally restrained by her baker's cap, bouncing around her shoulders. We dispensed with formalities and hugged warmly. I really liked this lady and I was looking forward to getting to know her and her family better. Mauro, looking more and more like Jonathan Pryce, followed her out of the door, bidding me to come in. Crossing the stone steps, the cats having moved away to facilitate access, we entered a cool dark and impressive hallway furnished with large pieces of antique oak furniture. To the left was a sweeping stone staircase and to the right a doorway leading into the kitchen, from which was emanating the most wonderful smells.

Having become used to Stefano's rich and flavoursome cooking I was looking forward to trying someone else's! I was shown into the kitchen and offered a seat at the large table where Luisa's mother was shelling peas. We were introduced and she smiled a welcome to me. A coffee was offered - and accepted - as Luisa returned to the cooker and the array of saucepans thereon. She explained that we were having several types of pasta and then cold roast beef and salads. Was this ok with me? I laughed and said of course it was. She grinned and said that she had wanted to use my visit as an excuse to try out some new pasta recipes. I wanted to say that I was more than happy to be a guinea pig for them, but I had no idea what guinea pig was in Italian, so I nodded conspiratorially wondering what gourmet treats lay in store.

The other members of the family popped in and out, sitting for a moment, then rushing off to do something else. I was struck by the fact that, although the house looked imposing and somewhat formal from the outside, inside it was welcoming and familial. Luisa asked if I'd like to have a look round it but that unfortunately she couldn't show me the Oratorio as that was undergoing repairs. Of course I said yes and was whisked off on a whirlwind tour, starting with their living quarters on the ground floor - the upper floor being inhabited by Roberto, Mauro's brother, and his family - but also the cellars and some of the garden. What struck me, apart from the elegant yet simple beauty of the house, all facing south west and with wonderful views, was the enormous amount of cantina space set aside for the mechanics of everyday life in a great house. There were meat slicing machines, great glass jars of preserves and a bottling machine for the wine and shelf upon shelf of bottles, jars and containers all stuffed full of comestibles of one sort or another. Sauces, dried fruits, jams; cured meats hung from hooks and there was a massive oak bread chest. All full. I asked Luisa how on earth she managed to find the time to do all of this with the produce from their land, as well as work in the Bakery. And not just work front of house, but actually make the pasta, cakes, tarts, bread and biscuits EVERY DAY. She shrugged eloquently as if it was all second nature and I was absolutely filled with admiration for her. I turned as the door opened and saw it was her mother who had decided to join us as she wanted to prepare the walnuts for the *Nocino*. She set to with the green unripe nuts, much as I had with Luisa R up at the Hamlet, sitting at a low table and deftly slicing them into quarters, taking care that the juice did not stain her hands or clothing. She said that she liked it down here, it was cool and she could gaze out of the small barred cellar-type windows at the garden and watch the cats chasing butterflies.

"It is also peaceful" she said, and looked at me knowingly. I surmised that she meant that when all the family were in situ she relished the opportunity to come and spend some time in the great cellars, alone with her thoughts and that beautiful view outside.

Luisa and I continued with the tour of the house and its attendant buildings. We wandered into the garden and again I wondered how on earth she found the time to garden, for it was beautifully maintained and she showed me, with understandable pride, her various plants and fruit trees. My botanical knowledge isn't good but I did manage to understand what each of the plants were and what were their uses. We

368

returned via the front courtyard and the cats came wandering up to wrap themselves around my legs, purring noisily as I bent to stroke them. Luisa remarked that this was most unusual as they were normally suspicious of visitors. I replied that I seemed to be some sort of cat magnet and told her about Geisha, Mimi and the farm cats.

"You are lucky there, Stefano is a good man, he will make sure you are all right." I agreed and told her that I had already been introduced to Paolo and with whom I hoped to be working on selling the properties. She knew Paolo well, his family had always lived in the village and his father had been the postman. "He's a good man too" she said. I remarked that all the men to whom I had been introduced seemed to be good men and she nodded.

We walked back inside and she hurried back to the stove to check on the progress of her 'experiment'. I returned to the kitchen table, now joined by Mauro and Roberto a wiry man with an open friendly face and kind eyes. I'd met him with Paolo as he had a stunning old barn, a cowshed complete with stalls, with views to die for which he was wanting to sell and I'd been up to have a look at it. With imagination and a good architect the potential was incredible and I sort of wished that I'd got the money to buy it, convert it and spend the rest of my days, surrounded by cats, writing (a long cherished dream of mine) and drinking in the view. It had a uninterrupted view of the Pietra di Bismantova some kilometres distant, it was also overlooked by the powerfully brooding Monte Valestra and yet was only minutes from the village - and the Bakery! I told him so. He asked me why I didn't buy it, I responded that I didn't have the wherewithal,

369

at which point the whole family looked amazed. I think they had assumed that I was well off and were surprised when I told them I wasn't!

They were too polite to ask, yet curious to know my story so I told them snippets. When it came to my leaving home for Verona and the subsequent vagaries to which I had been subjected they were outraged. I was praised for my bravery and asked how I'd coped without family to rally round and support me - something inconceivable to them. I tried to tell them about the legendary British stiff upper lip but it did not translate well and they looked bemused. I think they thought that I was describing some ghastly genetic mutation - a bit like a cleft palate - to which stoic Brits were prone!

Luckily my inelegant attempts to describe the condition, were happily interrupted by the arrival of Mauro and Roberto's mother, who still lived above the Bakery. She'd been picked up by Roberto's son, who worked away from the area and who was on his way back to the family home for Sunday lunch. He was a personal trainer and fitness instructor and certainly looked the part. I reflected on how lucky I was to have been invited to join them. They, for their own part, were welcoming, friendly and interested in the stories and experiences of someone from another country. I was asked how I found Italy - I told them I loved the people but hated the bureaucracy! They all laughed heartily and nodded in agreement. I didn't tell them that I was going to have to leave.

Crockery, cutlery and glassware was beginning to appear and I offered to help lay the table. Not a bit of it, I wasn't allowed to lift a finger, other than to carry two serving dishes heaped with delicious-looking pasta while Valentino carried bowls of steaming and fragrant sauce. The dining room was spacious and airy with great windows overlooking the countryside. I think it also served as a sitting room on less formal occasions because at the far end there were a couple of comfy chairs and a sofa. But I had learnt that what the Northern Europeans used as their main living focus - the living room - was secondary to the main focus of the Southern Europeans - the communal table. Life quite rightly revolved around sharing food, drink and companionship, whereas us northerners tended to eat on our knees in front of the tv and not always at a table. My heart preferred the Southern European way of life but my back didn't like being sat on dining chairs for any amount of time. I recalled that, over the years, and in several countries, I'd had some momentous lunches and dinners - seated inside at great long candlelit tables and those outside, eating alfresco under the stars - and I remembered them all and the people with whom I'd been breaking bread, with great fondness. I was definitely Southern European in that respect!

My hosts indicated that I should sit near the top of the table with Mauro and Roberto while Luisa sat near the door, close to the kitchen and the children sat beside their *Nonnas*. The food appeared, plates were piled high and I was exhorted to try absolutely everything. Which I did and with enormous pleasure. Mauro produced several bottles of wine and Sunday lunch *a la famiglia* proceeded apace. Being the guest I was of enormous interest to the Grandmothers who couldn't quite figure out why this foreign lady did not have a husband!

I explained that my life of constant travelling meant that I had lost my husband somewhere en-route and I joked that I couldn't remember at which airport I'd left him! They laughed till they cried and I grinned, knowing that the real story, as to why I preferred being alone, would do nothing other than confuse them even further!

In order to refocus the conversation I asked about the house and its history. Mauro and Roberto between them told me a little of its history, about the great landowning family that had built it and many other houses in a wide geographical area around Reggio. I'd never heard of the family in question, unsurprisingly, but was fascinated by their story. Roberto excused himself for a moment and reappeared with a huge and fascinating-looking book - about the family, their history and their holdings. We decided it might be best if I looked at it after lunch as I was in severe danger of liberally dousing it with Luisa's incredible chocolate spaghetti sauce.

Roberto and Mauro said they were surprised at my interest, I told them that I was very drawn to this area and in order to be able to promote it to interested foreigners, I'd wanted to know more about its history, myths and legends. That kick-started another fascinating conversation and I was transported back in time to the last battle between the Liguri and the Romans at the foot of Monte Valestra where, to this day, beside yet another abandoned and disintegrating village, situated just below the main road, ancient armour and weapons were still being found. I made a mental note to ask Paolo if we could visit it, not just to see the village, but also because I would dearly loved to have found an artefact. Of course it would have had to be declared to the Ministry of Culture - the *Sopritendenze per i Beni Architettonici e il Paesaggio* - referred to by everyone as the *Belle Arti* - which among other things is in charge of archaeological heritage and landscape.

Taking advantage of being sat with a family of bakers I wanted to ask about the many types of breads they produced in the area, for on a daily basis, the wooden shelves in the *Forno* were stacked high with a dizzying array of different breads and I was sure that some of them were specific to the area. Roberto replied and patiently explained the differences in types of flour and yeasts. For 50 years their family had been exclusively producing bread with natural ingredients based in long held traditions and using the *'lievito naturale pasta madre'* mother yeast dough, without stabilisers and chemical additives.

He said that you could tell a good bread by its smell. I said something fatuous along the lines of "there's nothing like the smell of freshly-baked bread" and he looked fiercely at me. "No, you misunderstand. If you go into any one of the supermarkets in town and buy their freshly-baked bread it is industrially produced and not artisan. I can, we all can, smell the difference." I was intrigued and asked him how. "You learn the olfactory signature of the various components." I got the olfactory reference, having seen it in action with *oenologists* when assessing grape varieties for wine, also in France near Grasse with the *Maitre Parfumiers*, which reminded me of the amazing film, Perfume, the story of a murderer. The sense of smell is always so underrated, yet a whiff of newly mown grass or liquid tarmac transports me instantly back to my childhood, or a particular cleaning fluid used by the cleaning lady in a flat I'd stayed in once in Greece that it still makes me nauseous every time I smell it!

I was so moved by these generous and talented people, who wrought miracles of the baking kind every day. I'd read somewhere that the collective noun for bakers is 'tabernacle' and that seemed most appropriate. I liked the formal name for a tabernacle - sacrarium - for what took place in a bakery was definitely sacred; the interaction of earth, air, fire and water.

We'd eaten everything, drunk everything and now my metabolism wanted, nay needed, nothing more than to sleep. A wave of tiredness swept over me and without wanting to be rude, or give offence, I needed to take my leave. Somnolence seemed to be catching for both the *Nonnas* were nodding off and Mauro stifled a yawn. I got the hint - Sunday afternoon was for resting. Luisa read the signs and brought proceedings to a close by rising from the table and asking if anyone wanted coffee.

Twenty minutes later, having been bade farewell by the whole family, except the now-sleeping *Nonnas*, I was on my way home, with the beautiful big book of the well-to-do family on the passenger seat. Roberto, having seen my interest, had quietly taken it into another room, written an inscription on the fly leaf and shyly presented it to me as I took my leave. I'd been genuinely moved and very touched by such a generous gesture and told him so.

I reflected on the lovely time I'd had in the home of my new friends - but how on earth was I going to return their hospitality? Somehow a large tin of shortbread fell well short of reciprocity.

Chapter 27

Castles, choirs and supper

A couple of days later, en route to Castelnovo for a much-needed lymphatic drainage massage, I popped into the Forno to give Luisa some British compotes that I'd found in my stash of comestibles. I thought she might like to try the Damson and the Apricot jams and explained that while they were 'industrial' in their production, they were considered good and I'd welcome her opinion. She laughed and tried very hard not to look dubiously at the proffered jars. I realised the futility of my attempt to find them something delicious to try - for how can you improve upon perfection? She did, however, rave about the shortbread, which they'd tried with their coffee and *digestivo* on Sunday evening. I told her that it, whisky and smoked salmon seemed to be Scotland's main gastronomic exports. "I'd love to visit Scotland" she said wistfully. "Well if you ever do, let me know and I will be your guide!" We grinned conspiratorially at each other and briefly I envisaged us both, curls blowing in the wind, doing an Anglo-Italian version of Thelma and Luisa!

I told her that I desperately wanted to reciprocate their lunch invitation but that would all most likely end up in hospital with food poisoning if I attempted to cook for them. She looked genuinely mystified and I explained that even by English standards (which to an Italian is already embarrassingly low) I was considered a bad cook. That I could just about manage to produce pasta *al dente* but that any sauce would be from a jar. "But what about *rosbif?*" she asked, pronouncing roast beef the Italian way. "Luisa I live alone, rosbif is for family lunches on Sunday..." I got the impression that she was convinced that we Brits lived on rosbif and English pudding and warm beer. It would take aeons to convince her otherwise!

Changing the subject hurriedly before she offered me cookery lessons - reminding me of the lovely super-tidy lady in Pantano - I asked when Mauro was next singing in the church as I'd missed seeing him on the evening of the concert.

"Ah, *già*! He and his *coro* are singing at a festival in Scandiano on Friday. Would you like to join us?" I told her I'd absolutely love to and we arranged that they'd swing by The Hamlet and pick me up. The bell over the door pinged as a customer came in and patting me briefly on the arm, Luisa turned away to serve them.

I headed off to Castelnovo. Some weeks previously I'd been in a lot of pain from my swollen legs and Googling massages in the area I came upon a small business called *Estetica Chiara*. I phoned and an efficient-sounding lady answered, pausing for a nano second when she heard my accent, but assuring me that, yes, she could do manual lymphatic drainage. Would I like to pop in for an assessment? I'd done as she suggested and had been so impressed with her knowledge of the requisite massage technique and professionalism, that I'd immediately booked a series of 11 sessions - for the price of 10.

Chiara, for it was she who owned the business, was Castelnovo born and bred. A pretty and vivacious brunette, she offered a huge range of beauty and well-being treatments from her elegant and tasteful premises. Her customer service was second to none, she

378

ensured that her clients, big, small, beautiful or not so beautiful all felt welcomed, comfortable and at ease. Summing me up in a nano-second she had realised that I was actually pretty self-conscious about my condition and ensured that my sessions were always on the main massage couch in a calm and shady room of its own and adjacent to the small bathroom. The decor in this room was natural and she always burned the most wonderful-smelling oil, her own mixture, having first ascertained that I wasn't asthmatic or allergic to any of the ingredients.

Thoroughly professional yet friendly and welcoming, I liked her immediately and, as my sessions progressed, we became friends. We would talk about all sorts of weird and wonderful things as she gently massaged my poor legs. I'd lie there feeling like a beached whale, but a happy one who had floated off with the fairies on a cloud of exotic incense. I always felt wonderful afterwards and the pain had magically disappeared. She even helped me haul my compression stockings back on again at the end of a session, remarking that she really loved the fact they were in myriad bright colours. She particularly liked the tie dye ones! I explained that since I was going to have to wear them for life, I was most certainly not going to be wearing medical beige! "I wish more people were like you" she said. "You have a big health problem but you laugh about it". "Well crying about it isn't going to make it any better, so I might as well embrace it". *"Brava!"* we'd returned to the pretty reception area and booked in my next appointment.

I always loved my visits there for her salon was almost next door to the artisan sandwich making lady I'd come across months earlier.

So a couple of hours before my treatment I would pop in and after a mouth-watering discussion and a few slivers to taste, I would decide upon my panino and, a few minutes later, bearing her latest gastronomical creation and armed with paper napkins etc I would get back in the car and head to the car park below the Pietra where I would sit in the sunshine, rakishly sporting my floppy Panama hat and gazing out over the mountains, eating my lunch slowly and savouring every bite. Allowing a good hour for digestion prior to my session with Chiara, having I'd eaten I'd move out of the sun to one of the wooden picnic tables under the trees and relax or spend some time catching up with my Facebook friends - for even here, surrounded by mountains and trees and the great rock of the Pietra, the Wi-fi signal was excellent.

Friday afternoon arrived and, having spent a busy few days photographing the exteriors of the properties that Paolo and I had visited, I was looking forward to some time away and Scandiano, which I didn't know at all, was going to be interesting. Mauro and Luisa arrived exactly when they had said they would and I climbed into the car, Luisa having insisted that I take the passenger seat while she moved into the back. Mauro also drove an Audi and we swapped notes about our respective models. He asked me why I'd bought one and I explained that I'd needed something reliable and comfortable which could take a lot of luggage for the long drive down from England but that also my job had necessitated a lot of driving including all the way down one side of Italy and back up the other side. A trip I'd absolutely loved, even when I'd got lost in the outskirts of Naples!

"*Caspita*! You must know Italia better than we do!" Mauro looked impressed, doing that downwards movement with his head that most Italian men seemed to do when something wowed them. "I probably do. But what a wonderful thing to be able to do; drive around this beautiful country, stay in small hotels (that the company paid for for), eat regional foods, drink regional wines and meet the very different peoples that constitute the Italians. And all in a right hand drive car" I added naughtily, to guffaws of laughter.

I was pleased that I knew the roads that Mauro was taking and it was only when we got into the suburbs of Scandiano did I realise I didn't have a clue where we were going. I looked around interestedly because it meant I didn't have to concentrate on driving. From what I saw, Scandiano looked much like every other small Italian town, until Mauro turned right off the main road and pulled up in front of the most enormous pale brick and stone castle, literally just sitting there in the piazza. It was getting dark and the imposing facade was floodlit. I could see that the original edifice was very old with successive generations of owners having added features such as architraved windows and other such embellishments which did nothing to detract from the magnificent brooding presence of the original fortress. A long low bridge, spanning a long-vanished moat or river, led up a gentle incline to the imposing entrance, great doors and gates now stood welcomingly open but I shivered as the ghosts of those who has been unfortunate enough to be sequestrated there, behind the portcullis, hovered at the edge of my perception. There was a cruel energy emanating from the stones and I was glad we were going there to hear music, as if that would somehow ameliorate the echoes of the moans of the desperate.

Having got out of the car and equipped ourselves with water bottles, shawls and cushions (for the seats were, apparently, notoriously uncomfortable) we walked through the great entrance to be welcomed by a sprightly elderly man, his wrinkled face wreathed in smiles, totally at odds with the foreboding and brooding entrance. As Mauro signed us in - as family and friend of a choir member - I looked around me. The interior had been thoroughly redesigned by successive owners and now very much resembled the interior of a German or Austrian palace with elegant staircases, niches full of sober-looking statues of bewigged gentlemen in 17th century clothing, rooms with glimpses of frescoes and a general air of sophistication and culture.

I picked up a small leaflet which explained that the original structure had been built in the twelfth century by the Da Fogliano family, but that the name, Rocca Dei Boiardo, came from the Boiardo family who had occupied it from 1423-1560 and who had converted it from its original military purpose into their home.

Originally constructed as a fortress, it had been built complete with moat and drawbridge, battlements and two high watchtowers, only one of which remained. It was brutishly beautiful though I actually preferred the medieval architecture of the exterior to the overblown ornate interiors of the Baroque period.

At the invitation of the elderly man we moved through into a massive internal courtyard, dominated by an iron sculpture of what looked to me to be Don Quixote, though what he was doing in a castle in Scandiano remained a mystery! Many chairs were laid out facing a makeshift stage and people were rushing around busying themselves with sound systems, metres of trailing cables and all the paraphernalia of an open-air concert. Mauro made his excuses and headed off to join his co-choir members, while Luisa and I took a proffered glass of Spumante, went and put our stuff on three chairs near the front and headed out across the courtyard and into a small and really pretty piazza on the other side of the castle. Surrounded on three sides by medieval houses, painted in bright colours and a beautiful church with ornate marble carvings and a wide ledge on which we sat and drank our Spumante, the energy of the rear entrance was so different from that of the dark and forbidding main one.

Looking around me I remarked to Luisa how pretty it was and she agreed, telling me that the houses were known to be extremely expensive when they came on the market - which was rarely. There was not a sign to indicate that we were in the 21st century, so perfectly preserved was the little piazza and I reflected how good the Italians are at protecting their heritage. It was absolutely charming and Luisa told me that on another side were the gardens and the remains of the fortifications where gastronomical events, *feste* and even weddings were held. The Baroque heyday of the castle had been when the Este family, one of Italy's greatest families, had taken possession and made some stunning alterations. I decided I'd like to come back sometime and have a tour of the place but now, we were being hailed, for it was time to go back indoors and be seated for the start of the performance.

The courtyard had filled up and every seat was taken with people even standing at the back. I was glad that we had claimed our seats earlier because my back was beginning to trouble me and I needed to sit down. The performance was a sort of duel between Mauro's choir and one from another area. As was the case in the church concert they would be singing a Capella. I asked Luisa what register voice Mauro had. He was a baritone but could also sing tenor if required. His choir were the first on stage and having all changed into their choir polo shirts looked extremely smart. There was Mauro, at sanding at the back to the Conductor's far left. Someone gave the note, without using any form of device such as tuning fork and they started signing as one. Again I was enchanted, moved and transported. I found it difficult to understand the words for although they were in Italian some were hard to comprehend; possibly because they seemed to be singing a form of Melophonetics where sound, diction and expression are used to great effect. This was not just singing, this was alive somehow and once again I was holding back the tears at the beauty of the music, the voices and the oddly-excellent acoustics of the courtyard. Each choir sang their chosen repertoire. Songs about love and loss, songs written by soldiers in far away countries longing for their loved ones and one particularly beautiful one had been written by a soldier to his mother, where he knew it was unlikely that he would ever make it home to see her again. It was so deeply moving and even the amusing songs, sung in slang, written in the rural areas by shepherds or farmers or in the camaraderie of the *taverna* were gorgeous.

I was reminded of the time when, as a little girl, I used to stay with my grandmother and we would attend the Oundle Music Festival. Choirs from all over the UK and even some from abroad, which in the early 1960's was quite something, would compete. It was a whole day and we would take the bus and a packed lunch - our sandwiches - wrapped in greaseproof paper and tied with string and a thermos of Lemon Barley Water to drink. I would sit enchanted for hours listening to the various choirs and even today, over 50 years later, I can remember one particular performance that was my first experience of having goosebumps as a result of hearing music.

The second choir was also excellent but, not as good, to my mind, as Mauro's. Their repertoire was equally interesting and they performed one song with some superb and very funny characterisations which had the audience in gales of laughter. But for sheer quality of goosebumps, Mauro's choir won hands down. Actually I don't remember who won, I think they both did, there were speeches by the choir masters and the local dignitaries and the Mayor of Scandiano, resplendent in his *Tricolore* sash, and someone from an artistic foundation. It was heartfelt, it was glorious and I reflected on how very very lucky I was to see this side of Italy - a side that not many Italians, let alone tourists and visitors would see.

The recital finished with a joint performance by both choirs which engendered yet more enthusiasm on the part of the crowd which had turned from a respectful and somewhat congregation-like gathering of mostly middle-aged people into a cheering and whistling cacophony of thoroughly delighted and over-excited adults. It was glorious!

The music over, we all pitched in to fold up the chairs and clear the *cortile*, great rooms either side of the staircase were opened and in went the chairs, the trestle tables and all the cabling and electronics of the sound and lighting. Hovering near the door with a couple of folding chairs in my hand I was astonished to see that this wasn't a storeroom at all, but one of the magnificently decorated state rooms of the castle, it's walls still adorned with enormous important-looking paintings. The accoutrements for the concert were neatly stacked in an area in the middle of the room, well away from the gilt-framed portraits of the Great and Good of Scandiano's history.

Finding Mauro, who was grinning with happiness, we walked back to the car where I was informed that we were now driving to the choir's clubhouse - where they practised every Thursday evening - for dinner and, hopefully a sing-song. About ten minutes from the castle the clubhouse was at the end of a lane. It looked a bit like a village hall and upon entering I saw that it had all the same characteristics as the local village hall at home, back in England. Happy and on an adrenaline high, the choristers were now clutching bottles of beer or glasses of wine and several ladies who appeared to be part of the village hall staff, were putting the finishing touches to long trestle tables and, beside a hatch, massive trays of lasagne and meat and vegetables were steaming.

Yelling at the top of his voice, the Chief of the choir told everyone to grab a seat before the food cooled. They did, for of course, in Italy,

386

one does not eat lukewarm pasta! I was seated away from Mauro and Luisa which at first caused them a little consternation, but I told them I was fine and that I was sure the charming men either side of me would look after me. This elicited howls of laughter from everyone - not least the 'charming men' who turned out to be very naughty, great fun and gently solicitous of my every need. I was plied with wine, with food, with water and with questions. It seems that everyone wanted to know who I was and how had I managed to get into a choir-only dinner. There was no unpleasantness about it at all, they were just genuinely curious. Mauro stood up and introduced me to even noisier howls of approval from his friends. "She's English? Does she speak Italian?"

"Ask her yourself!"

"I am and I do" I responded raising my glass to them all. Thirty odd glasses were raised in response and I saw Luisa laughing delightedly.

The food came thick and fast, plates heaped high with the most delicious things and every time I cleared a space someone filled it with yet another morsel of some local delicacy. My glass never seemed to empty and the good-natured teasing and laughter of the choir members and their families continued apace. The man opposite me was devilishly attractive in a Marcello Mastroianni sort of way and pleasingly attentive, the naughty gleam in his eye eliciting all sorts of ribald encouragement from his friends. The Brexit question was posed and my response, that I'd have to marry an Italian in order to stay, was greeted with howls of mirth and many unprintable suggestions! This was Italy at its best. Pure unrestrained joy and I just sat there, flirting outrageously with my companion, chatting to others and letting the whole joyous experience wash over me. But the Gods hadn't finished handing out their gifts that night, for once the dessert plates were cleared the singing began.

One man, by now a little the worse for wear, started singing in a slow deep rich voice, others joined, in counterpoint, their voices blending and swirling and as the tempo picked up, yet more joined in. I have no idea what they were singing, I'm not sure some of them did either, but the whole musical maelstrom that roiled and broke time and again was more than enough to please Apollo and Orpheus and the Muses. The talent in this room was off the scale and when there was a lull for coffee and cigarettes, I asked my new found friend why the choir didn't record their music.

He smiled and shrugged eloquently, telling me that it wasn't something they'd really thought about. I told him that was a pity because if singing monks and singing army wives could make albums then why couldn't these choirs. He looked thoughtful and said he'd talk to the other members. Meanwhile they were busy practising for a forthcoming visit by a Russian choir. They were going to be performing a song in Russian for them and were finding it fiendishly difficult getting the pronunciation right. I told him that I had learnt Russian at school and that if I could help in any way, I'd be absolutely delighted.

"Why did you learn Russian at school?"

"I've no idea, but it was at the time of the Cold War, so maybe they thought it might come in useful."

"*Cara*, forgive me, but that was some time ago…"

I nodded, "It was a very long time ago, but I can still remember it…"

He smiled and reached across the table to pat my hand. Having thanked me for the offer, he stood up and, taking a deep breath, started another song. Others joined in and for those of that couldn't, we just sat there in a happy stupor.

Many minutes later the music stopped and as if by some magic prearranged signal, everyone started clearing away and looking for their coats. There was a lot of laughter and hugging and kissing and high spirits and I wondered whether half of them should be driving, immediately chiding myself for being such a '*rompi coglioni*', 'ball breaker'!

Looking around for Mauro and Luisa I saw them heading towards the door so bade a fond farewell to my dinner companions and was rewarded by a resounding kiss on both cheeks by my Marcello Mastroianni lookalike and a proffered business card with his name and number. Lorenzo…

"If we need help with the Russian I will let Mauro know and he can bring you to a rehearsal…but call me any time - if you want…"

"*Va bene!*" I smiled and kissed him back and, with a soft touch on his arm, followed Mauro and Luisa out to the car, reflecting on the extraordinarily wonderful evening I'd had.

We drove home a different way, one which I also knew and when Mauro swung the car round a steep hairpin bend to take a small side road, I remarked "Aha, *intelligente!*" for the route he was taking was a little-known shortcut used by the farmers to get to the area close to the Hamlet without having to go through the village, thus saving Mauro a round trip.

"Is there nowhere you don't know?" he asked me.

"Not around here I don't think. Remember that I spend days driving around here getting to know the area and Paolo has also taught me many shortcuts. I feel at home here. I like connecting up the different bits - like a...." And I realised that I didn't know the word for jigsaw, so used the word for puzzle instead. They knew what I meant.

Having thanked them profusely for such an amazing evening, I clambered out of the car. It was very late. I looked up at the sky and saw millions of twinkling stars. Paolo had promised to take me to the little observatory that had discovered Tincana and I could think of nothing that I'd like more than to look heavenwards through the clear unpolluted skies.

Chapter 28

Florence, Cantuccini, Vin Santo and a sobering meeting

The day dawned when we had to head down to Florence to meet the property lawyer, and for me to meet my *Commercialista*. I was dreading the last appointment and had a notebook stuffed full of questions to ask him. I hoped that the meeting wouldn't take too long because Paolo would have to wait for me before commencing the long journey back. Speeding down the A1, I thought of how many times I had driven this road, especially the tract between Bologna and Florence where the fast three-lane motorway gives way to a perilous dual carriageway which twists and turns its scenic way through the Appenines, offering stunning views when not plunging through long dark tunnels where the trucks keep to the right and everyone else, irrespective of their horsepower - or driving skills - tries to overtake them. The first time I had driven that road, in the late 1980's, I'd been terrified. Many many years of doing the route regularly had honed my driving skills and being what the Italians call a *Ferrarista* - someone who drives fast - I'd actually relished the drive.

Not having been down to Florence for years I was astonished to see, that in my absence, a second fast *superstrada* had been built and one was offered the option of the scenic route (the original one) or the direct route with longer but more modern and better illuminated tunnels. The last time I'd returned from the South I'd taken the Via Aurelia - the coastal road, originally built by the Romans which had also been upgraded into a superstrada - and had turned off onto the

A15 Motorway running between Livorno and Parma, to join up with the A1 heading north. This, the *La Cisa*, is my favourite motorway because it loops through Matilda country over the Passo de la Cisa passing evocative places such as Aulla and other small towns of the spookily atmospheric Lunigiana.

Paolo and I made good time and decided to park adjacent to the medieval walls of Florence near the Torrigiani Gardens. Our meeting wasn't until 4pm so we decided to walk into the city via a less touristy route, thus avoiding the crowds around the stunning Ponte Vecchio, Florence's famous bridge which is covered with jewellery shops selling wonderful, sparkly and wildly-expensive things!

Many years earlier I had spent a lot of time in the city; I'd been in a loose relationship with one of the handsomest men I'd ever seen and from time to time he would call me and wherever I was I would go to meet him. In between bouts of passion we would walk the city streets together and he would tell me of its history. He was immensely cultured and knowledgeable and being with him was always utterly fascinating. Paolo asked me how I knew the city so well and I told him. He laughed "Are you still in contact with him."

"Yes. We've been friends for years."

"Do you want to go and see him? I can find somewhere for lunch and meet you later."

I roared with laughter. "No! But thank you for the offer. He is not the sort of person one meets for an hour or two... we talk too you know!"

He grinned and I changed the subject for I was getting hungry. Florentine cooking is legendary and rightly so. I was looking forward to finding somewhere with *cucina tradizionale* and hopefully without tourists. For although I am a foreigner, to my mind there are degrees of foreignness! While I do not deny that a visit to any of Italy's great cities with all their incredible cultural treasures is something that everyone ought to experience, I liked being as invisible as I could make myself, in order to properly savour whatever the area had to offer. So we looked for a Trattoria with the menu in Italian, as opposed to a multilingual one with little flags denoting the different languages spoken within.

We were not disappointed and spent a very happy couple of hours gorging ourselves on *Crostini* - little slices of toasted bread liberally spread with chicken liver pate, or chopped tomatoes and basil - then a couple of *Crespelle* - rolled pancakes stuffed with ricotta and spinach and covered in a Bechamel sauce. I eschewed the main, meat course, but the owner, a welcoming, amusing and very cultured man, persuaded Paolo to try the *Trippa* - Tripe (which I loathe) - which he ate with great relish and pronounced to be '*ottimo*' excellent. The dessert menu was then proffered, although tempted I wanted nothing more than to round off my lunch with *Cantuccini* and *Vin Santo*. The hard, dry, twice-baked almond biscuits which are traditionally dipped into the incredibly sweet and alcoholic *Vin Santo* - literally Holy Wine - a dessert wine made from the local varieties of grapes - Trebbiano and Malvasia. Aged for at least three years, though some producers prefer to wait for five or even ten years, the high sugar content of the wine, ensures that even if stored for such a long period, it does not turn to vinegar.

The *Cantuccini*, originally from the Tuscan city of Prato, seventeen kilometres to the north west of Florence, are ancient in origin. Pliny the Elder (the Roman author, naturalist and philosopher) boasted that they would be edible for centuries, they were a favourite of the Roman legions and, it is said, that Christopher Columbus carried them on his voyages, because they didn't spoil.

I thoroughly enjoyed my portion and asked for more of the Vin Santo which was particularly good.

A couple of Espressos later and carrying the gift of an excellent bottle of local wine, we hurried towards our rendezvous with the *Avvocato* and the *Commercialista*.

The meeting with the *Avvocato*, Matteo, a charming and very educated man in his early 40's, did not disappoint. He would be willing to work with Paolo on a reciprocal basis, that is if Paolo had clients who wanted to buy in Tuscany then he would happily look after them and if he had clients who were interested in what we had for sale, then he would pass them on to Paolo. Fees would be split. He didn't know our area well but was pleasantly surprised when we showed him the photos I'd taken and also those taken from Daedalus. He agreed that there was enormous scope for the redevelopment of the villages and was very up-to-date with the necessary legislation. It appeared that the Italian government and therefore the *Regioni*, were very keen to attract inward investment - even offering advantageous tax rates for certain criteria, such as working from home and running an Italian-based business. Not for the first time was I proud to tell someone of the superfast Broadband that we had in our area. He was impressed.

He asked how we were going to manage the fiscal aspects of our collaboration, given Brexit. I told him that I would be able to answer him better once I'd spoken to his colleague, Giorgio, my *Commercialista*. Under Italian law, the vendor pays the Broker, *Geometra* or Estate Agent, a commission of 3% on the sale price, while the purchaser pays the person acting for them, in this case, me, another 3%. As Paolo was a *Geometra* his Association forbade him to act as an Estate Agent - these being allowed to act for both vendor and purchaser, thus earning 6% on each transacted sale. But he was entitled to the 3% which he said was more than suitable and was happy for me to earn 'my' 3% for my role in the proceedings. Obviously if we worked with the Florentine office then we would have to fee share but we agreed that this would be approached on a case by case basis.

In the back of my mind were the nagging doubts of my situation. I would have to register as a *Libera Professionista* and pay the associated national insurance contributions and taxes. It all sounded horribly bureaucratic and expensive. I looked at the time, saw that I was due in my other meeting and left Paolo and Matteo to meet with Giorgio.

He was young, very bright, very efficient and spoke incredible English. I had apologised at the beginning of the meeting and requested that we conduct it in English as I simply didn't have the proficiency in Italian to understand legal and commercial jargon. He was charming and agreed immediately, commenting drily that most Italians had difficulty with the more arcane aspects!

We went through my parlous financial situation and as we talked I realised that I had no alternative but to find the wherewithal to move back to the UK. Not being Italian was turning into a disadvantage and every time I came across some bureaucratic hurdle I felt sick and scared. If things with Paolo turned out to be successful I would soon find myself in deep deep water financially for, as a *Libera Professionista, he confirmed that* I would be expected to pay all sorts of things and not having any form of financial cushion, disaster could strike almost immediately.

What on earth was I going to say to Paolo? I asked Giorgio how many days a year I needed to be in Italy in order to be able to do what I needed to do without becoming part of the fiscal system. I explained that if I earned anything from the venture, it would be payable in the UK as the clients were likely to be predominantly British and that I would therefore pay British taxes on any earnings. My only connection with Paolo being informal as we were not forming a company or legal joint venture. We we working together for individual benefit by pooling our resources.

He said that as long as we kept it like that then what I did in the UK was between me and Her Majesty's Revenue & Customs. I was allowed into Italy as a non Resident for up to 180 days a year under current EU rules but after Brexit, no-one knew. Especially with regard to the existing double tax treaty between the two countries.

Given the uncertainty and my position, his advice to me was to cancel my Italian Residency, go home, become UK resident once more and put my *Carta d'Identità*, of which I'd been so proud, into a drawer. I agreed. Then told him I couldn't afford to get home, that was the problem.

"Do you not have any savings?"

"I'm living on what I have left, so no, I don't".

"Do you have a private pension?" I told him I had a small one in the UK. He suggested that, without delay, I call my Independent Financial Advisor to see whether I was entitled to draw down a lump sum. I asked him if he'd mind if I did it there and then, so that he could be present if my IFA asked any questions I couldn't answer. He looked amused but agreed. I don't think he actually understood how terrified and vulnerable I felt and, at this moment, all I wanted to do was go home and feel safe living and

working within a system I knew and understood. I now realised that I was too old for such adventures and wanting nothing more than to live a quiet life on my terms, free from fear and worry.

With my heart in my mouth I dialled my IFA, and to my amazement he answered almost immediately. Good start. I explained where I was and what were my circumstances. He asked to be put on speaker so that he could also hear what Giorgio had to say. I pressed the button and waited for a moment while he looked up my file. After a minute or so he came back saying that yes, I WAS entitled to draw down a small lump sum from my pension, as I was now over 60 and not a UK Resident but that as soon as I became one again I would not be able to draw down anything further. How small I asked, mentioning a figure that I had quickly calculated would get me and my stuff and Geisha home and give me something to live on and some breathing space once back in the UK.

Telling me that I could have a little more if necessary, he said that it could not be paid into a foreign account and that it would have to go into my UK bank and then be transferred to my Italian one. It could be quite expensive on bank transfer charges. I almost laughed with delight, telling him about a wonderful App I had, called TransferWise, which guaranteed to be cheaper than traditional bank transfers and which was extremely efficient. I gave him my bank account details and we agreed that within the next two weeks, once I'd been to the town hall in Verona and ceded my Residency, upon receipt of signed paperwork to that effect and which I should courier to him without delay. He would then make the transfer, there would of course also be forms which he would email forms for me to print out and sign and that I to return hard copies to him, via courier as fast as possible. I recalled that there was a DHL office in Castellarano near Sassuolo.

He sounded pleased, Giorgio was smiling and I just wanted to burst into tears of relief.

I thanked both men profusely, ended the call and leaned over the meeting table to shake Giorgio's hand. "There is just the small matter of some tax that you owe for last year…" I glared at him and in that wonderfully eloquent way that the Italians have with their body language, he shrugged and spread his hands, basically saying, "what can I do, this is how it is…"

He was right, at least I knew this would be the last of the nasty and quite terrifying financial surprises to be sprung on me. I could see why there was such an active black economy in Italy, for how on earth did people survive if they weren't in full-time occupation? A little job, off the books, here and there were obviously lifelines for most people. It was ingrained into the very psyche and culture of the country and I felt that the authorities were wrong to try and stamp it out. It was surely necessary for the continuance of life!

After thanking them and taking our leave of Giorgio and Matteo, Paolo and I hailed a taxi and climbed in.

"*Dove andiamo?*" Where are we going? asked the taxi driver. Paolo looked blank and I laughed, knowing that he hadn't a clue where we'd left the car, for it had been me that had directed him to the car park.

"The parking by the Torriagiani Gardens, the north end please" I said, grinning at Paolo's look of astonishment, how did I know where north was?

"I have a photographic memory for maps and once I've seen something I can remember it. Which at times has been pretty useful" I explained. The taxi driver guffawed. Who had heard of a woman with a sense of direction, let alone a photographic memory for maps?!

The journey home was interesting. Paolo was all fired up about the possible collaboration with Matteo and his team. For my part, I was glad that there was the potential for collaboration for I felt, very much, that I was abandoning Paolo and letting him down. I took a deep breath and mentioned this. I explained what had happened in my meeting with Giorgio and suggested that, since people didn't tend to look for second homes in the autumn and winter (unless they were buying ski chalets) that I spend the winter months in the UK building a client base and when the spring came, I would come back out for a few months (well within my 180 days) and we would show the properties and hopefully sell some!

Paolo thought that this was an excellent solution because the winters could be pretty terrible, cold, wet and depressing and half of the more rural properties would be impossible to visit - especially if there was snow, which most years there was. He told me that I was wise to go home, that nothing would suffer in my absence, that we would continue to progress matters on FaceTime and I could spend the winter putting my life in order. We had enough stuff to do in any case and I could take Geisha home to England, knowing that everything would be here when we came back again in the spring. I also suspected that Paolo would quite like a break from me!

At which point the accumulated stress of the past months dissolved and for the first time in a long while I felt secure as Paolo drove through the darkening night northwards towards home - my Italian home.

Chapter 29

'All things must pass'

Whilst I was relieved that I had found resolution to my situation and would be returning to England, I was also ineffably sad, for I had come to really love the Hamlet, the area and the people. I had been welcomed, without judgement, by so many people and every time I went into Carpineti, someone always greeted me cheerily.

My days were about to become a whirlwind of administrative activity. But first I would have to sit down with Stefano and explain what I would be doing. Paolo and I had agreed our *modus operandum.* I would come out in late April or early May and stay until September, always counting the days to make sure that I didn't stay more than the allowed 180 - and that included those spent driving to and from the Italian border. No one seemed to know whether this applied to time spent in the whole EU or just Italy. It usually took me three days to drive down and so, to be safe, I would subtract six from my total and make sure that I was back in the UK by day 175 or 176 at the absolute latest.

Feeling somewhat tearful I had broached the subject the morning after I had returned from Florence. We were sitting outside at the glass table having our morning coffee. Stefano knew something was afoot because I was on edge. With his ever-present unlit cigar in his mouth, he regarded me, silently inviting me to get on with it and say whatever it was I was so clearly needing to tell him. I took a deep breath and plunged straight in.

"You know that I had to visit my *Commercialista* to try and sort out my financial affairs here?" He nodded, waiting for me to continue. "Well I did, yesterday. His advice was that for financial reasons and because of Brexit I cannot live here permanently and so I should cede my Residency and go home, back to the UK where I would once again become a British Resident. However, under current EU legislation I can come back for up to 180 days a year. Paolo and I have discussed this and feel that we can continue our collaboration with me in the UK for the winter and here in the spring and summer. I would of course continue to pay the rent on the *Tavernetta*, and leave most of my things in situ, I just wouldn't be here for part of the year. Would that be acceptable to you?"

He looked at me for a long moment and then nodded his head "It would". It had been as simple as that and I was profoundly grateful.

His acceptance finally brought the enormity of what I was about to do home to me and I threw myself into organising the myriad things associated with a half move.

What to leave, what to take with me. When, how and with whom? I also had to make sure that my tenants in England were served proper Notice on their tenancy. It was due to expire in November anyway but there had been murmurings about them extending it or even renewing it. While that had seemed an ideal solution at the time, their rent being my only source of income, now all I wanted was my house back. I organised a Skype call with them, explained my situation and was profoundly relieved when they told me that they'd decided they wanted to buy a bigger house so would be leaving at the end of the tenancy. In fact would I mind if they left a month early? I was delighted and said it would be fine, that I'd organise it with the managing agent and we agreed that the house would be empty from the beginning of October.

Meanwhile I had to get up to Verona fast. Wrestling with the *Comune di Verona's* website and faced with incomprehensible myriad choices within various departments, I felt the familiar sick feeling in my stomach. There was nothing about a '*Denuncia*' of *Residenza*. There was plenty about applying for one, or changing *Comune*, but nothing about actually leaving the country. Maybe it was incomprehensible that anyone would actually want to depart, having gone through torturous bureaucracy to obtain the desired Residency including having to be at home on an unspecified day at an unspecified time to receive a visit from the local Policeman to confirm that you were who you said you were (proof of identity required) and you lived where you said you did! This was one aspect of life in Italy that I most certainly was not going to miss!

In the event, I was lucky, I phoned the *Comune's* helpline and a very chatty lady told me that she rarely had questions about abandoning (her words!) Italy. She put me through to another less chatty lady who, in an efficient and a matter of fact way, gave me an appointment for the following week telling me to bring all my original paperwork, my *Carta d'Identità* and my British passport. Luckily the time slot she'd given me was 10.00 am which meant that I wouldn't get stuck in the rush hour traffic going into Verona.

I phoned Aurora, with whom I'd spent that magical first Christmas Eve and we arranged to meet for lunch. It was odd, she was less than two hours away, but it seemed like another world. We'd spoken often about her coming down to the Hamlet, but it had somehow never happened. Now it didn't look as if she'd make it before I left, which was a pity because I would have loved to have shown her 'my' corner of Italy and to repay her hospitality.

The appointed day arrived and I left ridiculously early, not wanting to get stuck on the motorway if there was an accident - which happened all too frequently - I could be held up for, literally, hours.

Driving back into Verona I felt stressed and anxious and I simply hadn't realised how much the constant battle for survival had affected me. It was, however, lovely being back in that beautiful city - of which I had so many happy memories and as I drove towards the requisite office, through ancient streets, mostly medieval, built upon Roman foundations, I realised that I was also going to miss the city. I'd been very happy there in the first flush of excitement and with a steady job. The *'Anagrafe'* the registry office dealing with such matters, was a stunning modern building cleverly built into a part of the old medieval and probably Roman walls surrounding the historic centre. Parking was usually impossible but I was lucky and found a disabled space close by. My UK Blue Badge, with the EU flag on it was still valid but for how much longer? Brexit was getting closer every day.

Which is what I told the efficient woman when, having only had to wait a few minutes, my number had been called and I was sitting in front of her, signing forms and handing her my documents for

404

copying. She'd asked why I was leaving and nodded sympathetically at my response - I cited Brexit - swiftly and efficiently bringing my brief sojourn as an Italian Resident to a close, handing me back copies of all my documentation and, to my surprise, my *Carta d'Identità*. I said nothing because it would be nice to keep it as a memento of my Italian residency.

I left the office feeling quite emotional and sent Aurora an SMS to say that I was on my way. We had arranged to meet in the restaurant under my former office and as I walked in I was greeted like an old friend by the staff and Lucia, the wonderfully glamorous, cynical and very funny woman who ran the bar. She and I had hit it off immediately when I had first started work and I would pop down for a quick coffee and a chat when I needed to escape the madness upstairs! Working in an office with very thorough and efficient colleagues had been a joy, for they had somehow managed to combine great professionalism with natural exuberance and when the smokers gathered on the balcony (eight floors up!) for a swift nicotine hit, the guffaws of laughter emanating therefrom were at odds with the stress of their individual roles. I was delighted to see some of them already at their usual table and went over to be greeted with hugs and a lot of teasing. I realised that I missed the interaction with them but definitely wouldn't swap it for my bucolic existence. I was asked whether I had fallen in love with a farmer yet and what had brought me back to Verona. I said no to the former, making them howl with mirth when I told them about the man at Valentina's who had offered to marry me so I could stay on. When I told them why I'd come to the city they looked thoughtful and nodded mournfully. "Did you vote for Brexit?" asked one.

"No. I think that those who did were misguided and they certainly don't understand Europe but the result was very close and now we have to make the best of it."

"How do you feel about leaving?"

"Sad. Very sad, but nothing is forever and who knows what adventures might await me in England?!" I wondered whether I'd ever see them again, this group of young, hard-working and very very good-looking people. They had welcomed me, their gentle teasing enabling me to feel accepted and part of the team.

Aurora materialised at my elbow and, having hugged and kissed everyone goodbye, I followed her to our table for a good chat. She was unsurprised at my decision and announced that she would come and visit me in my cottage as soon as Geisha and I were settled. I told her that I would absolutely love that and that I couldn't wait to show her around the beautiful area in which I lived.

Driving back down the motorway I felt as if another huge weight had lifted from my shoulders and as Monte Valestra became visible in the far distance, the phone rang. Being on hands-free I answered.

"Hello, is that Cassandra?" asked an English voice. I answered in the affirmative. "My name is Mark Stevens and I'm a friend of Jonathan's" referring to an old friend of mine back in England. "He tells me that you are dealing in real estate and I wondered whether you might be able to come and have a look at our house in northern

Tuscany? We have been trying to sell it with a local agent but without success."

I didn't tell him I was about to leave the country, because I was pretty sure that between Paolo, Matteo in Florence and with me hovering electronically in the background, we might be able to help him. I asked him a few questions as to location and timings, gave him my email address and told him that I'd be home later on and would respond to him properly then.

I was amused that this had happened now, but I was grateful for it seemed to indicate that there was some potential not only for our area but maybe a little further afield. I didn't want to encroach on Matteo's territory but this seemed to be at the very limits of his 'range' and was actually only a couple of hours' drive past Castelnovo, so practicable from our point of view.

I decided to come off the motorway before it joined the A1 and drive home across country instead. A pretty, but somewhat annoying drive, as it was peppered liberally with the ubiquitous '*Auto Velox*', the speed cameras. Happily my SatNav beeped each time I was about to pass one and Ben's disembodied voice would gravely inform me of my speed and that of the speed limit. I loved this route despite the intrusive cameras as it led through small villages, around towns and past great tile factories, all shiny and interesting-looking. There were *Trattorias* and *Pizzerias* and *Gelaterias* beside the road and a fabulous emporium selling local charcuterie and cheeses. There was also much less traffic and I didn't have to trawl through the depressing outskirts of Sassuolo.

Having successfully evaded the dreaded flashes of the speed cameras, I was soon winding my way back up the mountain, no longer officially a Resident and now just a tourist - albeit one in a car with Italian number plates - the changing of which, back to UK ones, was another thing to add to my ever-increasing to-do list.

Geisha greeted me affectionately, I could see that Farah had been in and given her more food and changed her water and no doubt there had been a few minutes of cuddles too. We sat on the sofa with her purring contentedly on my knee and when I told her that we were going home soon her ears twitched and she turned to look at me, talking in her Siamese way. I swear she understood! She had loved our house and I knew that she hadn't been too impressed with the flat in Verona, so I was glad that I was soon able to return her to her real home.

But first, emails. As promised Mark had sent through details of his house which looked lovely. A group of two adjoining *case coloniche* had been sensitively restored to provide year-round holiday accommodation for the owners and their friends. A swimming pool had, of course, been built in the pretty garden and the property was on the edge of an interesting-looking small town, close to Aulla! I was finally going to be able to explore this intriguing area, one which I'd raced past on so many occasions, promising myself that on the next trip, I'd stop and have a mosey around. Something which, of course, I'd never done.

I emailed Mark back, and in a swift exchange we agreed that I would go the following week when he and his family were going to be there. This gave me plenty of time to research the area and similar properties online. He had mentioned a sum which they hoped to realise and I needed to know whether this was in the right ballpark or not. Hence the research. There was a lot of competition, some houses looked truly fabulous, some less so, but it was an appealing area, easily accessible by motorway up the coast from Pisa airport and also Genoa, at a pinch. It was equidistant from the sea near Livorno and also the Passo Cerreto, the mountain pass with its ski lodges and nature trails, which led into the area beyond Castelnovo. It should be an easy and delightful drive. I was looking forward to it.

The next day, being sunny and a little cooler, with a cloudless blue sky, I decided I'd had enough of making lists and doing moving admin. So I headed off into Valestra to take photos of the village, general views, for the particulars I was preparing. I'd parked the car up at a small parking area, lyrically named Piazza del Pane, at the crossroads to the Hamlet and the tiny borgo of Magliatica. The *Comune* had erected a small wooden shelter in the middle of the piazza, where in the evenings the elderly would sit and watch the setting sun beyond the mountain.

I'd bought a wide angled clip on lens for my iPhone which actually was brilliant for landscape shots and I was busy snapping away, standing somewhat stupidly in the middle of the road. I heard a car brake sharply and come to a halt beside me and turned around. To my astonishment, it was an English-registered BMW coupe, inside which was sitting an elegant couple.

" Oh I'm so sorry, let me get out of your way…" they gazed at me in open-mouthed astonishment as I'd spoken to them in English! What were the chances of coming across a compatriot in the middle of the road in a tiny Italian village in the middle of the Appenines?!

"You're ENGLISH?" their evident delight was unexpected but I smiled and admitted that, yes, I was indeed English. "Oh good! Can you tell us where the Parmesan Factory is?"

I could and I did, suggesting that as it was down a lane why didn't they follow me, indicating my car parked just a few metres away. They agreed enthusiastically and we drove in convoy the short distance to the *Latteria* San Pietro. They would never had found it if I'd not been standing in the middle of the road, for *Latteria* means dairy and there was nothing about Parmigiano on the signage.

Parking in the car park I showed them the entrance to the small shop. They thanked me and asked if I spoke Italian. I told them I did and they asked if I'd hang on for a few minutes to help them with their purchases should the need arise. I said of course and watched as they made their way to the entrance, they could be nothing other than British. The man was wearing cream chinos and a striped linen shirt, with deck shoes on his feet and a Panama sun hat atop his head and his wife, or girlfriend, was wearing baggy linen trousers and baggy over shirt, with expensive looking gold leather sandals, and a pretty straw hat perched on her artfully cut blonde hair. Both wore impenetrable black sunglasses. How the hats stayed on their heads when they were driving with the top down was a conundrum! They looked smart and well off and indefinably British! Both were tanned and yet there was something, apart from the giveaway GB plated BMW, that marked them out as Brits.

I waited by the car and within a minute or so I was asked whether I could help. They were confused as to which sort of Parmigiano to buy. I briefly explained the differences without going into culinary detail. They also wondered whether the Ricotta would last the journey back to their holiday villa. I discussed this with the lady behind the counter and she said that she'd pack it in ice as well as vacuum seal the Parmesan so that both survived the trip - I explained that the Parmesan was going to go back to England with them, so she doubled her efforts and presented them with a huge, well protected package. They were astonished at the price and queried it. I asked if there was a problem. No - other than the fact that they couldn't believe how inexpensive it was compared to the delis and supermarkets at home! They had a point and I made a mental note to buy a LOT of cheese to take home with me.

We stood by the cars and chatted. They were fascinated as to what I was doing living in the middle of nowhere. Was my family with me? I explained that it was just me and my cat. They were intrigued by this and asked lots of questions about the area. I told them about my collaboration with Paolo and asked whether they or their friends might like to buy a house in the area. Or even a project. They looked very interested and we exchanged numbers. I said that we didn't yet have a website and that things were at a very early stage, but if they were at all keen on exploring things further we would have much to see the following spring and summer. I was devastated that I couldn't show them details immediately, but it was way too premature, we didn't yet have prices or written instructions from the vendors, so it would have been wrong to do anything other than take their details and promise to keep in touch. I asked them where they were staying and was astounded when they told me - the very area I was going to be visiting the following week.

They'd read about our prizewinning cheese factory and had spent a very pleasant few hours driving over the mountains to get here. What a coincidence!

We chatted for a few minutes longer then they said they had better leave as they wanted to head into Modena to see the famous carved Baptistery doors of the Duomo. I suggested that rather than schlep back over the mountain roads, they return the fast way, via the motorways, the A1 and then the A15 La Cisa, and take the Aulla exit. They thanked me and said that was excellent advice and that it had been lovely meeting me and they would definitely be in touch as they were very taken with this area. Wishing me luck with the new venture they somehow managed to shoehorn their massive package of cheeses into the ridiculously small boot of the BMW and with a throaty roar, headed off down the road I'd indicated to the valley and Modena.

I stood in the car park for a few minutes longer skating my head in disbelief. What were the chances of bumping into an English couple in the village who just might be interested in buying a property in this area. Talk about synchronicity! I couldn't wait to tell Paolo!

Chapter 30

The eleventh hour of the eleventh day of the eleventh month...

Best laid plans and all that! Mark Stevens called me a couple of days before I was due to meet him and told me that he was very sorry but his plans had changed and their trip over was delayed indefinitely. I came clean and said that actually it was something of a relief as I was preparing to return to the UK for the winter and that I would be much better placed to meet him sometime after Easter next year if that still suited him. I explained that it was unlikely that eager house hunters would be lining up during the colder months, he concurred and we agreed to be in contact the following spring.

Paolo and I had also started winding down our activities - he needed to focus more on his *Geometra* work as he had some demanding new clients and we both felt that we should spend the winter months doing our respective things! He knew that I was going to face an uphill task getting my house back in order and genuinely wanted me to have time to myself to do it. I was grateful for that but we agreed that we would remain in contact nevertheless.

Dear Farah had been devastated when I'd told her. We'd become such good friends and had both enjoyed our evening chats in the cool shade of the portico. I was really going to miss her and the children. And Hussein who, with his dry sense of humour and endless acts of kindness, had also become a friend.

I called Ugo and told him what had happened. He was, unsurprisingly, most supportive and happy that I would be back in the

Spring. I also called Luisa and said that I was really sorry, but the Ladies' Matilda trip was going to have to be next year - which would actually give me the time to read the books I'd bought and put together a really good day out. She agreed and asked how Geisha was going to manage the trip.

Stefano and Carlo - and the boisterous Asi - had all left the Hamlet and returned to their respective homes. I promised Stefano that I'd pop down the mountain and say goodbye before I left. Farah was busy shutting the house up for the winter and Mimi prowled around looking somewhat disconsolate. The preparations for the coming winter were well underway. The *boscaiolo* had delivered huge loads of wood for the main house, Hassan and his brother, aided by Suleiman, had overseen the storage and also brought our wood into the woodshed for their use. It was sensible that we had three separate caches of wood, thus ensuring that we were responsible for our own supplies and not running down the others'.

Hassan told me that the farmers had pronounced that the coming winter would be a harsh one with a lot of snow and that I needed to leave as fast as I could. I told him that the timing of Geisha's rabies jab and other necessary injections for her unhindered entry into the UK (we were rabies free) was dictating when I could leave. There had to be waiting period after the first shot and she had to have the last shot not less and not more than 72 hours before we crossed The Channel. Which meant that I would have to drive like the wind up through Italy and France in order to get her through in time. Otherwise we would have to find a vet in Calais and repeat the process.

I'd twice taken her down to the vet in Cerredolo. He'd been delighted to see her and crooned at her in a mixture of Italian and his American-accented English. She had been stoic and borne the indignities to which she'd been subjected with great aplomb. On our last visit and clutching her Certificate of Vaccination with her updated and stamped Pet Passport I thanked him and bore her off to the car - but not before all the people in the waiting room had had a chance to pet her! Her aristocratic good looks had enchanted them, even the gnarled old *contadino* - farmer - in the corner who had looked wonderingly at her blue eyes and pronounced her to be "*bellissima*". She had purred graciously for a few moments, basking in the adoration and then curled up and gone to sleep in her furry carrying bag, for there was already a nip in the air.

For the last time I took the scenic route back to the Hamlet, instead of turning off the main road towards Levizzano, I'd got into the habit of turning off closer to Cerredolo and driving up through tiny hamlets and ancient churches - all bearing Matilda signs - via Debbia (church built by Matilda), San Cassiano (ugly modern church but a great family trattoria) and on to Cost'Alta, past the driveway to the intriguingly-named *Agriturismo Sole Luna* - Sun and Moon. I'd asked Paolo about it and he'd said that it was in a stunning location with incredible views and that it had a small pool and several rooms in some beautifully restored farm buildings. It prided itself on its sustainable architecture and approach to living - taking as little from the land as it could and serving zero food miles organic food. It

415

sounded like a good template for our abandoned villages and I decided that I would visit when I returned.

Turning onto the road to the Hamlet, I encountered Red Tractor and waved at the driver, who waved back. We inched past each other, him skimming the bank on his side and me trying not to look down at the terrifying drop on my side, it was only a field but the slope was sheer and I had visions of Geisha and I rolling over and over as the car plunged down the hill. How the farmers managed to plough the almost vertical fields was beyond me! But I would see them, their shiny vehicles perched precariously at impossible angles, a far cry from the huge flat fields of home.

As well as the bureaucracy associated with returning home I'd also had to consider what belongings I needed to send back. Obviously the car would be packed to the gunwales with our immediate needs, but all my bedding, winter clothing, kitchen equipment and many books were still in the *Tavernetta*. I'd decided against calling the removal company that had already been and taken the antiques etc. and which had

had them in temperature controlled storage in the UK. So I looked online for a man with a van. There were international ones who, it seemed, ploughed up and down the motorways of Italy on a regular basis and who did whole or part loads.

Farah, Hussein and I had boxed up as much as we could and she and I had started vacuum bagging clothes, bedding and the like. I needed to provide approximate dimensions and weight to potential couriers in order to get an accurate quote. Apparently the French police loved nothing more than stopping British registered vans and subjecting them to bureaucratic hell by insisting that everything was documented down to detailed descriptions and exact weight. So Hassan and I were very very thorough and each box, bag and suitcase was weighed and measured.

I had decided to leave behind all my summer-weight bedding and clothing, suitably bagged up, and Farah had said that if I piled it all into the sitting room, she would light the *stufa* once a week to keep the damp out and to maintain a minimum temperature. I was grateful for her forethought.

Having finally ascertained the volume of the goods to be returned to England, I put it out for pricing on an amazing website I'd found, Eurogearshift. I had an answer almost immediately, yes Gordon was available to come and pick up my stuff, but not until after I'd left! This didn't actually matter because he was going to be quicker than me getting back and I wasn't moving back into my cottage immediately because it needed new carpets, so I had rented an Air BnB nearby for a week. Gordon and I spoke several times, I sent him Google earth screenshots, map co-ordinates and Farah's mobile number. I explained that everything would be ready for him to load but that she didn't actually speak a word of English - he said his Italian was basic so I told him that I'd be on the mobile (Geisha and I would actually be in France on the day of the pickup) the whole time in case I was needed to translate or answer queries etc. The price was extremely reasonable and the testimonials on his website reassuringly glowing. What a wonderful service! No more mad Brazilians taking time off work and no ridiculously expensive Italian *uomini con furgoni,* the likes of which I'd remembered encountering on my attempts to move from Verona!

Things started falling into place. I'd planned the trip, booked cat-friendly hotels along the route with a necessary respite of two nights in one place so that Geisha could recuperate from being in the car for so long. Luca the ironmonger had sold me picnic stuff, plates and a thermos for necessary coffee. Money had arrived into my account from the UK thanks to my extremely efficient IFA and I was starting to say my *arriverdercis* - until we see each other again - to Mauro and Luisa, to Roberto, to Ugo, Alberto and Luisa R, to Valentina and the Sisters in their Trattoria and of course to Paolo. Everyone had wished me a safe journey - most thought me deeply eccentric to be leaving with my cat to plough up through half of Europe alone in a car packed to the gunwales with my life! But without exception all of them had told me I was wise to avoid spending the winter in the Hamlet. The forecast was

looking somewhat worrying and I was thankful that I had a schedule to stick to, for the snows were due to arrive literally the day after our departure.

I popped into the bank to tell them that I was heading home for the winter but that I would be back in the spring. I'd paid Eolo 9 months in advance for the Wi-fi - which would remain unused unless Ugo wanted to stay and use it in my absence. I'd checked with Alberto that no *bollette*- bills - were unpaid and I'd prepaid Stefano his rent to the following May. I had already shifted into Anglo-Saxon mode it seemed! My somewhat lackadaisical Italian persona was already being replaced by a frighteningly efficient British one! It was definitely time to go home.

The night before our departure I rang Stefano and bellowed down the phone at him. Bless him, his deafness was getting worse but he was happy to hear from me and I told him to be good and do what his doctors told him and we would see each other in the spring. It was chilly as I walked around the Hamlet mentally taking my leave of the ghosts and the Beings that I was convinced inhabited the grounds and the fields. I shivered and reflected that I was pleased we were leaving. A winter snowed-in at the *Tavernetta* would probably have driven me mad and I was longing to get back to England, my DNA was positively fizzing at the thought. Besides I wanted Geisha to be snug in our centrally heated home without my having to wake up in the night to feed the stufa. She and I already smelt of woodsmoke!

Returning to the *Tavernetta* I found Hassan waiting for me. He'd had dinner and was now ready to help me load the car. We'd both looked at the pile of stuff, suitcases of winter clothes, bags of documents, some kitchen utensils and cutlery, all the paraphernalia of everyday life. My pillow, Geisha's beds and travelling cat box, food and food bowls, cushions and blankets and torches and food and water all had to be fitted in. Where did I amass so much STUFF? All of which was, seemingly, vital.

Having moved many time in my life, mostly for work, I'd become extremely adept at packing cars. In fact when I'd left Greece I'd managed to pack an enormous amount of stuff into a tiny little hatchback, much to the astonishment and approbation of the movers, which I'd then had to unpack on the quayside of the ferry terminal as the Customs man wanted the drug dog to check the car. Why on earth he thought that I was taking drugs out of Greece was beyond me, but I'd unpacked and repacked the car and he hadn't lifted a finger to help!

Hassan and I managed it with no difficulty whatsoever, we even managed to create a cushioned viewing platform for Geisha in the middle just behind me, so that she could see where we were going and also benefit from heating or cooling from the air vents. The travelling cat litter tray fitted neatly into the footwell of the passenger seat, and her carrying case lay on the seat in case we were stopped by police, for having a loose animal in the car was very very illegal, although everyone did it. Geisha of course was far too sensible to try and distract me when I was driving and would sit quietly either on the passenger seat beside me, or on her viewing platform, hunkered down amid fleeces and blankets and protected from the rougher edges of the myriad bags, boxes and cases. These blankets would also double as emergency warmth should we break down in the forecast snow and I had had Amazon deliver foil emergency blankets - just in case - as well as a mug that heated soup and water by the cigarette lighter plug and several bottles of still mineral water, instant coffee, instant soup and tea bags. Farah had made me a huge supply of *panini* with her wonderful bread and two whole pizzas, cut into slices and put into a Tupperware box. I'd added chocolate, protein bars, loo rolls and cat treats! We were all set.

I slept badly that night. I just wanted to get away. My head was already in England and there was nothing for me here until the spring. Hassan had checked the oil, the water and the tyre pressures, I'd filled up with petrol in town which although expensive, was far less expensive than the exorbitant prices they charged at the motorway service stations. My Via Pass would ensure that we sailed unhindered through the *caselle* on the motorway and beside it was another which worked in France!

By 8.00 we were ready to leave, having bade a tearful farewell to Farah, promising her that I'd check in every night and when we finally got home. I think she was more worried for Geisha than for me! I know she was also concerned about the arrival of Gordon the man with the van and I told her to call me when he arrived.

It was just getting light as I pulled out of the drive and headed towards Levizzano and down the mountain. The *padana*, far below, was still in semi darkness and far to the north I saw a great dark mass of cloud, presaging the anticipated snow. I was thankful we were heading northwest and not towards it.

We reached the A1 just as it started sleeting. Pulling out into the main carriageway I knew that this was going to be a long and arduous drive home. Our first stop was Aosta, on the Italian side of the Mont Blanc tunnel, several hours' drive and not wanting to miss the turn offs onto other motorways, I was glad that I'd programmed the Sat Nav - Ben's reassuring voice telling me that I had to continue for 101 kilometres before taking the exit onto the A21 towards Piacenza. The sleet was becoming heavier and staying in the slow lane resulted in me being sprayed by the slush created by the wheels of the great 16-wheeler lorries that ploughed and up and down the motorways - except on Sundays. So, locking my arms, gritting my teeth and switching my headlamps up a notch, I moved into the middle lane and stayed there, just keeping pace with the traffic. No faster and no slower.

In a way I was glad that the weather was shitty for it meant that I wasn't pulled to look longingly at the mountains to my left, the mountains I'd called home for a while. I peered through my glasses into the ever-increasing gloom and just prayed for the kilometres to Piacenza to be swift and without incident.

They were. Almost as soon as we turned off, the weather changed and it was bright and cold. The sun shone from a beautiful blue sky with the thin line that marked the already snow-capped Alps just visible in the distance. We left Piacenza behind and headed for Alessandria and then Ivrea where we stopped at a service station for a bathroom break. Normally I would have put Geisha into her carry bag and taken her into the building with me, Italians are used to seeing little dogs being carried by their owners, but not cats! She was asleep and when I called her name she opened an eye and looked at me balefully. I told her that I was going to do *pipi* and did she want to come. By way of answering she looked at me as if I was an idiot, sighed and snuggled deeper into her nest. I locked the door and hurried inside not wanting to leave her too long alone in the car. I needed chocolate and so on my way back to the car, negotiating the torturous shopping aisle that every service station now comprises, ensuring that clients are unable to continue their journey without purchasing a

Greatest Hits CD of some famous Italian pop star, or kilos of 'artisan' pasta, or half a mortadella or bags of overly sweet biscuits. I loitered briefly looking for my winter fix of Ferrero's inestimable Pocket Coffee and Mon Cheri. The former are liquid espresso encased in crisp dark chocolate while the latter are dark chocolate with a whole cherry in liqueur inside. Both are addictive and both have saved me from exhaustion on many many occasions.

Luckily this service station had massive boxes of both, as well as the smaller versions. I opted for the former - one of each - and loaded up headed for the car. Geisha was still fast asleep and we set off again, me biting into the pocket coffees I was stuffing into my mouth and savouring each hit of espresso. I reflected that the Italians do make some amazing confectionery! Amazing food, amazing wine, amazing clothes, amazing music and literature and culture - just not amazing bureaucracy! At least not in the complimentary way!

We arrived in Aosta after another short stop near Pont Saint Martin where I'd munched my way through several slices of Farah's pizza and drunk one of the bottles of water. Geisha had sniffed at the pizza but eschewed the proffered anchovy. She knew that I'd feed her as soon as we'd settled into our room. Looking at the map - the old-fashioned but up-to-date paper map I kept in the car in case of global internet outage, or satellite failure - I'd mused on the place names of this area, all French and not at all Italian. Bard, Verres, Monjovet, Chatillon. Yet still in Italy. Proof of the geo-political vicissitudes of the country, necessitating the redrafting of maps and displacement of the populace. The Aosta Valley, had apparently formerly been the

Aoste *arondissment* of the Doire Department in the First French Empire, but had become part of the Kingdom of Italy, more specifically Sardinia (which was nowhere near Aosta!) in 1861. I reflected that, until the unification of Italy - the *Risorgimento*, under Garibaldi, in 1848 - Italy had long been under the rule of many foreign powers. The South had belonged to the Normans and the Ancient Greeks before them, the area around Naples had belonged to the Kingdom of the Two Sicilies (where was the second one?!), Rome and the east around Ravenna to the Papal States and the north to the Kingdom of Lombardy-Venetia. In the middle of all of this was the Grand Duchy of Tuscany, Matilda's fiefdom. Various parts of the country had come under the rule of the Greeks, the Normans, the Spanish, the Byzantine Empire and the Holy Roman Empire (Germany) to name but a few and it was a miracle that the Italian-ness of the country had survived through such turbulent history.

Which is probably why I loved it for each area was different, with its dialect, its cuisine, it's myths and legends. Even under the unifying influence of Ancient Rome, as evidenced by the Battle of Valestra, the indigenous peoples, the tribes, had fought to try and retain their independence and identity and not be absorbed into the homogeneity of one all-encompassing society.

The next morning, we left Italy, driving slowly through the tenebrous depths of the Mont Blanc Tunnel and onwards up the seemingly endless French motorways past names associated with, to my mind, great wines. For two days we ploughed northwest, ending our continental journey in a suite in the extremely smart and very expensive Novotel Suites at Coquelles, right by the Eurotunnel, which Geisha absolutely loved and where she had the entire reception and restaurant staff wrapped round her elegant paw. I phoned Farah. Everything had gone smoothly with Gordon and I knew that somewhere behind me - or maybe in front of me - my stuff was wending its way homewards.

Early on the morning of the 11th of November, following a slightly worrying SMS from Eurotunnel at 6.30 am warning of possible closure to the Tunnel due to maintenance concerns, I took Geisha and her passport to the Pet Reception Building where, heart in mouth, I waited while the slightly officious and worryingly coiffured veterinary officer checked her chip and her documentation.

" *Bon, tout est en ordre, vous pouvez partir...*" Good, everything is in order, you may depart. I thanked her and almost ran to the car to make sure that we got through the tunnel before the mooted closure.

40 minutes later, we emerged from the tunnel at Folkestone. It was exactly 11.11 am on the eleventh day of the eleven month. An historic day, both for having seen the cessation of the Great War, the First World War, and for the fact that we were finally home.

Manoeuvring away from the stream of traffic emerging from the covered Eurotunnel wagons, I pulled into a parking space by the side of the road, turned off the engine and sobbed and sobbed, finally letting the tears wash away all the buried stress and fear and the long-submerged feelings of being alone and vulnerable. Geisha climbed onto my knee, the first time she had ever done that while in a car, and nuzzled into me, we sat there together for quite some time. We were back.

To be continued…

Postscript

This book only tells half the story… my return the following Spring brought many more adventures - too many to include in one book!

So please look out for 'Further Tales from the Hamlet', to be published in mid 2022.

Here are the details of all the restaurants mentioned, I know the owners would love to meet new people. They may not speak English, so if you are likely to get stuck, take a phrase book with you!

All offer excellent traditional and regional cooking.

- Trattoria Vasirani, 28 via Cà Perizzi, (Felina), Castelnovo ne' Monti, 42035 RE. Tel: +39 0522 619429

- Cà Poggioli Ristorante, Via Lugo 18a, (Lugo near Cerredolo), Baiso, 42031 RE. Tel: +39 0522 844631

- Bar Trattoria da Gianni, Via Casette 60, Montefaraone (between Baiso and Carpineti), Carpineti, 42033 RE. Tel: +39 0522 893117

- Osteria Dei Cacciatori (Bikers Welcome), Via Ponte Dolo 83-87 (between Cerredolo and Ponte Dolo), Toano, 42010 RE. Tel: +39 0522 809415

- Foresteria San Benedetto, Viale do Bismantova 36, Castelnovo ne' Monti, 42035 RE. Tel: +39 0522 611752 (at the foot of the Pietra di Bismantova)

Il Forno, the bakery in Valestra, is run by Mauro, Luisa and their family. Their website is www.panificiodallari.it

You will see that their bread has been produced for over 50 years using natural yeast dough without the use of stabilisers and chemical additives. As they say 'as with good wine the bread of the Dallari bakery will never be the same as the previous year!'

Latteria Sociale San Pietro, the International multi award-winning Parmesan producer in Valestra. www.latteriadivalestra.it. Each individual producer is recognised by a unique code, theirs is 166.

Estetica Chiara in Castelnovo ne' Monti, for the best massages, beauty treatments and Reiki. Via Roma 15/B, Castelnovo ne' Monti, 42035 RE. Tel: +39 0522 611074. www.esteticachiaramagnani.it

And last, but not least, the wonderful Enoteca (wine and so much more) shop in Cerredolo. Enoteca Il Cantinone, Via del Lago 12, Cerredolo, 42010 RE. Tel: +39 0522 809138. www.enotecacantinone.adunmetro.it. They will send orders via courier to all over Italy and deliver free of charge to nearby municipalities (check on their website).

My website www.cassandracampbell-kemp.com has pictures of the area to whet your appetite and if you are interested, also has a link to Paolo Bonini's website for details of the properties mentioned in this - and the next - book.

Acknowledgements

These Tales originally started as posts on my Facebook page. The enthusiasm, encouragement and exhortation of my Facebook friends to write my stories down - has finally resulted in this book. Thank you all.

Thank you also to Ugo, Signor S, Alberto, Luisa R and her literary ladies and Farah, Hassan and the rest of my Hamlet 'family' without whose help and friendship I could simply not have managed. I'd also like to thank the friends I made in Verona, Valestra, Carpineti and beyond especially Aurora and Cheila in Verona, the generous and welcoming Dallari family of the Forno in Valestra and Geometra Gianpaolo (Paolo) Bonini of Carpineti, who took me at face value and offered me friendship and the opportunity to try and make a living in one of the most beautiful places I've had the fortune to discover.

I loved my time in Italy. It is a magical country, full of beauty, culture, great food and great people but like anywhere, it has its disadvantages. My struggles with the bureaucracy and coming to terms with some of the less than palatable elements of life there are in no way a criticism. They were what they were. I have many Italian friends and I hope that they are not dismayed by my retelling of my story. If so then please accept my apologies. As Oliver Cromwell said, "Paint me, warts and all". I have attempted to do this with my time in Italy and to recount the less than salutary experiences in a tongue-in-cheek way.

Last but not least I salute the indefatigable Matilda di Canossa, a woman whose single-mindedness, over 900 years ago, showed me that in the face of adversity you just keep going. Her legacy lives on.

Printed in Great Britain
by Amazon